"In this meticulously researched account her letters into the heart and soul of . extraordinary adventure of her mid-19t. which takes her, newly married, from her native Edinburgh to rural New Jersey and then far west to Kansas. The vicissitudes and fragility of church building, homemaking, and family life, lived out against the continuing threat of infectious illness, are all laid bare; and the author's lucid prose makes it a most pleasurable and thought-provoking read".

—JOHN FEEHALLY,
Emeritus Professor of Renal Medicine, University of Leicester, UK

"In *Ireland to the Wild West*, Marcus Paul has created a 'faithful record', drawn chiefly from letters, of a remarkable pair of lives, a remarkable partnership, lived out as young folk in Edinburgh and Ireland, culminating in church development, and tragedy, in the new world. It is an inspiring story, told with skill and with deep compassion. There are flashes of bright humour – bite off one of the Pope's toes as you bow to him! – and there is a sincere and gutsy picture of a couple facing challenges but maintaining trust in God's good purposes. Mr Paul has painted Christian lives, fully in their context and yet fully alive to the eternal need for dependence on God. The faith of Agnes and James Wilson lives splendidly in the pages of *Ireland to the Wild West*".

—DR JOHN GODDARD,
Teacher, Author, Traveller, Sydney, Australia

"Through diligent research, and poignant heartfelt letters I was transported back in time by *Ireland to the Wild West*. It was interesting to compare how things are so different now, but in many ways still the same. A very easy read, that I had difficulty putting down, and have returned to many times since my initial read".

—REV JIM AGNEW,
1st Presbyterian Church of Cedarville, New Jersey

"*Ireland to the Wild West* uncovers previously unknown first hand personal stories of life in the first years of the settlement of Wakeeney, frontier town in Trego, NW Kansas, in the days of the 'cowboys'. Tough resolve and missionary endeavour go hand in hand in this moving account which brings the 1870s Old West brilliantly to life".

—LARRY HIXSON,
Researcher and Local Historian, Trego County Historical Society, Kansas

"This is an extraordinary tale of love, passion and faith. The beautifully written account of the intertwining of two lives is both a gripping story of the opening up of the 'Wild West' and a truly astonishing love story. Told vividly and with candour, it brilliantly informs, challenges and inspires in equal measure."

—JOHN RICHARDSON,
Formerly Headmaster, Cheltenham College, UK

"It was our founding families that helped establish the towns out of the prairies of western Kansas. Families, like the Wilsons, lived through the early days of a growing community through the prosperity and the tragedies. It was the determination of the early settlers that proved to be the life blood of Trego County and Wakeeney. *Ireland to the Wild West* evokes the reality of the 1870s and brings the past vividly to life through unpublished letters, documents and photographs seen here for the first time. It's a book you won't want to put down".

—MARJEAN DEINES,
Director, Trego County Historical Society, Kansas

"A wonderful and engaging tale of love, faith, commitment and adventure, made real through the frankness of Agnes' letters – this along with a dose of rural development issues which include some fascinating references, particularly for this reader, of water and sanitation health challenges".

—DR RICHARD FRANCEYS,
Formerly Water and Society Course Director, Cranfield University, UK

IRELAND

to the

WILD WEST

A True Story of Romance, Faith,
Tragedy, and Hope

MARCUS PAUL

AMBASSADOR INTERNATIONAL
GREENVILLE, SOUTH CAROLINA & BELFAST, NORTHERN IRELAND
www.ambassador-international.com
Celebrating Forty Years of Getting the Word Around

Ireland to the Wild West

A True Story of Romance, Faith, Tragedy, and Hope

Scripture taken from the King James Bible. Public domain.

ISBN: 978-1-62020-959-2
eISBN: 978-1-62020-985-1

Cover Design and Page Layout by Hannah Nichols
eBook Conversion by Anna Riebe Raats
Edited by Daphne Self

AMBASSADOR INTERNATIONAL
Emerald House
411 University Ridge, Suite B14
Greenville, SC 29601, USA
www.ambassador-international.com

AMBASSADOR BOOKS
The Mount
2 Woodstock Link
Belfast, BT6 8DD, Northern Ireland, UK
www.ambassadormedia.co.uk

The colophon is a trademark of Ambassador, a Christian publishing company.

To my wife Elaine and wonderful children Naomi and Laurence; to all family members, past and present, and especially those who gave their lives on 'the front line' in the service of others.

ACKNOWLEDGMENTS

Thanks are due first to June Can and the staff of the Yale Collection of Western Americana, Beinecke Rare Book and Manuscript Library, Yale University for curating the letters of the Wilson family and for their encouragement in this project. Secondly, thanks are due to Rev Jim Agnew, minister of First Presbyterian Church Cedarville, New Jersey, for allowing me access to the church's archives; also, to Jim Howell of the same. I would also like to thank the staff of the National Archives of the Presbyterian Church (USA) at 42, Lombard Street, Philadelphia for their help in discovering presbytery minutes and other sources. Larry Hixson of First Presbyterian Church, Wakeeney, Kansas, I would like to thank for his research in the archives of Trego County, Kansas, along with Marjean Deines, Museum Director there. The British Library was also most helpful in providing a variety of documents. I owe to my son, Laurence, a central idea for the first two chapters of the book and for suggestions throughout his careful reading of the manuscript.

CONTENTS

FOREWORD

I am very glad to be able to write a few words at the start of this unique and fascinating story about my grandparents' extraordinary adventures. The events took place on a frontier that was for many both the fulfilment of a dream and a testing-ground where dreams turned to nightmare; but, in so many ways, the story sheds light and hope on today's world — so much in need of faith, perseverance and courage.

The author has painstakingly researched the lives and times of James and Agnes using the archive from Yale University's Rare Book and Manuscript Library in the USA, as well as the British Library in London. He has brought to light a "true life adventure" which you will find hard to put down: a story of faith, hope and love; and yes, some sadness, too. But its ending is a truly joyful one, one from which we can all take inspiration and renewed hope for the future.

—JAMES KINNIER WILSON,
Emeritus Fellow, Wolfson College, Cambridge

PREFACE

THIS IS THE STORY OF a love affair, one that is all too human yet also divine; revealed in letters and lived out on the prairies; a romance that is also a tragedy; a disaster that is yet a triumph of faith; in one sense an interlude, but in a larger sense a complete story played out on a grand stage. It would be no surprise to our greatest playwright for he knew the strange pattern of things, fought out in this instance by those who could recognise the hand of Providence in a mysterious universe. Shakespeare would hardly have altered a line of *Romeo and Juliet* had he read this story first: the two tales were in many ways one — until the writing of Act VI, an Act full of grace, that Shakespeare could not allow himself.

When, after three generations of dusty darkness, the Kinnier Wilson letters were sold, the cost was high: lovers' secrets suddenly laid bare for the cold and minute attention of scholars or the merely curious; no longer the preserve of their previous keeper; no longer known to none save their writers and recipients, those long ago buried in America, Ireland, and Scotland.

The sale of those secrets produced a surprising result. No one had expected the rather scruffy collection of yellowing pages to elicit the interest which they generated. The Swann Galleries in New York were pleased that Yale's prestigious manuscript library, the Beinecke, paid considerably more than many expected. It was not known, of course, who put them up for auction, but someone had at one time treasured them for they were numbered and neatly annotated in places. The faded ink on the fragile page was sometimes further obscured by being overwritten as palimpsest: in the 1870s there

11

was not much paper in a tiny community three hundred miles west of Kansas City in the Great American Desert. Perhaps they told a unique story: letters from a previous age often do for they reflect states of mind that no modern documents ever can. In fact, the humble letter, so carefully folded into its protective sleeve, so vulnerable to every opportunity for loss, so prone to delay of every kind, has long been a window to the human heart as few other forms of writing have. That age is past and future historians and literary critics will bemoan its passing, for today no such revelations are made in digital form with anything like the pent-up passions of the long-awaited, carefully composed letter in the post. The loss of anticipation in our age is a real and significant one.

From the potato fields of County Monaghan and the soirées of Victorian Edinburgh to the sod-houses of High Plains Kansas, this love story and adventure of faith opens up a world long faded from view but which shares many facets with our own and reflects brilliantly on today's world — still a place of heartache, longing, faith, and sometimes apparent tragedy. A place we can understand better, as we reflect on the struggles and triumphs of our forebears in the faith.

CHAPTER ONE

A DIVIDED CITY

MR JAMES KINNIER WILSON, BACHELOR of the County Monaghan in Ireland, twenty-seven, and lately scholar of Princeton, New Jersey, was due at 8, Merchiston Avenue, Edinburgh, the house of Rev Dr William Arnot, on December 30, 1872. He had received a formal invitation to the party on embossed headed notepaper, and as a student at the Free Church's prestigious New College in Edinburgh, was pleased to receive it. For Arnot was minister of the Free High Church, a vibrant place where the music and preaching were excellent; he had published a number of popular theological works and had twice been sent as a delegate of the Free Church to America. Dr Arnot was also the editor of a fashionable magazine for godly Scottish families: *The Family Treasury of Sunday Reading*, a monthly magazine with a title which is oddly revealing of its context. Strict Sabbatarianism was taken for granted by conservative Presbyterian households; so, on the one day of the week when there was no work but when most normal recreations — even including visits to friends, or "walking out for pleasure" — were forbidden, to read of the high adventure and romance of missionary heroism, of hardship, foreign travel and survival (or perhaps death) against the odds was a welcome diversion.

James kept the invitation for it became important to him in ways he could not, at the time, foresee. The house to which he was invited was already a place of some pilgrimage, and able and sociable young people liked to be there. One such was Agnes Hately, a single lady in her twenties, attractive, opinionated, and blessed with an exceptionally fine soprano voice which had been trained in Leipzig, the "City of Music", famed throughout Europe. Agnes, at that stage, could never have guessed that one day she would be contributing her own articles for Sunday reading to *The Family Treasury*, from a distant and sometimes dangerous foreign field.

A month later, James, having clearly made a good impression on his first visit, received another invitation, this time from Mrs Jane Arnot to speak to the

Hately family with Agnes far left

children gathered in the hall in Exchange Square where they would "be ready for Mr Wilson's address". The talk James gave must have gone down well for Arnot, keen to continue his links with America and to support the cause of Presbyterianism at home and abroad, was to be instrumental in preparing this robust and able young man for the American mission field. He found out quickly enough from James's brogue that although he had spent much of the last decade on the East Coast of America, he was an Irishman (though of Scottish ancestry) and came from a staunch, but gentle, Presbyterian farming family with a long history.

The family had been in Ulster since 1623 when a certain John Wilson had come over in the Plantation of that time when James I had sought to bring the Province more under his control by importing Protestant settlers, mainly from South West Scotland. James's parents were much revered in their local community and had contributed significantly to the building up of the First Presbyterian Church in the parish of Clontibret, where a funerary monument erected in 1897 in polished limestone indicates that "the Wilson family may have been important patrons of the church".[1] Late in life, James's cousin, John, (there was one in every generation) had been in danger of his life when 1920s Monaghan, though in the Province of Ulster, was largely Catholic and had gone through revolutionary times leaving the Protestant community a marooned minority. On one occasion local men, bent on harm, had surrounded his house by night. But the Wilsons were saved by the memory of one man in the crowd who recollected that long years before, the couple had sent food to his starving family while he was a child, so no hair of old John Wilson's head was to be touched by any revolutionary mob.

James, given his mother's maiden name, Kinnier, at his baptism, had been born in 1846 during the years of the Great Hunger, the Irish potato famine, in which as many as a million people died and a million more emigrated, reducing the population by some twenty percent or more. Thousands died in Monaghan which, according to an 1837 topographical dictionary of Ireland, was "mostly good arable land under tillage" and therefore suitable for potatoes (until the blight) — though there were many small loughs in the county and 4,000 acres of bog. As is well known, the English government's failure to assuage the famine of this, their own people, permanently changed the political landscape and America was seen, more than ever by the Irish to be 'the land of the free', the place where twenty years later the bloodiest civil war would be fought over slavery — a condition which millions of Irish peasants felt they could identify with.

---

1   See *Buildings of Ireland: National Inventory of Architectural Heritage.*

Originally, James had gone to visit friends in Philadelphia but like so many of his countrymen had stayed for economic reasons. Perhaps he had read John Stuart Mill's famous treatise *On Liberty,* or later, even his 1868 tract, *England and Ireland,* which advocated radical land reform to Ireland's advantage.[2] But there was the widespread view that the Irish prospered in America where land was cheap and a labourer's wages were high — just the opposite of Ireland "where wages were less than a shilling a day, and where the purchase of land was a luxury wholly beyond the peasant's reach". In America "a day's labour would earn two or three dollars, and . . . one dollar would suffice to purchase the fee-simple of an acre of land". As a result, it is estimated that some three million Irish had emigrated by 1868.[3]

It was not, however, on that December evening in 1872, the teaching, the talk, or the children, which had most impressed James at Arnot's house. It was Agnes. By her mid-twenties, having now lost both parents, she was a young woman who knew her own mind and spoke it — quite forcibly if necessary. She was proud of her appearance and liked to be fashionable. Money was not easy to come by, but she was very capable with a needle (she had had to be since her mother died so young) and her artistic temperament led her to choose her clothes well. She was also nice looking, the youngest child of handsome parents, and she could sing, dance and play the piano enchantingly. Her voice was especially good, and she was in training: every week she would sing in one of the fashionable choirs of the city and was not averse to performing solo or in duets and trios, when invited, at the concerts and soirées. She was now earning her living by giving singing lessons. More than this, Agnes had travelled, was intelligent and well-read.

---

2   The Wilsons were an able family. James, from farming stock, would later attend four theological colleges; James's cousin had a son, Thomas, who was honoured in 1937 by the new King George VI for services to Government; James's son, Samuel, became perhaps the greatest neurologist in world medicine.

3   For an extended discussion of these issues at the time, see *The Irish Church* in *Quarterly Review, Vol. 124,* pp. 538 -580, esp. pp. 538, 542-3.

We do not know exactly what happened that evening but the chemistry between the two must have been quite strong. James, rather lonely as a student from abroad at the New Free Church College, would not have had the sort of company which his southern counterparts enjoyed in the collegiate system of the old English universities. It was remarked at the time that at Edinburgh University students "usually feel themselves as much strangers and aliens at the end of their four years' course as they were at its commencement".[4] There is no reason to suppose New College was very different. Agnes, her father having died six years before, was in need of a husband both for security and company, not to mention status. She had no intention of becoming a maiden aunt to her siblings' children.

Agnes came of strong stock and from a distinguished family. She lived in a capital city of wide renown. The city of Edinburgh in the mid-nineteenth century was a leafy place where a west wind could bring the scent of the heather in August from the Pentland Hills. Much building remained from the Middle Ages: Cowgate and Canongate had still the air of antiquity, but there had been rapid change as well. Princes Street with its trim three-storied houses had become the place to promenade, rather than the High Street of a generation before. The Town Council had extended the burgh in many directions and gas lighting brightened the streets. Hackney carriages crowded the thoroughfares and the canal to Glasgow had increased trade and travel between the two cities. There were new University buildings and the Medical School had, for thirty years, been reckoned the best in Britain. The wars with France, having closed off the continent had served to open up Edinburgh to the rest of the Kingdom who found it a focus of culture. National schools of science, philosophy and letters, a distinguished Bar and Bench, a new library and old traditions of high learning and continuous controversy served to make the city justly famous. High Street and Bank Street, being home to no less than seven newspaper presses, ensured that whatever was latest in

---

4   Ibid. p. 418.

the news was soon on the lips of a people engaged with their world. One further facet of Scots society in general was that in both town and country there was a widespread musicality, hardly to be found in England. As early as 1806, Stark in his *Picture of Edinburgh* noted that music was "a part of modern education, and few are to be met with who cannot sing or play upon one instrument or another".[5]

While its ancient university founded in 1582, its agriculture, schools, medical school, and hospital were in the front rank of institutions and practice anywhere in the world, its churches were seen by many south of the border to be hide-bound by the past, haunted by the acrimony of generation upon generation of secessions and strife. Robert Louis Stevenson in 1875 recalled with regret that his land had "echoed for three centuries with the uproar of sectarian battles".[6] But without some understanding of the Church in Scotland it would be all but impossible to understand Scottish history or the Scots. Since 1643, with the signing of the Solemn League and Covenant, the Church had long sought to direct the details of daily life and encroach on the responsibilities of secular government in contrast to what was happening in most of Europe, exhausted by religious wars. The prosecution of witchcraft and hanging for heresy continued until the end of the century and in Scotland in 1695, a mere lad of nineteen, Thomas Aikenhead, was hanged in Edinburgh on grounds on which the Inquisition would have acquitted him.

For the next two centuries in Scotland, faith and religious partisanship continued to be central to daily life and the Scriptures were indeed as the psalmist said, "a lamp to the feet" — a relevant and powerful metaphor in a dark and rugged country. The Church therefore — its leaders, doctrines, activities, preaching — was an intimate thing, integral both to society and the individual, touching life at all levels, fit for debate, the most living thing

5   Quoted in Millar Patrick's *Four Centuries of Scottish Psalmody* (Oxford University Press, 1949), p. 201.
6   Quoted in John Buchan's *The Kirk in Scotland 1560-1929* (Hodder and Stoughton, 1930), p. 68.

a Scot could conceive. What part of the Church you belonged to *mattered* and Church teaching coloured the outlook of everyone, including the few sceptics, for since the Reformation, there had been little literature that had not been dependent to some extent upon it. John Bunyan's *The Pilgrim's Progress* with its graphic depiction of the narrow dangerous way to salvation was by every bed or fireside.

Not only was the Church pioneering in faith but also in popular education, in politics, and in social service. For centuries it had been through Presbyterianism that a citizen could make his voice heard on matters of public debate. It was "a system by which any one, first of all the common man, had his recognised place, his defined position, his ascertained and guarded privileges, his responsibilities . . . "[7] When Episcopacy disappeared from the national church after the revolution of 1688, there was a chance for each to have their say in how churches governed themselves and with the ripples of Methodism reaching north in the next century such democratic leanings became strengthened.

But democracy is not a perfect system and it promotes argumentation — in many ways its very life blood — with the result that the Scottish church was deeply fissured. By 1843, after ten years of especially intense conflicts of opinion, two factions of the Church of Scotland had finally fragmented into two distinct Church groups. Edinburgh was, therefore, a divided city. The fragmentation was not something done in a corner, momentarily catching the interest, as today perhaps, of those who attended the kirk. There were scores of churches in the city and many thousands attended them. Social and intellectual life revolved around their activities. They were places of song, scholarship, news, the interchange of ideas, debate, and constant endeavour to do good works, in equal parts. Mission, the expansion of the Church both at home and abroad, was a natural topic at the dinner table. David Livingstone, a household name by the 1850s, was one of the most famous sons of the kirk

---

7   Principal Rainy, quoted in Buchan, Op. Cit. p. 66.

and his journeys through Southern Africa had gained international attention. The conjunction of Christian idealism and hard-headed practicality in his character was the epitome of Scottish heroism. Today he still stands as one of the world's greatest explorers.

It is into this cosmopolitan yet religiously fragmented city, the Edinburgh of 1843, that we must plunge to meet Agnes's father: Thomas Legerwood Hately. From the age of nine Thomas had to earn his keep among the seven children who his mother, early widowed, could barely feed. James Ballantyne, the famous printer, who in 1822 alone had produced 145,000 volumes of Sir Walter Scott, apprenticed the boy "in his tenth year" and one of Thomas's tasks was to rush the proofs between Sir Walter's house in Castle Street and the printing press, in days when the turnaround time between writing and publishing was a fraction of that today. On one occasion in the drowse of summer he'd fallen asleep in the great man's porch — he'd had to wait so long.

As a young man, Thomas had witnessed the most important day of nineteenth-century Scottish history and had been central to it. He was, at the time, a manager of the famous printing firm, Constable's in High Street, and on the eighteenth of May there had been, all morning, a strange and solemn hush in the streets. Street vendors of all sorts of wares, horse traffic, and the whole bustle of commerce had all been silenced by the gravity of the situation. Whatever the outcome, life would have to change, but for the Hatelys only one result would be acceptable for it was the historic moment when the Church had the chance to be free — free of government interference, free to arrange its own affairs. Thankfully it did so as one third of the clergy and half the laity, in protest, streamed out from the General Assembly of the Established Presbyterian Church on to George Street, and processed down the hill to Tanfield Hall at Canonmills. In our day, imaginative children at school are caught up by recordings of Martin Luther King's "I have a dream" speech (a defining moment of the Civil Rights Movement) with its climax:

"Free at last . . . thank God Almighty, we're free at last". For children of 'The Disruption' (as it was aptly named) there would have been a similar catch in the breath as their elders told them the story of that great day. It was a story that Thomas would later tell his children often. Eventually, 474 ministers out of about 1,200 signed the Act of Separation. W.E. Gladstone, one of Britain's greatest statesmen, called the action "a noble and heart-stirring spectacle" which it was when so many put their conscience before their security of employment in determining that the law-abiding affairs of their church, their leadership, their beliefs, should not be subject to interference by governments.

The impact of the new Church was soon to be felt, both in Thomas's family and throughout Scotland. Across the country there was a constructive spirit about the impetus that was unleashed. In its first year the new body built five hundred churches; schools were founded, prestigious colleges set up and a new direction given to the nation's religion. The whole enterprise was entirely self-supporting and collected money at the astonishing rate of one thousand pounds a day.[8] Every overseas mission joined in and the ripples of that tide can be seen in historic churches planted globally from America to the East. Its leaders were the ablest theologians of their day; it enjoyed the most popular preachers; its youth was the flower of their generation. Thomas's daughter would remember with pride that she met "many of the Disruption fathers and worthies".

Thomas's life also took on a new direction. Though then working for Constable, the publisher, he was a man devoted to music and used his gifts in the service of the new Free Church. James Love in his history of Scottish church music considered that "he gave the first great impulse in recent times to the cultivation of church music in Scotland".[9] In singing-schools up and down Scotland he taught up to 1,000 children at a time and

---

8   John Buchan, Op. Cit. p. 79.
9   James Love, *Scottish Church Music*, (Wm. Blackwood, 1891), p. 157.

today, some of his many compositions for the Psalms are still remembered and sung.

That lively energy he passed on to his daughter, Agnes, who, with James, is the central focus of this history. But, as so often in those days, death came early to Thomas's family and Ann, the wife who had borne him three children, died after only eight years of marriage in 1847. He was now alone with his "wee bairnies", Mary, Walter, and Agnes, the youngest, who had been born in 1845. But coming from adventurous Border stock meant he and they would be tough enough to face this adversity. Agnes, especially, would need courage and faith in equal measures.

Rev James Kinnier Wilson

Her 'coming of age' was the moment she boarded ship (albeit with her father) for Europe: it must have taken some courage to go to Leipzig, the famed 'city of music' to study singing and piano aged no more than sixteen in 1861. Besides preparing, as she imagined, for a life of music-making she would be able to practise and improve her German and learn to deal with the unfamiliar summer heat. This training in Leipzig and subsequently in Edinburgh qualified her to give singing lessons to others — her main source of income through her twenties, just as it would be an important part of her life in America.

"I was very young", she wrote much later, "but I shall never forget the glees, motets, choruses we sang then" — at the meetings of the Scottish Vocal Music Association. She was proud to be invited to sing, too, in the Sacred Harmonic Society in Queen Street Hall which, she boasted, "included all the best amateurs of Edinburgh, and was very fashionable". Meeting young men therefore, for all the strictures of the Victorian period, was not unusual or difficult for Agnes. To be sure, being alone with one was a different matter but snatches of conversation and meaningful glances, as ever, could always be managed by those intent on romance — even where the faithful had gathered for the most noble purpose of instructing children. It was not long before James and Agnes were exchanging letters.

CHAPTER TWO

A DIVIDED COUPLE – ROMANCE AND EXILE

THE FIRST LETTER THAT AGNES sent James suggests that their mutual attraction was unabashed for within a short time Agnes was writing intimately to "My Dear Jamie" that they should defer their intended visit to a friend and instead meet secretly at Moray Place, especially since Walter's mother-in-law did, " not know of . . . " as she chose to put it. This rather coy refusal even to name the nature of their relationship even in the most private letter, suggests a playfulness and spirit more buoyant and boisterous than many would have guessed of her. She signs off: "I am ever Dear Jamie, your own loving Nanny". The wording reveals how clearly she is assured not only of her love for James, but his love for her, and is taking the initiative in what the next move is — namely how and where to meet privately. Agnes also enjoyed pretending an ironic displeasure in a transparently false anger, writing, "if I find you here when I come home I shall not be very angry". Her postscript was playful too: "I am looking forward with fear and trembling to the scolding you will give me" for her having failed to get on with her letter writing as she promised.

At this point it is worth drawing attention to the beginning of the correlation between these lovers' story and that of Shakespeare's tragic pair in "fair Verona" more than three hundred years earlier. Edinburgh, like Verona, was a divided city. The factions may have been less violent than the feuding between Capulet and Montague households, but the two-party factionalism was, nevertheless, fierce at times. The two lovers came from opposing shores rather than opposing families, but Agnes's thoughts and language would echo Juliet's not only in her forthright declarations of love and her passionate opinions but in her premonitions of disaster. Already in this letter, her teasing of James was reminiscent of Juliet's "O Churl" to Romeo for dying before she did. The seeming secrecy of their love for each other was an obvious further parallel.

From March 1873 they corresponded constantly for a year before their marriage when James's 'exile' — a mixture of wanderlust and training for his work — kept them apart. To be fair to him, the plans for his travel must have been made before he set eyes on Agnes. He was ambitious and capable and if he was to provide adequately for a wife, he needed to be fulfilled in his educational ambitions as well as his marriage.

After having known each other for only two months and with restricted chances to meet, James was in London, listening to the famous evangelical preacher Charles Spurgeon.[10] To hear this news inevitably made Agnes long to be with him. As it was, she could only look often at his photograph and doing that made her "deserted and forlorn". "Everything in the place reminds me of you" she wrote, expressing the common denominator between a forced separation and a bereavement: grief. The loss of separation may not have been permanent but it was still experienced as loss and resources had to be mustered to cope with it. The essential difference was hope for better times, and hope was creative and energising.

But Agnes loved a joke, especially a straight-faced one, and between a couple so briefly acquainted, some would inevitably misfire. "You stupid Jamie, I meant it was your thirty-seventh birthday". James had mistaken a joke about his age (he was actually twenty-seven) for a quirky reference to the day of the month. "All these blunders", Agnes protested, "just prove to me how very

---

10   Spurgeon would preach to crowds of 10,000 people for up to two hours and hold them spellbound. He has more work in print than almost any other Christian writer. When David Livingstone died in this year (1873) a copy of one of Spurgeon's sermons was found among his very few possessions with the comment "Very good".

superficially 'somebody' reads my letters — even burns them!" The result of this was that though he had asked Agnes to write at length, she chastened him with: "A very long letter . . . he certainly shall not have". "So there is a bit of scolding for you Master Jim" she continued. "How do you like it?" Clearly this would be at times a tempestuous relationship. The reality, rather than the teasing, was that Agnes would become easily the superior partner in writing at length. She liked, however, to take control of the situation at the end of the letter: "Don't forget to answer all my questions and let me have a nice long screed on Monday" she concluded.

Agnes also liked to paint pictures of herself that would elicit compliments from James, not just about her looks but about her courage and the pleasure she took in being mildly shocking. On one occasion when asked to sing, Agnes mentioned that her final rendition was "O whistle and I'll come to you my lad" which "I'm afraid was very improper and shocking of me" — but of course she is really pointing not to the impropriety, but to the fun of it. In the summer of that year she was due to sing at the Sacred Harmonic Society again but could not forbear to point out that at the end of January when they were together, "a certain individual wore white muslin with a blue sash". In a later letter she said she always wanted to "look pretty and nice in my husband's eyes" and for him "to look handsome and strong". This attitude is not without its moral difficulties for no respectable young girl at such a time in Edinburgh would have been entirely without the knowledge that "Favour is deceitful and beauty is vain" as the Book of Proverbs said, and as Mrs Arnot tended to remind her rather too often — so much so that Agnes felt "really I have been angry at her almost". When James was in Rome, he visited the Colosseum by moonlight and a choir was performing there. Agnes's response was to want to remind her lover that, had she been there, "the singing would have been much finer". Whether the primary sense of that was that under such romantic circumstances they would, had they been together, have heard the music differently, or whether Agnes more boastfully meant she would have sung better than the voices Jamie heard, we can only guess. In the same letter she reflects that she and Walter were both going to study music in Florence, but an end was put to that idea by the arrival of Miss Gray to whom Walter became engaged. Perhaps there is a little *frisson* of resentment here. It would be hard for her not to compare her own situation in which, unlike Walter, her betrothed did not change his plans for the lady's sake.

Perhaps the intention was to make her absent sweetheart less complacent and so provoke him to more frequent letters and declarations of love, for in the summer Agnes described at some length her night out at a coming-of-age party for the oldest of Mrs Lownie's eight sons "at which there was a great deal of dancing and I think I scarcely missed one". She "had the honour of opening the first quadrille with the hero of the evening". She also wore earrings for the occasion which some of her elders would certainly have frowned upon. She performed a number of the songs (including such light numbers as *Pat Molloy*[11]) and did not return until four a.m. — the latest she had ever been out — brought home by Willie Lownie himself. One reason she had the confidence to adventure in this way in the strictest circles of Presbyterian Scottish life in 1873 was that she had an engagement ring on her finger! With her sister and brother both already married and having started families, Agnes must have felt it was time she shared their status. This prolonged absence of her fiancé was therefore doubly difficult for her. Moreover, while she remained, seemingly gaily enjoying the social life of Edinburgh, James had embarked on a version of the Grand Tour.

Historically the preserve of the wealthy landed gentry, such a tour was also undertaken, by enquiring minds who could afford it, as an educational rite of passage. It involved taking a ferry to Calais or Le Havre and then visiting Paris and as many other cultural centres, especially in Italy, as time and money allowed — from several months to several years. Geneva was on the

---

11   *Pat Molloy* tells the story of an Irish boy who (like Jamie) went to London; he caused some chaos, ending up before a magistrate. It's a highly humorous song.

tour because it was the cradle of the Protestant Reformation and this was an obvious stop for James who wrote a letter to *The Presbyterian* on April 12th. The fact that James put this ahead of spending the summer with Agnes reveals that he had both money and a desire for discovery and learning. He had been only seventeen when he first took sea passage for America in 1863, in order to visit friends. That visit extended itself into business enterprise which lasted several years. But as Agnes later wrote, "About this time the whole purpose of his life was changed and he entered upon a course of studies" — theology. James had been dramatically converted — perhaps by the extraordinary ministry of D. L. Moody in Chicago at the Illinois Street church and YMCA — and by 1869 he was enrolled at Princeton. From 1871 until we see him in Edinburgh at New College he attended Presbyterian College of the North-West in Chicago for further theological training. To pay for and pursue these three courses and then to travel in Europe as he did suggests both a talent for making money and a vigorous intellect — the latter being something which he and Agnes passed on to their children in full measure.

James visited the principal cities of France, Germany, and Italy and stayed away so long that Agnes began to fear she might not see him again. Venice, Naples, Bologna, Rome, Milan, and Pompeii were all mentioned in the letters and Agnes was keen to trace his wanderings on the map in her brother Walter's house. Such an action, especially if shared with other family members brings a sort of closeness to a world so infinitely more distant than is imaginable today. A world in which not only was travel more time consuming, but also more dangerous. It is little wonder then that Agnes's fears for James's safety, repressed in public as they had to be — if her faith and indeed decorum were to be kept up — surface in her dreams and are expressed poignantly in her letters. She loved to remind him of what he should be seeing, of wanting to be with him; she playfully told him too that she was aware that he was not very good at looking at paintings and other artefacts. One thing he would have to see, she insisted, was Leonardo's mural of the Last Supper in the Santa Maria convent in Milan while he was there, staying at the Hotel Royal. This sort of desire for James to edify himself with high art contrasts with Agnes's unabashed sense of humour and fun. While he was staying at the Hotel d'Allemagne in Rome she suggested that Jamie paid the Pope a visit, bit off a piece of the pontiff's toe (to use as a relic) as he did obeisance and give him her compliments. This sort of ludicrous jest betrays how the younger generation at the other end of the theological spectrum from 'Romanism' were allowed or encouraged to see the Papacy. This was in part because in 1870, three years earlier, that the First Vatican Council under Pope Pius IX had made such moves as to define dogmatically the Pope's infallibility which would have been seen in Presbyterian circles as compounding error upon error. To a Scottish or Irish Protestant evangelical family the imposition of such doctrines placed the Catholic Church at a greater distance from historical gospel religion and diminished their respect for it.

Such matters, however, could not long distract Agnes from the dangers of the long absence to their relationship, and the journey, to James's health. These sometimes overwhelmed her and she had to share her worries along with her nightmares which demonstrate so clearly her deep insecurities about their relationship.

In a letter of April 28th, Agnes dreamt that her good and kind friend, Mrs Arnot had come to her with the most terrible news. "James," she said in the dream, "will never come back to you. He has sent word that he has forgotten you". Still dreaming, Agnes looked down at her hand and realised that her ring finger was bare: there *was* no engagement. The nightmare was a ghastly fright which any lover can identify with, but Agnes's faith enabled her to reassure both Jamie and herself: "God", she wrote, "has taken care of you hitherto — and I am sure He will continue his goodness. I pray constantly for you," she continued, "that you may be preserved from danger and be blessed in every way".

The delays necessitated by an overland postal service using railway and coach produced feelings of longing and impatience and frustration which are caused by other communication issues today. But in 1873 when there would be week's delay between the posting of a letter to Italy and its arrival there gave ample occasion to Agnes for complaint. In May, when a sixpenny stamp took her letter to Pompeii, Agnes longed for a letter to cheer her up. "My heart was so heavy I couldn't sing" she wrote, complaining that if he loved her, he would write at least once a week rather than every ten days. "You once said you'd do anything for me" she reflected. Her depression was compounded by the fact that she now knew that James would return to America, and that she might not see him again before he went, thereby bringing about a year-long separation of which she was very scared. In addition, she knew that crossing the ocean was far from safe. Writing her letter after midnight she confessed: "I dread more and more the idea of crossing that dreadful Atlantic". The fears now were not solely on Agnes's side. James asked, "Nanny, do you think of me?" To which she replied: "I think of you morning, noon and night — I don't know the time when I don't think of you". In a later letter, dated August, it was Agnes's turn to ask, "Do you think of me, and what do you think of me?" The agony and the ecstasy are parallels to Juliet's "Dost thou love me? . . . If thou dost love, pronounce it faithfully". But there were other fears. The travelling for James was not without difficulty. On a number of occasions, he was ill; at other times, plagued by headaches, he felt he had "more 'downs' than 'ups' in life". He was of a quieter disposition than Agnes; rather than loving to show off at a party which she did, James's view was that "the pleasantest recreation is good conversation" and that is not readily available when travelling alone, moving from place to place.

These two characters, strong in different ways, opposites in some respects, occasionally felt a chill fall over their friendship. In July Agnes was openly angry that she had not been receiving letters as she thought she should, but then had a sudden misgiving that this might be because Jamie was ill. ("What a beast was I to chide at him" says Juliet). She resolved therefore to put her hurt pride and resentment behind her and write frankly to him: "I just poured out my whole heart in prayer for you, body and soul". Her fear was that illness had prevented him writing, " — but if that is not the case, then you have vexed me by your indifference, that is all". There is no escaping the fierceness of temper and the absoluteness of opinion in Agnes's letters: she expected a great deal, but she gave a great deal of herself in exchange. In an earlier letter Jamie had complained that some of her letters were cold — and oddly enough Agnes accepted this criticism, and must have known she was very demanding, though, unbeknown to her, part of the problem was her naivety about how certain things look in writing when there is no tone of voice or body language to help interpret the words. Did she ever think, for instance, how James might respond to this statement, written when she heard he had met up with an old American "sweetheart" in Rome: "I demand an explanation Mr J K Wilson"? The mock formality betrays the teasing tone, but it could have gone badly wrong.

It was now three months or more since James and Agnes had seen each other. They had been apart longer than they had been together, so the exchange of letters and the single photograph that Agnes had of James's "kind, good, manly face" (now apparently sporting "hirsute appendages") became an increasingly tenuous, sometimes slightly desperate, lifeline for them. "The days when your letters arrive are white days to me" she told him — days for celebration. In between, however, there are black days: "When I think that I may not see you for many long weary months, my heart sinks in spite of myself". The original of his photograph "I long to see more than anything in the world". Agnes, nevertheless, put a brave face on it, allowing that she was as happy as she could be "under the circumstances". She attended a party in honour of Professor Calderwood, recently returned from the United States who was "talking a great deal about it". She thought she might be invited to go there and had half a mind to do so. (Dr Arnot was to return to USA towards the end of August.) Perhaps this was the result of her singing at the party where "Mrs Hughes and I made quite a sensation". As ever, Agnes desired to show James that she still cut a figure. "Mrs Hughes wore green Irish poplin with white roses in her hair. I wore my white dress with the blue ribbons". The two ladies complimented each other afterwards:

"Mrs Hughes, I think you were the best looking person there".

"Miss Hately, I looked round the room and saw none as pretty as you".

The exchange could have come straight from the pages of Jane Austen. One of the songs Agnes chose to mention was a far cry from *Jack Molloy*. It was *Mistletoe Bough* in which the bride of Lord Lovell, weary of dancing on her wedding day decides to hide in the Baron's castle. She climbs into a self-locking chest, never to be seen again till her mouldering remains are found years later. A strange choice to our ears but perhaps unconsciously chosen as a reflection of Agnes's turbulent feelings. It is also reminiscent of Juliet, locked in a living death in her tomb, awaiting Romeo. Other expressions of love and grief in the letters at this point remind their reader of the play. The lovers are conspiratorial about "a great secret which you mustn't tell to anybody" and the dramatic irony of Agnes's declaration "If you were only to live a week I would marry you for that week", if not a verbal echo of Romeo's ecstatic heedlessness of danger, certainly betrays the same sentiment as his passionate: "Love devouring death do what he dare; it is enough I may but call her mine". "Your last letter made me very happy indeed" Agnes wrote on July 21st so perhaps at this point James had suggested a date for their marriage thereby giving Agnes an end point to her loneliness and fears that this engagement might never reach fruition. By August 19th the matter of their marriage had become a topic for discussion: Agnes was expecting a silver tea service from the congregation (which she got) and she expected the wedding to be a big affair since Mary was given one hundred and fifty presents and as the younger sister, she would not want to settle for fewer than that.

Curiously, and without warning it seemed, James had suddenly arrived back home in Clontibret, County Monaghan in Ireland where he was unwell and may have needed a spell in the hospital. Agnes recommended sea bathing to him. The upshot of this is that, as far as we know, James never managed a visit to Scotland that year — to Agnes's "bitter disappointment". In August she told him "Many a bitter tear I have shed" but her faith under duress was strong. "God is good, as you say in your letter, and will not lay more on you than you can bear. And if this trial only brings us nearer to that dear Saviour who suffered so much for us, it will not have been in vain".

As usual, Agnes's piety did not prevent her from enjoying a joke or requesting longer letters from her future husband. It being the summer she had been out playing a great deal of croquet and with some glee told him she had "had some vicious games". She also told him that an unattractive visiting minister had been preaching at church — and the pews were largely empty as a result. "I suppose the people are away from home just now", he said. To which, George Young, the beadle noted for his acerbic tongue, replied, "'Deed Sir, I think God Himself is away from home the noo".

CHAPTER THREE

PREPARING FOR AMERICA

WHAT HAPPENS NEXT IN THIS intensely felt love affair in which the lovers have not touched or seen each other or even heard each other's voices for so long is that Agnes was to send her letters no longer east, but west across the Atlantic. James enrolled at Auburn Theological Seminary in New York State, one of the oldest religious institutions in America, and remained there for two terms until the spring of 1874. This was to further his studies he had begun at Princeton in 1869 and continued at Chicago from 1871 to 1873. Auburn Seminary, founded in 1819, was a Presbyterian training college in a town set attractively in the heart of the lake country of Western New York. The town had a sizeable Irish immigrant population and factories which were to produce agricultural implements on a scale almost as large as anywhere in the country. On all these counts therefore, James had found a place well suited to him. He had also found his vocation — in the New World — and expected Agnes to join him.

Agnes, however, in her first letter to America, dated October 8th, had a grievance. Without alluding to the cause of the problem, she told Jamie: "You ask me to forgive you if you have vexed me in any way — you have vexed me more than I can tell — but I do forgive you — but I will say no more on this subject". Did Agnes feel excluded from Jamie's decision to take up his place at Auburn? The letters do not tell us but they reveal Agnes's character so well. Practical as ever, she told Jamie:

I have begun my preparation for America. How strange it seems.
Well, I think the very first thing I will get ready will be a nice little
cane to whip you with when you are bad. But I forgot — you have
a great big stick which you bought in Edinburgh, which will do
well enough.

It would still be six months, to the day, until they were married and only
after that would they start their lives together en route for New Jersey. It
seemed early to be making preparations but making your own dresses for a
foreign shore both hotter and yet sometimes as cold as Edinburgh took many
evenings of sewing. Agnes needed to be busy — and she had to learn a new
skill: how to use a sewing machine.

Underlying the tensions, however, there was also relief that longer-term
plans had begun to take shape. Agnes was confident that they were both
"happy and full of hope". There were several factors contributing to this. The
end of the long exile or separation was in sight; Jamie's vocation seemed clear
at last — what Agnes in a December letter called "the noblest calling on this
earth"; job opportunities in America were seen to be plentiful; stipends were
higher than in Scotland or Ireland, and there would be, crucially, a role for
Agnes. On October 22nd she wrote: "I feel I would rather spend my life in
doing good among people who need it, than in just living comfortably and
doing nothing in particular". She also liked the idea of being able to criticize
her husband's sermon drafts when he read them out to her (which she had
done before). She could not forebear, however, to add: "You know I will need
to give up a good deal in leaving my country and my kind friends who love
me so much and going away among strangers who perhaps won't care for me".
A sense of self-sacrifice was an important component in Agnes's DNA.

It is at this point in the archive that it breaks in on the reader that, despite
James having spent so long in the United States, it had probably not dawned
on Agnes, until that October that James would want to live there permanently
when married. It was of course possible that he too had not realised this until

this juncture. God does not often reveal His purposes for us long-term far in advance. Perhaps Agnes's affront in the earlier letter had been the result of being presented with a *fait accompli*. She continued to exhibit signs of insecurity as she contemplated the reality of living so far from the community in which she was well known:

> I don't feel at all as if it were such a dreadful thing to go to America — it is getting so common now.

> I hope you have not been telling all sorts of stories to Dr Patterson etc. If you make him fancy that I am pretty, and stuff like that, I will be very angry at you, for you know I don't think so myself at all, and they will just be disappointed when they see me . . . I wish you would just tell them "I'm better than I'm bonnie" to use a Scotch saying.

This does not sound as if she was fishing for compliments but rather that she was genuinely apprehensive about her acceptance in an utterly strange environment. The vanity in the apprehension was that of someone looking in a mirror, not to admire themselves but to ensure that they looked presentable enough to face those they would meet. Agnes continued to prepare little things for their home "somewhere in America" on the understanding that James would provide the furniture. She was sewing much of the time and would soon have the loan of Mary's machine in her own home. Thoughts of all her industry reminded her to repeat playfully to James: "you'll have to become awfully tidy and orderly, Jamie . . . in fact if you're not a good boy generally, I'll maybe change my mind at the last minute, and not go with you to America at all".

Glimpses of the everyday life of previous ages are almost invariably interesting to historians. When those glimpses are of people one has come to know they are even more so, as we empathise not just with the great or shocking events that so often envelop humanity but with the humdrum and commonplace — especially when we know that these are the prelude to circumstances which will shake their subjects to the core. Much later in life, thinking about her father and earlier forebears, Agnes wrote:

> The past is cut off from us, swept away behind silent horizons; but faithful records, illuminated by a sympathetic imagination, will bring before us the spirits and personalities that lived and moved in that past.

She was using an image redolent of her days in remote Kansas, a world that she could not begin to envisage as she began to prepare for married life in the cold dark autumn of 1873 in Edinburgh.

"I dread the coming of winter" Agnes complained. She had always been someone who loved the comparatively warm and dry summers of the East Coast and sat out in the garden to sew or read when she had leisure. The bright lights of a winter party were, in consequence, a particular pleasure for her. It was a disappointment therefore that she was away in September and thus missed Miss Arnot's marriage — especially as there had been a lively reception party after it. Somehow, she knew that the bride's allowance, or "pin money" as she called it, would be no less than £400 a year for her sole use. This, to someone of Agnes's means, was an enormous annuity, given that the tiny stipends of the ordinary clergy and ministers at the time were frequently in the region of £200 to £300 a year. At another social gathering Agnes, with misplaced levity (or so it seems) delighted in telling James: "I had a nice time flirting with James Gray" — Jeannie's brother. She reassured her fiancé that "it was only flirting" but seemed unaware that her betrothed would hardly take this kindly. At this distance we have to assume that Agnes's use of the word connotes something different from today[12] for she was enjoying the look of the engagement ring on her finger and thinking about how she would make their future "parsonage" pretty with books, pictures, and ornaments. She was also taking new singing pupils, practising her music, and learning new songs.

---

12   In *The Century Dictionary* (1899) the central definition is given as "To practise coquettish behaviour". Insincerity is also mentioned; today the term includes the idea of "toying with someone or something".

Every Tuesday night she sang with the Sacred Harmonic Society at the little hall in George Street. In November, Mr Mackenzie, its President, asked Agnes if she would sing in a duet at the next concert, probably, he told her, to be held in January. It is hard not to smile at what she next wrote: "I think I will keep all Mr Mackenzie's notes now — Dr Chalmers' son-in-law you know!!!!" The four exclamation marks show that although she was immensely proud to have been asked — doubly so because of the connection with a figure as significant as Dr Chalmers[13] — she knew well enough that pleasure in the social cachet attached to such an invitation did not fit well with her required Christian humility.

In America, James was searching for a job: "I am so glad to hear of your good prospects", Agnes told him. "If you get that church of Cataragna, it will be very nice". The stipend would be much better, she noted, than he could expect back home. Cataragna was the site of a famous battle against the French and 'Indians,' now known as Kingston, Ontario, in Canada. "If you always love me . . . I will go with you anywhere to do God's work" she added. Fears and hopes and dreams continue to weave their way through each letter. Hopes that James would settle on a church; fears for his health; dreams of their new life together one day. "Many a night when the gas is lighted in the parlour, I wish the door would open and you would come in as you used to do — last winter . . . I know God will bless and prosper us if we seek to please Him. You must tell me about the new sermons you write . . . Here is something for you XXX". The letter was posted to "2018 Frankford Avenue, Philadelphia, Pa. (Care of Dr Patterson)".

Agnes's fears about James's health were prophetic, for when she next wrote in November there are indications in the letter that he had been seriously ill. The letter is addressed simply to "Auburn Seminary, New York" with

13   His entry in *The Century Cyclopedia of Names* (1894) calls him "A celebrated Scottish divine and author . . . professor of moral philosophy at St. Andrews". In *Encyclopedia Britannica* (Eleventh Edition, 1910-11) the entry on Chalmers runs to some 2000 words.

the afterthought "Lock Box 56" at the base of the envelope. James had been preaching on two Sundays in Pittsford, an agricultural settlement close to the south shore of Lake Ontario in the north-west of New York State, where he was hoping another church might want his ministry:

> Jamie, I am sorry more than I can tell you, to think that you are ill
> sometimes yet — it vexes me very much and makes me so afraid
> sometimes, so afraid of looking forward. Today I have felt a load
> on my spirits which I can hardly shake off, and it is just because
> I know from your letter that you are afraid about yourself . . . O
> how earnestly I hope and pray that you may be quite well again
> . . . O dear Jamie, do all you can to get well, for my sake, as well as
> your own, for I do believe my heart would break if anything came
> over you.

Agnes's imagination, left to its own devices and without news of her beloved, raced ahead of her. Like Juliet, for her "in a minute there are many days" and like her imagining the death of her beloved, she could say, "O God, I have an ill-divining soul!" and found herself fearing the worst. Deciding no longer to dwell on it Agnes declared she would say no more about health matters and so reverted to two of her favourite topics — fashion and romance. She had enjoyed the American papers she had been sent (three in one week on one occasion), with their fashion pictures and she was characteristic in warning Jamie, "when you go visiting ladies with Mr Johnson, you mustn't fall in love with any of them because I know a lady in Edinburgh who would be very angry with you if you did". The topic, of course, reminds her of her own flirtation which Jamie had not let pass. His reply gave occasion for her to explain more of what gave rise to it:

> You say you suppose I must have had a fine time flirting up at the
> Grays'. Jamie, that was about the saddest time I ever had in my
> life for my mind was full of anxiety about you — I thought you
> had acted so strangely and unkindly in the way you had left me
> and I was angry at you and very miserable — but as I said before
> I have forgiven you all that — though I know I had good cause to

be offended at you — if I did flirt with Jim Gray it was just to keep myself from thinking".

It is tempting to speculate about the tone and nature of this exchange. How ironic is Jamie's phrasing ("must have had a fine time")? How transparent is Agnes being when she says her flirting was to take her mind off her misery? What exactly had James done to make her so miserable? Did she feel, at the time, almost jilted, and was that an over-reaction? Whatever the answer is, it is clear from the rest of the letter that the couple passionately love each other and, of course, if there had been anything underhand in Agnes's behaviour with Jim Gray, the last thing she would have done would be to tell James about it. Moreover, she wanted to be with him in America: "I often say to Aunt that I would like to live in a climate where the sky is always blue and the sun always shines . . . I often try to fancy you in the Seminary — but you see I don't know at all what the place is like" — a coded way of asking him to write describing it (which she reinforces at the end of the letter by wanting to know about "your lessons and your friends and your sermons, everything".) This led Agnes to say it is too painful sometimes even to look at the places in Edinburgh where they used to walk together, so full were they of shared memories. Such thoughts had been triggered in part by the fact that Dr Arnot, recently returned from America, had baptised (in the house) her sister Mary's baby, Thomas Hately Macfie. He then stayed for tea and talked at length about his experiences there, "and about the voyage, and all the jokes they had". Passage across the Atlantic would once again be preying on Agnes's mind but she was far from completely alone and went fortnightly to Walter and Jeannie's house for the evening; the alternate weeks they came to her. She was frequently at Mary's home as well.

Like James, ill-health was also suffered by Dr Arnot's son, Willie, who had had to return from Chicago because of it. Towards the end of this story both Willie and James were to share this misfortune again in a place much further from home.

Any personality as exuberant, forthright, and yet fundamentally kind as that of Agnes is liable to suffer from bouts of remorse. Having spoken her mind too forcefully she would, on occasion, suffer bitter remorse and wish she had not spoken, fearing the untold damage that her words might have wreaked. Such an occasion arises in her letter of the twenty-seventh of November. The letter is worth quoting at some length if we are to understand Agnes better, and indeed ourselves. She began with her reaction to his last letter:

> I hardly know how to begin — or to tell you how I feel about it — I have been like to cry over it. I am sure you know, dear Jamie, that I would not willingly hurt your feelings and I hope you will forgive me for having done so — when I wrote that way about the trial of leaving home and friends I really felt it and I'm sure you would think me strange if I didn't. I love my friends, and feel sore at leaving them, but then I love you better and that makes a great difference. If you had written to me in that way I think I would have said, "Yes Jamie, I know that is all true, but I will be so good to you that you will never regret leaving them". I am not afraid to go to America, I am as willing as ever I was to go with you anywhere because I love you and I know you love me — And I think you are getting dearer to me every letter and even paper that comes makes me long for you more and more. Sometimes I sit and think of you till I can scarcely keep from crying. And, Jamie, that was only a joke of mine about you being tidy etc. I was thinking about "our home" at the time and I meant tidy and orderly in the house — it was only said for fun — and the same when I said I perhaps would not go to America at all — that was just for nonsense — just as I sometimes used to joke with you — and you with me . . . I am not afraid of your not loving me, I know you do, truly, and I ought to have thought that you would feel wounded by my speaking so much about leaving home etc. But, indeed, I did not mean to vex you — and now you will forgive me won't you? Oh, how I wish you were here, and we could talk it all over with our own lips.

This might be dismissed as a commonplace enough lovers' quarrel, but the distance between the lovers, both geographically and in terms of how long an exchange of letters took to cross the Atlantic both ways intensified the emotion on both sides of the ocean. In America, James was beginning to have misgivings about their suitability for each other. He seemed to be engaged to a woman who may not have wanted to emigrate and who perhaps had an eye for other men. In Scotland, Agnes felt frustrated that James did not understand her tone of voice, intentions, unswerving loyalty, and suffering in his absence. Having each made their complaints clear they had to agonise for a minimum of several weeks over whether they were right to raise the matter at all and whether or not their expression of it would be misinterpreted yet again. At times, their mutual misery was simultaneous.

All of this tempestuous doubt was made more complex by the feeling evoked in Agnes by James's reports about his health. This seemed strangely at odds with her insistence in several places elsewhere that he was a robust, manly, and energetic figure. The next part of this most revealing letter affects the reader like a rumble of distant thunder in *King Lear* or one of the premonitions in *Romeo and Juliet*. Do such things exist in real life and if so, are they merely a recognition of previously observed patterns or are they signs from a world beyond? Perhaps they are pure imaginings, yet they remain powerful markers both in literature and life.

James had raised the matter of his poor health again (it would prevent him taking up the offer of ministry that he had hoped for at Pittsford). He also, perhaps unwisely, wrote: "I had certainly looked forward to this summer as my wedding summer, but I can hardly think that it will be now".

Agnes's anguished reply was:

> You can guess how I feel this, when you had been making me again and again to prepare for this, and when I was counting the months till summer, when I hoped to see you again. I can bear a good deal and have borne a good deal of sorrow already since I knew you, in parting from you twice and in anxiety about your

health but I can imagine something happening to me that would just break my heart. Maybe I am wrong in feeling this way, but I can't help it.

It is all too obvious what Agnes envisaged, namely Jamie's death, even before they were united in marriage. Given that a mere six years later, almost to the day, she would lose James precisely as she feared, it seems not untoward to call this a premonition of just such a disaster.

She continued: "God is good and will not lay upon me more than I am able to bear". The words may, to a modern ear, sound like a platitude but this would be a complete misreading. To give that advice solemnly to another might sound complacent; to give the advice to *yourself* when it is made in the face of terrible adversity is a mark of strength.

There is so much to be gleaned from this laying bare of Agnes's heart. She was emphasising to James that she could not avoid, at his direction, preparing for life, as a couple, in America; she betrayed (in the near finality of "I hoped") that she now felt she might never see him alive again and that she was at the mercy of her feelings; she showed just how much emotional capital she had placed on a summer wedding; and she referred to their double leave-taking for a long absence, which in the context seems, as it does today with any loved one, like a little death suffered twice over already. Truly, this was a letter which exhibited as well as any, what we have lost in no longer writing them.

"Perhaps you were too hurried when you said you would come for me next summer" she continued. "Remember, if necessary, I would go to you, alone" she bravely added. Her underlining, as always, strained to convey her tone of voice and bring her that fraction nearer to him. The last page of the letter spoke of hymns she sang the previous Sunday and it seems almost predictable, almost the stuff of fiction, that it was "God moves in a mysterious way His wonders to perform" that stuck foremost in her mind and which reminded her more than most hymns of Jamie singing it with her. She would have cause to reflect on those words many times before much time elapsed. Nevertheless, for the present, she was to Jamie, "ever, ever yours".

Aggie (as she signs herself) wrote again on December 11th (expecting the letter to arrive about Christmas Day), still concerned about James's well-being and wondered why he wouldn't go into hospital. "I dare not look forward" she said until she had assurances that her fiancé was restored. When she picked up her sewing projects for America she had to throw them down again and started to cry. She found out in his response to her previous letter that he had to turn down the call to Pittsford because he was not well enough to accept it. Naturally her anxiety levels were further raised by this and confessed "anxiety and suspense is so hard to bear". On the lighter side there was a marvellously feisty passage in the letter about a couple whose husband expected his wife simply to stay in the house, act as housekeeper and look after his every need. Aggie made clear her feelings of dislike about him.

Three days before Christmas, Aggie wrote again to James a long and heart-warming love letter, some eight pages in length. James had not received an expected missive and Agnes reassured him that she replied without fail either the day of the letter being received or the next day. In hoping he had now received the letter she also hoped he had the mittens she knitted and sent to go over his gloves in the winter cold of New York. "Be sure to tell me that everything reaches you safely". The writing conveys a much more settled assurance than some earlier letters and Agnes felt confident in sharing her feelings without restraint:

> . . . you are always growing dearer to me. And this last letter to me is so kind and loving that if you were here beside me I'm afraid I would spoil you altogether. With love like that to support and cheer me how gladly and willingly would I go with you, my own dear laddie, anywhere . . . I hardly ever go down the street week day or Sunday without thinking how often your feet trod these stones on your way to see me. You were a good and attentive lover always — I don't think you ever once broke a promise or failed

to keep an appointment — And I'll have no lover coming to see me this winter, no kind Jamie to talk to and sing to and tease . . . I sometimes think it is worse for me than it is for you Jamie because everything about me reminds me of you — the armchair you were so fond of, the fans in the mantel you used to play with, even the very scratches on the marble chimney piece, where you used to put up your feet, — I often look at those scratches and would be willing to have it scratched far worse, to have you back again. And then when I go out there is the canal bank where we used to walk and The Links close at hand, and the very cars we rode in — but why need I go on — everything and everywhere makes me think of you, Jamie, and I am thinking of you always . . . But I hope we shall meet again, perhaps sooner than we think. If only it could be next week, or even next month — but God knows best — and I'm not the least afraid but all will be well with us yet.

Agnes then went on to ask for a portrait photograph of Jamie, and for it to be sent soon:

"I'm wearying to see how you are looking now, my own Jamie, — whether you are much changed or not — I'll perhaps get mine taken . . . I wish I was beautiful. But I'm not, only I know that I'm not ugly either. But I don't think we care for people for their looks, we soon get accustomed to that. It's themselves we like, the soul, the existence inside the body, don't you think so?

On this night week, Jamie, it will be exactly a year since we met at the Arnots' party. How I'll think of you that night, and on New Year's Day. I'm going to Lauder on Friday 26th, and I'm glad to be away from here at that time, for I would only make myself unhappy — thinking and brooding. I'll be glad when New Year's Day is over. I was so happy last N Y Day and now it is so different. But I'll be thinking of you and praying for you, my Jamie, and do you the same for me.

James had told Agnes about his visit to an orphanage where he had been asked to speak and Agnes, always imaginative, could see him there speaking to the children. "I'm so proud that you are a minister," she tells him, "It is the noblest calling on this earth".

Although pouring out her heart in this way Agnes was not blinkered by her passion to the events of the wider world. Indeed, in later life, the width of her reading and intellectual interests is astonishing. The next section of her letter refers to a headline event, a catastrophe at sea, to which she was given a particular insight and which she must have identified with as someone anticipating a sea voyage to America.

Today, when an airliner goes down, although we know it is one of the safest forms of travel, it gives pause for thought and can cause trepidation among those flying the same route soon afterwards. The *Ville du Havre* disaster, now forgotten, produced a *frisson* of fear among travellers due to follow her across the Atlantic. The only (unrealised) echo of the event today is in a hymn: its words beloved by generations of churchgoers. Mid-Atlantic, a week into its two-week crossing from New York to Le Havre, in water three miles deep, the ship sank. In early 1873 she had just been re-fitted and re-named, given an additional mast for more canvas and the paddle wheels replaced by screw propulsion. On 15th November she had sailed from New York with 313 passengers and crew on board. In the seemingly empty darkness, in mid-ocean, at two a.m. on Saturday 22nd November the liner collided with an iron clipper, the *Loch Earn*, when under both steam and sail. Two of *Ville du Havre's* masts collapsed destroying two of the lifeboats; the ship broke in half during the mere twelve minutes which it took her to sink and, in the darkness and confusion, few could emerge from their beds to reach the remaining boats among the wreckage. In the horror of that night 226 lives were lost. Among them were all four daughters of Horatio and Anna Spafford.

Spafford was a prominent American lawyer and Presbyterian church elder; James knew Spafford's wife and almost certainly therefore knew him. He was a well-known and prominent figure in Chicago in the 1860s and 1870s and when, in 1871, the great fire there reduced the city to ashes,

Spafford who had invested heavily in real estate, lost nearly everything. It would have been the talk of the town — certainly the Presbyterian community — and since, as we have seen, James was a student there from 1871 to 1872 he would know about these events taking place at the time. Spafford was also a close friend and supporter of Dwight L. Moody, the famous American evangelist. Moody lost his house to the fire of 1871 and after this took to full-time evangelism. He visited Britain the following year with the gospel singer Ira David Sankey and by November 1873 they were in Edinburgh. It was reckoned afterwards that in a city of 200,000 almost every home had been affected in some measure by the gospel and thousands were converted, "chiefly through the influence of Messrs Moody and Sankey".[14] On 14th December Agnes had told James: "Mr Moody and Sankey are still quite the rage in Edinburgh". She also said she knew "a certain lady" (Agnes perhaps, having used that impersonal formula before) who attended every one of their prayer meetings.

On Monday 22nd December Agnes wrote that she had been listening to Sankey in church one evening telling the story of the shipwreck, or at least the tragic loss of the four Spafford children. "I heard Mr Sankey say", she told James, "that he knew that very lady you say you knew who lost her 4 children". Their mother, Anna, had been picked up by a rescue vessel, unconscious, and when she docked in England cabled her husband (who, of course, knew of the disaster) the terrible words, "saved alone". Agnes, imaginative as she was, cannot have missed in the pathos of the story that she too, in the next few months, would spend two weeks crossing the Atlantic herself.

One extraordinary outcome of the wreck was that Horatio Spafford turned his suffering into the famous and moving hymn, "It Is Well With My Soul". The poignant first two verses of the four refer directly to his loss:

---

14   https://christianheritageedinburgh.org.uk/2016/08/23/the-peak-years-and-the-moody-revival-1865-1900/.

When peace, like a river, attendeth my way,
When sorrows, like sea billows, roll;
Whatever my lot, Thou hast taught me to say,
It is well, it is well with my soul.

Though Satan should buffet, though trials should come
Let this blest assurance control,
That Christ hath regarded my helpless estate
And hath shed His own blood for my soul.[15]

The whole event was an utter tragedy but in the midst of it was Horatio Spafford's extraordinary resilience and faith in the goodness of God, even in the teeth of suffering and disaster. Agnes herself, all too soon to be plunged into disaster and tragedy, perhaps drew later strength from that example which would have been unforgettably imprinted on her memory as someone about to make the same journey.

Before the end of the letter there was naturally the need to change the subject and Agnes described how happy her brother and sister-in-law were together, while she had to try to enjoy life "as well as I can" without her lover. She was going away at Christmas, perhaps to her brother, and, shortly, also to the Mitchells at Lauder (near the Lammermuir hills, south of Edinburgh) where "the change of air will do me good and help to make this long dreary winter pass a little quicker. We will likely go out to tea a good deal to the neighbouring farmhouses".

Agnes concluded that she was reading *The Family Treasury* and would send James more of Spurgeon's sermons. "And Mispah be our watchword now and

---

15   The Spaffords went on to have three more children and emigrated to Jerusalem where they engaged in philanthropy among the people of all three of the city's religions. Their adopted son discovered the Siloam Inscription verifying the Old Testament account of Hezekiah's water tunnel. Philip Bliss who wrote the tune to *It is Well* was a colleague of Moody and Sankey and was killed on another tragic journey while attempting to rescue his wife from a railroad disaster in Ohio when a trestle bridge collapsed.

ever". This is a significant word to use at this point. It is both lovers' code and a signpost to their feelings. Taken from the Old Testament[16] the word is Hebrew for "Lord, watch over me" and signifies an agreement between two people who have the Lord as their witness. More than that, it came to mean an emotional bond between two people geographically separated. It was a highly appropriate code word for our two lovers, fearful about their separation and wanting to strengthen their ties. When Agnes next wrote it was from the Free Church Manse in Lauder. It was the last day of the year and she seemed to have learned the lesson that to suggest to James that she was "flirting" was not a good strategy. Having told Jamie she did not expect him to be calling on young ladies and taking them for a walk, she told him that she had been for a long walk with Mr Mitchell, "a very nice fellow but awfully little and plain". "Perhaps we'll have happy days again yet" was her rather wistful hope.

MARRIAGE

There are no further extant letters from Agnes to James written from this side of the Atlantic, but we know that sometime in early 1874 James returned to Edinburgh to marry Agnes. She would want to be married at home in Edinburgh and it would not be within the bounds of propriety either to leave Agnes to take ship on her own or to accompany her on board while unmarried. The banns were announced through March and the marriage took place at St. Cuthbert's church on 8th April 1874. Dr Arnot officiated. The Certificate of Proclamation identifies James as "Minister in Philadelphia" and Agnes as "daughter of the late Thomas Legerwood Hately, Professor of Music". A week before the wedding the President of the Sacred Harmonic Society had written to her in terms very expressive of the formality of an earlier age and the society of that day:

---

16   Genesis 31:49.

Dear Miss Hately,

I must send a line in reply to your note received this morning to express my own and Mrs Mackenzie's most cordial congratulations on the prospective event which it announces. Most sincerely do we hope that it proves conducive to your future happiness both temporal and spiritual. You do not mention the name of your future husband and I only wish I had an opportunity of congratulating him on the wife he has chosen and telling him how happy I expect him to be. But my pleasure in your account is mingled with regret at the thought of your leaving this country for so distant a land and of our losing so valuable a member of our Sacred Harmonic Society . . .

. . . I remain, with our kindest regards, Dear Miss Hately,

Yours most sincerely,

John Mackenzie

Mackenzie also mentioned how "deeply indebted" he was to Agnes both for her sympathies with the aims of the society and efficient handling of many occasions. It was a letter from a genuine admirer who would feel his loss of her. Agnes, as we have seen, determined to keep all the notes from the son-in-law of Dr Chalmers, but only two have survived.

Curiously, John Mackenzie made no mention of attending the wedding and had clearly not been invited.

The silver tea service presented to Agnes as a wedding present from Free High church members

Three days earlier he had written asking Agnes to perform in a duet in "the latter end of May". Perhaps Agnes's celebration was not as large as she had hoped when she spoke of wanting one hundred and fifty presents. To this day, two gifts remain from that time: a fine quarto Bible given to Agnes by Walter and Jeannie and the beautifully crafted and engraved silver plate, five-piece tea service which she had hoped for from the Free High Church.[17] A month later they would be packing their bags ready for their journey to the New World — taking both those presents with them; both objects went to the frontier, the infamous one hundredth meridian in Western Kansas.

---

17 "Presented To Miss Agnes Hately By Friends in Free High Church Edin. April 1874".

CHAPTER FOUR

TOGETHER AT LAST: THE ATLANTIC CROSSING

ROMEO AND JULIET IS FULL of nautical images; it is one way that Shakespeare made his audience aware of the dangerous course his lovers were taking: it was as risky as a sea voyage. Juliet says her "bounty is as boundless as the sea / My love as deep"; Romeo allows "I am no pilot" but dares to "adventure for such merchandise" as Juliet, and in Act One of the tragedy had commended himself into the unknown with the words: "He that hath the steerage of my course / Direct my sail". No known diary or letters survive from the Wilsons' voyage to America but one of the magazines that James frequently sent Agnes was *Harper's Monthly*. If he had sent Agnes the back number for August 1870 her fears about the voyage might have been considerably increased: it detailed some of the hazards of making the crossing.[18]

In 1863 when James first adventured to Philadelphia the days of sail were already numbered. By sail the journey would take up to a month and the season was limited: only April to October was considered safe. The power of new steam technology, however, had been cutting journey times year on year so that by 1868 sail was finally eclipsed as an economic viability. As early as 1850, the new ship, the *City of Glasgow*, left Liverpool on December 17th with 400 passengers and arrived in Philadelphia only ten days later — an extraordinary feat for which a steerage passenger (berthed in a converted storage space without privacy or proper sanitation) would pay eight pounds eight shillings — two

18   *Harper's New Monthly Magazine*: August 1870, vol. XLI, no.242, pp. 185-198.

or three months wages for a labourer. The early days of these huge new liners were far from entirely safe however. In 1854 the same ship simply disappeared mid-Atlantic with the loss of all 430 passengers. Another went aground and broke up off Newfoundland though no lives were lost. On April 1, 1873, when Agnes was writing to James on his way to Europe, a White Star liner went down in mountainous seas twenty miles south of Halifax, Nova Scotia, with the loss of 585 lives. The ship had used more coal than expected in the appalling weather and was diverting to re-fuel, its 967 tons not proving enough for the boilers to complete the voyage. The winter of 1873 to 1874 was a particularly bad one and, on one late winter voyage, the *Ohio* — only just completed in 1873 — lost two lifeboats and a wheelhouse to the battering of the waves over her deck. Soon after, she suffered damage to her bow and a fire broke out on board.

All these losses and accidents were, naturally, the subject of newspaper reports and investigations which led to improved safety and more robust ships, and as with transport today innumerable safe journeys went unremarked. Cunard boasted not a single loss of life in thirty years of liner journeys. There were fifteen shipping lines across the North Atlantic and ships left ports almost every day of the week but, by 1874, only The American Line sailed direct to Philadelphia from Liverpool. They ran one ship a week, on a Wednesday.[19] If Agnes and James had wanted to go to New York, as many did en route for Philadelphia, they could have sailed from Glasgow. But James knew Philadelphia and it was a city full of immigrants. Out of some three-quarter million inhabitants, a quarter were foreign-born and of those 100,000 were Irish.[20] By 1873 it also had the largest and newest ships operating out of its port which revived its place as a leading transport hub. The city's first steamship line was owned by William Inman (and Partners), a Liverpool Quaker, but the company ceased trading out of Philadelphia in 1857,

---

19 For further details of shipping schedules and routes see *The Picturesque Tourist: A Handy Guide around the World* (Adams and Co., 1877).
20 http://www2.hsp.org/exhibits/Balch%20resources/phila_ellis_island.html.

preferring the deep-water harbour of New York on a river that did not suffer from the five feet high ridges of ice that blocked the Delaware — the approach to Philadelphia — in some winters.

SS *Ohio*, along with her three sister ships belonging to the American Steamship Company — in all likelihood one of which the Wilsons travelled on — was the largest iron ship ever built in the USA. Single-funnelled and double-masted, her compound engine which delivered two thousand horsepower to a single propeller allowed her to average eleven knots despite her weight of over three thousand tons — heavier by a thousand tons than any previous ship built in America. She could carry up to a thousand passengers who through the 1870s enjoyed increasingly comfortable accommodation. Those in steerage class, the lowest, now had cabins which housed two married couples or four singles in a space six feet by six. Many cabins had bells to call for service; there were separate chairs at the dining tables, cabins for ladies, and the mid-ship saloon (which included a piano), and state-rooms were upgraded. The voyage from Liverpool might have taken twelve days. The journey to Philadelphia was two hundred miles further than New York and included the long curve around Cape May, (the promontory protecting Delaware Bay) and the slow progress up the winding Delaware to the city over one hundred miles from the ocean. Since James and Agnes arrived on Monday 25th May, they very probably left Liverpool on Wednesday May 13, 1874.

Embarkation was generally a solemn business for emigrants, but it would be mingled with excitement for this newly married couple and must have been unique in their experience. They were finally together; they were at last alone and anonymous among the crowd; they were embarking not only on board ship but on an adventure into the unknown. For Agnes nothing would be familiar: the epic journey; marriage to a man she desired above all else but whom she had known, save by correspondence, only briefly; a new role as minister's wife; life on a continent in many ways still untamed; the uncertainty of when and how James would find employment; the absence of her family on whom she doted and relied.

As James and Agnes approached the vessel alongside the quay, the enormity of its structure would have forced itself upon them. No ship this size had been seen at Leith or anywhere else Agnes had been. Three hundred and fifty feet long, its iron clad hull towered above the waterline and its single stack oozed dark smoke as the coal furnaces built up a head of steam in the giant boilers. The bustle of travellers anxious to get aboard — emigrants, tourists, and those on business — was mingled with the shouts of rough-looking stevedores loading cargo as a dozen heavy trunks were raised effortlessly by machinery into the air in a slip-noose net, swung across the deck and swiftly deposited in a baggage hold. As they walked the footway on to the ship, they might observe the massive size of the blocks and tackles attached to the rigging, the unusual height of the bulwarks and the strength of the guards around companionways, as well as the frequency of the bulkheads. Each spoke ominously of the forces these structures were designed to oppose. To those unfamiliar with such sights, their scale was inhumanly large.

Once inside, as with all travellers on a long sea voyage at that date there would be the need to direct which of their cases they needed in their cabin, a desire to grasp the layout of the ship's facilities and the discovery of how to reserve your place at a table by pinning your card to a selected chair. James had made at least four crossings already, but these new ships were a far cry from the one he had first boarded eleven years earlier when merely seventeen. We can imagine his delight in showing Agnes the things he was familiar with and in discovering the developments in comfort and convenience that were still new to him.

At some point the great bell of the ship sounded above the noise of the throng on deck and the steward's call "all ashore" would set relatives and remaining friends scuttling, perhaps tearfully, for the footway back to the pier. Already the screw would be starting to boil the water at the stern of the ship, and any remaining physical contact with shore removed, almost imperceptibly the journey began. The line of waving handkerchiefs leaning over the rail on the promenade deck slipped silently away from those left behind and those who needed to shorten the pain of parting turned away, aware of their own vulnerability and even more so, that of those on board.

A journey of twelve days across the vast emptiness of the Atlantic, without any of the navigational or rescue resources that we take for granted might well induce a sense of humility before the forces of nature. Despite the overall safety statistics, the high profile given in the press to disasters at sea could create an underlying vague fear that would surface especially at night. The *Harper's Monthly* article "The Ocean Steamer" of 1870 was graphic:

> Sometimes . . . at midnight the scream of the steam-whistle on deck is heard by the sleepless passenger in her berth, indicating that the fog and darkness without are so dense that the only safeguard from collision with other ships, or with fishermen on the Banks, is in sounding that alarm, and then listening for the response to warn them away . . . Against the still more imminent peril of an encounter with an iceberg there is no protection whatever.

> While yet all the time the steamer is driving on through fogs and mists and flying scuds of rain, and over foaming and surging seas, without the slightest abatement of its usual speed, the danger reaches the highest possible state of concentration; and it is not surprising that the sensitive and the timid are sometimes entirely overpowered by it.

> The truth is that . . . there is probably no other great thoroughfare of commerce or of human intercommunication on the globe so beset with danger and difficulties as the voyage from New York to Liverpool.[21]

---

21   http://www.gjenvick.com/SteamshipArticles/TransatlanticShipsAndVoyages/1870-08-TheOceanSteamer-HarpersMagazine.html#axzz4bflmbhID.

The reference to icebergs was prescient given what happened to *Titanic* forty-two years later. The standard shipping route was to work down the coast of Newfoundland so the article explained that the "fifty miles wide" warm Gulf Stream from the south meets the cold counter-current from Baffin's Bay out there beyond the Banks and created "a perpetual succession of fogs and mists . . . gales and squalls" and that icebergs and ice-floes were a constant danger, the worst time being the early months of summer — precisely when James and Agnes were travelling.

The use of a mere steam-whistle against such impercipient forces rams home the vulnerability of the ships and draws attention to the skill of the captains and crews using only a thermometer to gauge the likelihood of icebergs in the water, a barometer to presage any coming storm, the sextant, and chronometer to calculate the ship's exact position — when for day after day the only horizon was the restless sea.

It must have been with relief as well as growing excitement that, as dawn broke on Monday 25th May, Agnes leaning over the rail of the promenade deck before breakfast noticed the diminishing distance between her and the banks of the now narrowing reaches of the mighty Delaware River.

They docked in Philadelphia around about eleven a.m.

On that bright May morning, the wharves were full of the energy and business of a newly revived industry in a new and invigorating world. In 1873 two steamship companies, The American Line and The Red Star Line had invested heavily in the complex of new buildings around the railroad-owned pier at the foot of Washington Avenue where immigrants were processed in the southern part of the city. The *Ohio* was the first ship to be in regular service from that new immigrant station to and from Liverpool. From 1867 to 1873 the number of immigrants had been, on average, 1,013 per year. For the period 1874 to 1879 the average figure shot up to 7,051.[22] Trade for the railroad, for the port and for the city was starting to boom. Warehouses, sugar

---

22   http://www2.hsp.org/exhibits/Balch%20resources/phila_ellis_island.html.

refineries, factories, grain elevators, and freight depots all combined to make this a place of intense and purposeful activity. As adventurers from Europe were shipped in looking for new lives, out went food and materials brought up from the farms and factories, marshalled and shipped to Europe from the vast yards of the Pennsylvania Railroad Company.

Medical examinations were required of all incoming passengers, but these had already been dealt with eight miles downstream at the Lazaretto, so James and Agnes had, at this point, first to pass through customs inspections before moving downstairs in the new two-storey building towards the railroad ticket office and reception areas. Unlike most, they had no need to board a train. Dr Patterson, a distant relative and widower friend from James's days as a theological student, was there to meet them.

CHAPTER FIVE

PENNSYLVANIA: A NEW WORLD

IN THE 1870S, PRIOR TO all modern communications, it would have been hard for Agnes to prepare herself for the shock of the new, four thousand miles from home, though James must have, beforehand, shared with her what he could. As Agnes was whisked away into the bustling city, leaving James to get their "dreadful array of boxes" through customs and off the wharf, she was in some confusion. Two days later she wrote to her aunt: "You may fancy how strange and confused I felt as we went along in the street cars . . . looking at the strange foreign-looking city with its red brick pavements . . . and great wagons drawn by strings of mules, driven by negro drivers". On entering Dr Patterson's house in Frankford Avenue she was delighted to find a grand piano but rather shocked that the housekeeper sat with them at meals. Thus, begins a revealing theme throughout Agnes's American letters: social class and accepted proprieties. As a Scottish girl of good family, she had obviously made certain assumptions that what *she* was used to was what ought to happen. Where local practice fitted with her preconceptions, she approved it, and when it differed, she made the point unhesitatingly and to some effect.

Meal times were a revelation in another respect to Agnes and she knew they would be to those at home. Amongst other things she conveys not only the quality of the food but its quantity — oyster soup might not be a novelty (oysters were standard on many Edinburgh menus of the day) but strawberries in such profusion, along with peaches, pineapples, and other fruit were a luxury. "I sometimes feel as if I were living in an American story book", she exclaimed. Perhaps she had picked up a copy of *Little Women* (1868-1869) or been reading the short stories of Nathaniel Hawthorne, or even *Uncle Tom's Cabin* — the most popular book in nineteenth century America after the Bible.

Philadelphia was long known as the "immigrant" city. The second largest city on the East Coast, it now sprawls northwards between the Delaware and Schuylkill rivers extending from the ancient cobbled and red brick lanes set at right angles to Penn's Landing on the river up into the leafy domains of Chestnut Hill where, if you can peer through the wrought iron security gates, or catch a glimpse of the grandeur of the nineteenth century mansions behind them, you may see four or more gardeners manicuring the lawns of a single property. Between the two geographical extremes, Germantown Avenue today stretches through mile after mile of decay and dereliction. For much of its length litter is swirled by the prevailing wind into every corner; broken fences, collapsed verandas, and peeling paint tell a story of gradual decline. For Philadelphia now is not the city it was when James and Agnes first saw it together. Even then its population approached the one million mark for it was not only the arrival point for most immigrants, but an industrial, commercial, and cultural centre. This 'City of Brotherly Love' had been aptly named 'the workshop of the world.' In the production of cast iron, in engineering and shipbuilding the one-time largest, and capital, city was pre-eminent; it was Philadelphia money which built the national railroad network. In banking, publishing, and bookselling it also held first place for a time as well as in lighter industries such as cabinetmaking.

But these causes of industrial and commercial prosperity were also, sadly, the causes of its decline. As more suitable or economic sites were found for its industries the buildings in which they had flourished became derelict lots; the houses built for owners and workers alike losing value or being abandoned. Immigrant communities, divided by language and culture had tended to cluster together as the city's neighbourhood names indicate; these too easily became ghettoes, each preferring their own way of life above the desire to integrate with others.

As a cultural centre the city had a deserved claim to fame, and in this area, it has suffered less harshly. Pennsylvania Academy of the Fine Arts, founded in 1805, is America's oldest art museum. The Academy of Music (the country's oldest grand opera house still in use) dates from 1857 and hosted the finest performances and boasted the best acoustic. The Philadelphia Museum of Art, built two years after the Wilsons arrived, its classical West Entrance overlooking the Schuylkill, comprised two hundred galleries and, when seen from the river, could hardly be more imposing. If Edinburgh was the Athens of the North, then surely Philadelphia was the Athens of the West.

To Agnes every detail was of interest and worthy of report. To see Fairmount Park they hired a "covered waggonette with a black driver"; she loved what she perceived as the wildness of the park with the great river running through it. Later, she added, "Oh, that I could tell you of the beauty . . . the velvet turf, the great maples and chestnuts, the stately houses. Verandas draped with vines, and over all blazing sunshine and sapphire sky". On another occasion they went for a "delightful drive" going out by Germantown before returning through the Park. They had secured the loan of "a very spicy little turnout drawn by a pretty white mare".

Within the Park, and generally, Agnes noticed, obviously with some disapproval, "so many fast looking men and women". She was more comfortable in the Academy of Music which she declared to be the finest building she had ever seen. She was impressed not just by the auditorium (she thought it seated 5,000 but its capacity today is half that) with its ornate and steeply tiered balconies, Corinthian columns, and chandelier weighing five thousand pounds but by the nature of the speeches and quality of the hymn singing.

During the three summer months that the couple spent in the city, when because of the heat "many people give up their houses here", James was constantly looking for employment. Churches were growing at, or beyond, the rate of immigration. There was a need for ministers in a number of places but the process of appointment, as today, was slow. Sermons needed to be preached to allow congregations to make an informed decision — usually on more than one occasion. Several candidates had to be heard and presbyteries needed to give their approval; where there was not unanimity there had to be debate and time for reflection. A wrong appointment could be difficult to undo and cause long-lasting division and heartache. Moreover, as Agnes wrote to Aunt Jane: "All the folk here tell him not to be in a hurry but wait for a good church". James was in receipt of letters asking him to preach in a number of places including Pittsford, Summit Hill, and Mt. Holly. He was usually away all Sunday and part of Monday, but Agnes was enjoying herself. "I am well and happy, happier than I ever was in my life, everybody is kind to me, and it makes me glad to see how much James is liked here, and how many friends he has" she wrote. They were lucky to be able to stay with Dr Patterson so that Agnes did not have to "begin housekeeping in the heat" (it was eighty degrees in the shade as she wrote). Although money must have been short the Wilsons were, as a result, in an enviable situation given that the financial 'panic' of 1873, caused partly by post-civil war inflation and property losses in the Chicago fire, had placed many in economic jeopardy. Moreover, James would characteristically get ten dollars for every sermon he preached and "James can easily get preaching every Sabbath". Given the two dollars a day that many earned, this was a handsome sum. Not quite everything was idyllic, however, since Agnes confided to her aunt that they had expected to be at Pittsford soon after arrival — it was "the very reason we packed up so soon and hurried off". As it turned out, an acquaintance had misled James and had been "playing him false for some time" — the post was not, after all, available.

As might be expected from what we know of Agnes this delay was put to good use. A month after arriving and still having heard nothing from Scotland she wrote a third long letter — to her sister Mary. Despite the heat (it had now reached ninety-eight degrees in the shade), she told her "I feel so much at home

Agnes's older sister Mary, the main recipient of her letters

here". She was asked to contribute to James's completion of a section of a Centennial book on the lives of ministers from Philadelphia which contained a portrait of his friend Dr Johnston, and while James wrote sermons she sewed constantly, preparing clothes and household items for their first home together. One very hot day they took a picnic and enjoyed a day out by the river at Gloster to the south of the city. Agnes rather delighted in telling her older sister that she threw all restraint to the winds and wore no stays, or flan-nel petticoats, or even a slip but only one white *cotton* petticoat with a pretty linen costume and thread gloves. It must still have felt oppressively hot in such garb and they had need of the fans that all fashionable ladies carried in the heat. They crossed the Schuylkill River and explored the woods, enjoying the relief of the shade. "What a day that was!" she exclaimed.

Mrs Wilson liked to assess people — their appearance and character — in the light of her own fixed principles. She was aware that in cosmopolitan Philadelphia she had to remain fashionably dressed as best she could for "the ladies here look just as if they had stepped out of a fashion book". She noticed of other women "that their whole appearance is French — quite unknown in Edinburgh: dark hair and eyes and hair all frizzled out on the forehead, costly dresses and hats". It is difficult to avoid the sense that this is a showi-ness that Agnes both disapproved and yet rather envied; that her strait-laced upbringing and natural desire for self-expression were in conflict — albeit without her fully realising it. She was not above listening to some gossip for she goes on to say that the word on the street is that such women are "lazy, luxuriant, careless of home . . . very delicate and useless". Within a page, however, we hear that "shop girls, mill girls, servants are all alike stylish and gay" in the city and, I suspect, this happy egalitarianism and lack of deference had rather taken Agnes aback. She certainly did not approve the fact that apparently, "American women will not take exercise, so get weak and puny". Repeated reading of the letters at this point does become quite comical as we see the moral rectitude of a well-born Scottish lady of slender means being confronted with the carefree untrammelled attitudes of women (perhaps not unimportantly) ten years younger but seemingly well-heeled. Indeed, she proudly tells Mary, she was "determined to keep up my good Scotch habits". She was brushing up her German again by doing language exercises in the evening and "at meal times speak it all the time". Having firmly taken the moral high ground she felt strong enough to tackle her next target: Mary herself. It is unacceptable to her that there has been no word from home: "It is unkind and certainly not what I expected". It is hard to know how such a rebuke would be received. Was this what her siblings had grown used to and merely provoke laughter, or would it have been an affront? She signed off "I am ever your loving sister" — of which there was no doubt, but the signature is "Agnes L. Kinnier Wilson" which gives a considerable and perhaps rather cold formality to the end of the letter.

As the sticky months of July and August passed there must have been a degree of urgency about finding a living. It was with relief as much as pride therefore that Agnes could write in early September to Jane Crawford Brook that James had received three 'calls' from different churches: Pittsford, the romantically named Beaver Meadow, (where he had previously preached) "away up in the Blue Ridge Mountains" area, five or six hours away, "a wild mining community", and Cedarville in Cumberland County, South-West New Jersey. The first and last of these had been unanimous calls. Cedarville was three hours travel by railroad. For James's second visit there, the church requested Agnes to accompany him — in a small community, the minister's wife might be critical to the appointment's success.

> "So, on Saturday last", Agnes told her aunt Jane, "we first crossed the river to Camden, right opposite, and then took the cars to Bridgeton, where we had to change for Cedarville . . . At Cedarville an old gentleman came in, a member of Cedarville Ch., recognised James and was introduced to me. He sat down beside me and almost his first words to me were 'Do try to like Cedarville and get your husband to come.' He then told me how much they had been delighted with James the previous Sunday, that the leaving of their late pastor had caused some disturbances that they had feared would not be easily healed, but after that once hearing of James, they unanimously wished him to come. He said they all felt as if Providence had sent him — and much more of the same kind".

On arrival at Cedarville they were met by 'Squire' Whittaker in his horse-drawn carriage. They were to stay with his family until the manse was ready for them. The following day James preached in the church twice. "I have never heard him do better", Agnes announced. She had sung in the choir in the morning which would have pleased her greatly — and doubtless the congregation. To hear a professionally trained voice in Cedarville must have been a rare thing. On the Monday there was meeting of 'session' in which James was asked in writing to accept the post at a salary of $1,100 per annum — a considerable income for a pastor at the time, taking into account the low cost of living in rural America and the fact that they had the manse with a large productive garden attached. He accepted and they returned to Frankford Avenue that evening. Agnes reckoned that the salary was equivalent to £230 in gold.

The whole trip was clearly an enormous success and the young couple were much excited by their welcome and the prospect of the work there. They had seen everything they wanted to see in Philadelphia including the table in Independence Hall where the famous Declaration was signed in 1776 — in order to state, initially, that the thirteen American colonies were in fact sovereign states, independent of Britain. Today it is a World Heritage Site patrolled by Park Rangers, and crowds queue to see the inkstand used in the signing and the chair that Washington sat in as presiding officer. Perhaps one main difference now is the security checks that are required as you enter the building and, of course, the smart phones everywhere. In the year that the Wilsons paid their visit people would, even then, have come from most corners of the world. Two years later, the year of the Centennial Exhibition, the queues would have been as long as they are today.

CHAPTER SIX

NEW JERSEY

THE MOVE TO CEDARVILLE WAS made on Saturday 19th September. The day would have been warm for the prevailing wind was south-westerly and there are no frosts in the south until November. Cumberland County, bordering, as it does, Delaware Bay, does not suffer the greater variations of the Philadelphia climate and the state as a whole is more temperate than the same latitudes further west.

It was a journey full of history as much as it was of the future and anticipation. To leave the city and enter New Jersey, they had to cross the Delaware to Camden, a little upstream from where William Penn had first landed in 1682 to found the Province of Pennsylvania. As they took 'the cars' south on the West Jersey Railroad they would pass through Woodbury and Glasboro as far as Bridgeton, steaming through the counties of Gloucester and Salem and so into Cumberland. The 1869 map of the railroad shows it ending at Bridgeton, so the line on to Cedarville, Maurice River and the coast must have been new. Their new home lay just four miles short of the marshy mudflat shores of Delaware Bay.

New Jersey is just a little larger than Wales. In the southern half, the state is astonishingly flat. Seen from the air, when the atmosphere is less than perfectly clear, it is hard to tell where the land ends and ocean begins. The Coastal Plain extends over slightly more than half the state and only a quarter of this plain reaches one hundred feet above sea level. In the east, miles of tidal marshes lie between the long sandy beaches of the Atlantic Coast and the hinterland. In addition to the marshes, the eastward-flowing rivers of the Coastal Plain are fringed with large areas of swamp, often among forests.

On the western and southern borders, the Delaware provides a natural frontier, just as the lower waters of the Hudson form a north-eastern boundary. Other rivers in the State have quaint or exotic names, the sounds of which evoke a sense of strange indigenous peoples: Pequanac, Wanaque, Whippany, Ramapo, but the rivers of the south are mostly unimportant except perhaps the marvellously named Great Egg Harbour river, thirty-eight miles long and so called because of the size of the eggs found on its banks by the first European explorers. At May's Landing, what is known as a sizeable landmark to locals is the inn at Sugar Hill which stands all of twenty-nine feet above sea level: an unmissable vantage point.

This low-lying landscape was something of a meeting ground for many species, both flora and fauna, whose principal habitat was further north or south. Before the relentless European invasion, the entire state was a mass of dense forest but by 1,870 these areas were reduced by industry and agriculture to a mere 3,000 to 4,000 square miles. The greatest forest area was known as 'The Pines', a level area with a mixture of loamy, alluvial, and sandy soils which in its southern part contained over a million acres of woodland. Today it is federally protected. To drive now through these parts of New Jersey it is still easy to feel their draw. The seemingly endless belts of deciduous forest lining the road with strong sunlight filtering on to the forest floor through branches — still mostly bare in spring — makes the imagination hanker after the days when animals abounded here and were the target for the bows of the Leni-Lenape Indians;[23] or when, for the first time one of those hunter-gatherers glimpsed a pale face in a clearing with no idea of what that sighting

23   Also known as the Delawares, this was the European name imposed on them in recognition of the first Governor of the Province of Virginia. Interestingly, they were a matriarchal society: women managed the land, ruled the elders. Status was inherited through the mother's clan. They were also among the least violent of the East Coast tribes.

heralded. Red deer, black bears[24], grey fox, chipmunk, squirrel, raccoon, opossum, duck, quail, and woodcock were all to be stalked among the white cedar, pitch pine, yellow poplar, and a variety of oaks. Still today, mile after mile of closely packed mature seedlings, all struggling for light and air, keep their distance from the occasional forest giant which has survived the ravages of sawmill and charcoal burner. Among the trees, winter or summer, to get lost would be simple; even easier to stand invisibly, still and silent as one of the grey marsh herons in a patch of shadow. In the early days, both hunter and the hunted needed senses fine-honed and native-born to see a mortal enemy in time to avoid the soundless arrow or the crack of a musket.

Through these woods James and Agnes travelled to their new home. As they passed through the forest and its industries, and their train whistled and hooted past small farms on that September day, they could not have known that they were witnessing the felling of the very last of the primeval white cedar forest, the fine wood that gave its name to their destination and of which their manse, along with every other modest house in the area, was built. For Europeans, whose recorded history is so much longer than that of New Jersey, it is easy to forget that there had been two hundred years of development on this East Coast before 1870. As early as 1660 the site of Jersey City had come under English governance and by 1678 the first English sailors had made their way up the wintry Delaware and clambered ashore over the ice that blocked their progress upstream. The original inhabitants, the Navesink Lenape Indians had all but gone by 1715, though a few were still hunting and trapping in Monmouth County. The Wilsons would long have known that the revivalist preacher, George Whitefield, had ministered at the Presbyterian church in Newark in 1740 where "the Word fell like a hammer and like fire!" and that twenty years later the Presbyterian John Brainerd had ministered

---

24 Rather astonishingly, at least to the British, black bears may still be hunted with bows, and by children, in New Jersey. They have been seen in all twenty-one counties of the state.

to the Lenape at the Brotherton Reservation.[25] James would almost certainly have studied Jonathan Edwards's famous biography of John's brother David which has never been out of print since its first publication in 1749. The book much influenced John Wesley. James would also know that it was the Presbyterians who sought to reform the state's view of slavery. In 1787 the Presbyterian Synod of New Jersey called for measures to be taken to secure its abolition and the following year Governor Livingston urged the legislature for the same — a request which they chose to decline. In one county (Bergen) after all, slaves accounted for twenty per cent of the population. The Quakers had been the first to express profound opposition to slavery but by 1795 the Jersey legislature was still rejecting any sort of reform. It was only in 1804 that an "Act for the Gradual Abolition of Slavery" allowed the future children of slaves to be freed at age twenty-five (twenty-one for women). In the end, New Jersey was the last northern state to end the practice in 1846.

If life was unspeakable in earlier days for many slaves, it was seldom easy for those who, albeit not enslaved to their work, were bound to it without respite from dawn till dusk. In Cedarville, James and Agnes were to find a rural society where there were very few who lived in the grandeur of the mansions they had seen in Fairmount Park or Chestnut Hill, and where for many, life was gruelling: if it was daytime, it was work-time. New Jersey lent itself not just to agriculture but to industry. Employment in either one required long hours of intensely physical labour. The seemingly endless supply of wood meant that sawmills sprang up quickly; the lumber went to the making of warm durable houses, especially when cedar was used which is naturally resistant to rot and insect attack. But harnessing the water power in the forests allowed such effective industry that even by 1749 Benjamin Franklin was deploring "the wanton slaughter of the woods".

---

25   Weakened by European disease (smallpox, cholera), the few remaining Lenape in the state were removed by government order in the 1860s to Oklahoma ('The Indian Territory'), a place utterly alien to them in nature and landscape.

Another cause of the forests' decimation was the mining of bog iron ('black gold') which was found in river beds among the marl or greensand. When naturally deposited along river banks it oxidises with mud and hardens into ore. From the mines in the swamps it was taken to the smelting furnaces; each furnace required thirty square miles of timber to be clear-cut on a cycle of twenty years. Much of the iron ended up at Paterson, where by 1850, the locomotive factory was turning out one hundred engines a year. The demands of the railroads for iron were insatiable and it was the forests that suffered as well as the ever-retreating Native Americans.

The forests also lost their great trees to shipbuilding, as well as the lesser trees to the charcoal business. Oak, pine and cedar were all cut for transportation to shipyards on the estuaries of coastal streams. Less mature trees were used for shingles for roofs and staves for whiskey barrels or cranberries. The creation of charcoal was crucial to the glassmaking industry (which used the ubiquitous sand) and for the iron furnaces. Colliers would stay with their pits in the forest night and day, sleeping alongside the smoking fires to ensure that exactly the right temperature was maintained.

Alongside this labour-intensive industry was agriculture. Wherever trees could be removed and the soil tilled, a small farm would spring up. As early as 1806, one tree nursery catalogue listed sixty-seven different varieties of peach. A visitor today to 'The Garden State' might be perplexed by the very evident lack of gardens, but the title is, of course, a reference to the number and productivity of *market* gardens and nurseries. Not only fruit trees and vegetables grow in abundance but also cranberries, blueberries and grapes. By 1835 the first commercial cranberry bog was established in Burlington County. Cranberries are native to the Pine Barrens area and children as young as three years old would miss weeks of school in September and October as they picked berries or grapes throughout the day. While the harvests lasted entire families would live in a shack next to the harvest fields. Even the very mosses of the forest floor and the pine cones that lay on it were collected as means of eking out subsistence incomes. The capillaries of the sphagnum moss absorb up to five times its weight, so it was used, among other things, for nappies; the cones were sold to florists in Philadelphia or New York.

Cumberland County in the south-west had a fertile loamy soil, partly alluvial, and capable of sustaining a wide variety of crops — as James and Agnes were to discover in their own garden plot. But even in such a productive area, with profit margins so small, rural communities would always be vulnerable to economic depression, and so it was to prove. The little town of Cedarville would not be exempt.

CHAPTER SEVEN

CEDARVILLE: SETTLING IN TO RURAL LIFE

AS IS OFTEN THE CASE the world over, the country folk welcomed the strangers with full hearts and generous gifts. They had, after all, voted unanimously (it seemed) for James to fill the post and although it was subject to renewal after a year there was no hesitation or doubt in their response to the couple when they arrived that September Saturday.

The Wilsons would have been an attractive pair with a refreshing energetic youthfulness which the church needed. Though coming from a farming family which had no special pretension to scholarship, James was highly educated (at least theologically), widely travelled and had a good business sense. He was thoughtful, compassionate, and quite without self-importance. He was physically strong but vulnerable to illness which made him more aware of the frailties of others. He was energetic and committed. Having made his way in business as a very young man, by his thirtieth year he had a resourcefulness and fund of ideas for the furtherance of any enterprise he undertook. He was not new to America and his Irish accent could not have been novel to those who could travel to Philadelphia and back within the day. He had, anyway, first arrived on the continent twelve years before so it would not be surprising if in that time he had picked up many East Coast expressions and even their intonation.

Agnes was a very different character in many ways. A single woman until she was nearly thirty, daughter of a distinguished public figure in a capital city, she was also highly intelligent and musically very gifted. She was confident of her good standing in Edinburgh society and had the further self-assurance that an ear for languages can bestow. Now she was married to the man of her choice after a prolonged, sometimes anguished, engagement. At last, therefore, in Cedarville she would be able to organise her household affairs as she wished. Moreover, the move from a cosmopolitan city to a small rural town must have led her to feel that she could exercise her gifts with an even greater confidence than before. She was interested in people and liked to know about their background and hear their views — and pronounce upon them if she felt so inclined. Unswerving in her Presbyterian faith, and equally definite in her views about other things, she was dedicated to helping make James's ministry a success.

Today, Cedarville, its population a mere 776, lies in an area of productive farmland, copses, and scattered woodland, lakes and streams. Its wide streets are quiet and largely free of traffic. The pace of life is slow and people have time to talk to strangers and new arrivals. It was not so different when the Wilsons arrived.

Agnes first describes Cedarville to her Aunt Jane as:

> About four miles from the Delaware Bay — where there is splendid bathing. It has about two thousand inhabitants, mostly farmers or in the oyster trade — which is a great business down there. The whole surrounding country is rather flat and undulating, with splendid woods and trees. The soil is very sandy, that is the only objection I have to the place but that is nothing. Cedarville is much like Haddonfield[26] ... but is not quite as pretty ... the people are all Americans and came there from New England. There are two Pres. Churches, of which ours is the First, a Methodist and a Baptist church. "Our" church is a red brick building surrounded by trees, seated for 3 or 4 hundred with 4 rows of pews just like the

---

26 This was an early Quaker settlement to which the extraordinary and pioneering woman, Elizabeth Haddon, sailed alone in 1701. She proposed there to a Quaker minister, wielded great influence and named the town after her father. Today it still has many historic houses.

Free High, carpeted all over with crimson with a platform … and a white desk for the minister, a gallery at one end where the organ and choir are. Squire Whittaker leads the choir which is small but good and his daughter, Miss Minnie, plays the organ. Below the church is a very large and commodious lecture hall where prayer meetings and Sabbath School is held, there is also a small organ here. I had a class of nine girls last Sunday, all as big as myself nearly — their teacher, Mrs Robert Bateman, wife of a doctor in the place, and daughter in law of the old Dr we met in the train, died a fortnight ago and I am just going to keep the class. The membership is just over 200. I was introduced to a great number last Sunday, gentlemen and ladies who might have graced Free St. George's in Edin. as far as appearance goes. Well dressed, polite, refined looking people they are one and all.

Part of letter from Agnes detailing Christian work at Cedarville

Was Agnes pandering here to Aunt Jane's prejudices in these final comments, or dispelling her preconceptions, or indulging her own feelings that she preferred to think of herself living with those of a certain class? A further possibility is that she might merely be making an objective comment which simply remarks the appearance of those she met.

The greatest excitement which the new arrival shows is reserved for her description of the parsonage. Agnes had waited a long time to be mistress of her own household, and for someone as dominant and determined as she would increasingly prove to be, the prospect of a home for James and herself alone was a dream come true.

She continues:

> Then there is a parsonage, such a lovely one!!! As soon as James de-
> cided to go we got the keys, and drove over with the Whittakers to
> inspect it. It is about ten minutes' walk from the church, a frame
> house, like all the others, painted white two storied, with a nice
> shady porch in front, all of wood, and green Venetian shutters
> to all the windows. There [are] 8 or 9 rooms in it, but in a future
> letter I'll describe it all to you, when it is in order. They are going
> to paint and paper all the principal rooms for us — we will only
> furnish 4 just now.

The excitement is palpable here and with good reason. The uncertain en-gagement, the fear of the Atlantic, the anxiety about finding work through-out the summer were all now in the past and a brave new world was opening up. Agnes goes on to describe the garden:

> In the front garden there are maple trees and a great cedar and rose-
> bushes, one of them with white roses, two of which I plucked and
> now send to you. Behind, and to one side of the house there is quite
> a large garden with apple and pear trees, the pears lying about, sweet
> and luscious; 16 or 18 peach trees!! And a walk covered partly with
> vines now purple with grapes! We ate the grapes and peaches and
> pears as we walked about . . . Mrs Whittaker is going to preserve the
> grapes for me as they are quite ripe and would just waste.

Both the Wilsons came from backgrounds where any sort of waste would be seriously frowned upon and where husbandry was second nature. The fact therefore that the garden had such potential beyond its current yield allowed

James to surmise that they would not need to spend more than $500 of their annual salary and so "lay by more than half" their earnings. Moreover, Mr Whittaker, who had a furniture store as well as a farm, would give them all they needed at cost price. "We will furnish very simply and neatly" Agnes emphasised to her aunt. It is clearly important that everyone at home knows that frugality will be the keynote, despite being well catered for in so many respects.

But Agnes loved to describe people — in an age when photographs were only for exceptional occasions. It transpires that Dr Patterson, their host in Philadelphia, was to be married again and the bride was of interest:

> Miss Fulton . . . a very charming young lady, full of spirits and vivacity . . . exceedingly well read and a brilliant talker. She is very fair and has the finest hair I ever saw, golden, hanging far below her waist and as thick as a mane, but her features are almost plain. We must go, of course, to the marriage . . . I like Miss Fulton very much and she and I became good friends at once. She is frank and good-hearted and I am sure will do the Dr good, in every way. But her exceeding vivacity becomes almost oppressive, and her continual talking makes one feel more and more quiet and silent — it is too much. James says she'd talk him into dumbness if she were his wife. The marriage is to be in the evening (the fashionable hour here) in her father's church.

Agnes, too, had luxuriant hair and considered herself rather plain but knew that she was considered vivacious and talkative. It would seem that she felt upstaged by this new arrival (perhaps a caricature of herself) in the home of her first friend in America. It was less likely that she realised that her tone had distinct echoes of the mild satire Jane Austen points at a variety of characters. Miss Fulton's father, another Presbyterian minister, was a great admirer of Dr Chalmers in Edinburgh,[27] so on this topic, Agnes concluded:

> You cannot imagine with what avidity they listened to all I had to tell them about Edin. and the Disruption and Miss Chalmers and Mr Mackenzie — it was delightful to have such intelligent

---

27   Fulton's wife was a Chalmers and distantly related.

listeners — Miss Fulton is crazy to get to Europe, and I should not wonder if she and the Dr find their way there some day.

One further thing remained for Agnes to do in this letter and that was, if possible, to put things right with her sister Mary by whom she was so 'vexed' earlier. Agnes asked Aunt Jane: "Tell Mary I enjoyed her last letter beyond everything and long for another. She is the best letter writer I know". One wonders what sort of smile was on Mary's face when she heard the message.

The letters from the manse during that first autumn and winter allow a considerable insight into middle class life in the rural New Jersey of that day.

Their flock were kindly and generous, wanting to give the couple the best possible welcome. While they attended Dr Patterson's wedding (to which Agnes took her own wedding dress about which people were "in raptures") the manse was papered and carpeted, dishes washed and put in closets, saving the young wife "a world of trouble". They visited the Pattersons the day after the wedding, caught a train from Philadelphia around about two p.m. and arrived at Cedarville at six p.m. By the time they arrived the house was ready. The furniture had arrived from Mr Whittaker that day and they were helped with the hanging of pictures and with filling bookshelves. Before long, abundant quantities of food, including apples, cider and tomatoes, were brought to their door as gifts by "good, quiet, country people". Mrs Long brought a pan of oysters, Mrs Trenchard brought lard and pies; Mrs Payne's 'help' came from her mistress bringing sweet potatoes, milk and more lard. "The quantities of things we got — 12 great jars of preserves, dried apples, canned peaches, tomatoes, apples, bread . . . Then there was quite a crowd coming and going, and everyone bringing something — But oh!! James and I were tired that night! Next day I could not go to church in the morning or to Sab. Schl. I just rested myself and went to church in the evening".

On September 26th Agnes wrote to Mary: "I love this house already — it is so sweet and cheerful". The house was on "a broad country road, fringed with great trees, with grassy borders". The houses were (and are today) standing "at an easy distance from each other" separated by "low wooden palings painted white". From the start the couple received universal support, were popular, and clearly had plans both for the church's development and for their own lifestyle. Not only could they grow much of their own food, they also had their own deep well in the spacious house from which they drew clean water "with windlass and bucket". Either side of the roomy hall "laid with a wax cloth" were the study and drawing-room, each having "side as well as front windows, which you know, always makes a pretty room". Behind the study was the dining-room:

> The American dining-rooms are very different from those you have. They are mere eating rooms, always opening into the kitchen, and in fact much like the better sort of kitchen. Ours has a window looking to the back and two side windows looking into a sort of outer kitchen, where the water is. Side boards are unknown and unnecessary in this part of the world, instead they have capacious and convenient pantries. In our dining-room there are three windows and eight doors . . . A door opening into the hall . . . study . . . side kitchen . . . back kitchen . . . back staircase, cellar or larder and two pantry doors.

They bought a stove for the back kitchen in Philadelphia "with all the proper accompaniments" and Agnes described herself as a "dab" in the use of it. The food preparation took place in the side kitchen where all the cooking materials were kept, close to the well. She found it odd to have a well in the house — "but that is the way here, some have wells and some have pumps" and it was useful as a refrigerator: "today I made a cornflour shape for dessert and to cool it I just put it into the bucket and lowered it down the well. It soon cooled there I can tell you". Of course, the land being so low-lying, the water table was near the surface. Later, Agnes would be keeping local produce — grape, crab apple, strawberry and "citron" jams eaten "with a spoon out of little glass dishes, not spread on bread" — in the side kitchen, as well as pumpkin and custard pies. Unlike those at home, these were open and never had a crust on the top and Agnes declined to make these herself as she and James both thought they caused "dyspepsia" — indigestion.

It was the study, however, that they both seemed to treasure most. There were tall bookshelves that reached to the ceiling, a couch, a rocking chair, four further chairs and, in addition, a favourite chair that Agnes had brought from Scotland. James's writing-table was placed in one corner and above it hung their picture of the "Disruption" Assembly — the painting which included Agnes's father, Thomas, in the foreground.[28] "Here we have also my testimonial from my friends at the Free High Ch. and the class at the New College in which James was". They also had walnut furniture as a gift from Dr Patterson and paintings from other friends, but "Father's portrait has the place of honour over the mantel".

The staircase, facing the front door, led up from the hall to "quite a large square upper hall also laid with wax cloth". There were two bedrooms upstairs and an attic above them with two windows. A useful cellar, paved with red brick and with wide shelves, extended the length and breadth of the house. For a first house together, this was beyond expectations.

Agnes was clear that they would not have any servants — at twelve shillings a week for a maid the expense was too great in her view, "besides, I don't need one" — and practically no one they knew afforded servants.[29] "There is not so much to do for only two and for as long as I can I will serve myself". She also did not like the idea of a servant sitting with them at every meal — an understandable feeling when there were just the two of them and they had waited a long time to be alone together. James did the heavy work such

---

28   As Agnes wrote elsewhere, he was not in fact present at that meeting but was so central to all that resulted from it that the painter imagined that he had been. The original by David Octavius Hill currently hangs in the offices of the Free Church of Scotland in Edinburgh. From May — September 2016 it formed the showpiece of Tate Britain's 'Painting with Light' exhibition in London. The painting is eleven feet wide. TLH is left of centre in the foreground. There are over 450 individual portraits in the painting which took twenty-three years to complete.

29   This wage of course amounts only to about £30 a year out their £230 or $1100 stipend.

as bringing up coal from the cellar and chopping wood. He also often got up first in the morning to light the fire and make breakfast. Agnes did, however, give out her washing to be done for "two shillings" a week, while keeping the ironing for herself.

If Agnes felt lonely when James was away, she only had to go next door ("a large handsome house") for company where the Gandys had five children. They had a piano on which she could practice. She lamented that they were "horribly dear" in America and even the most ordinary would cost them over £100. There Agnes met friends of the Gandys who knew Agnes's acquaintances in Edinburgh. On another occasion Mrs Cassidy called, took them in her "waggon" to Fairton (three miles off), and introduced the couple to a Mrs Burt whom James discovered he had met in Rome at the home of Dr Elliott. Social life was clearly going to be more than adequate: "Every day we have callers" — who usually brought food.

At first, Agnes could not help making comparisons with characters in American stories she had read and was hugely amused by their speech habits and ways of behaving. "They say 'I hain't been to . . .' and so on and have rag carpet parties and quilting parties, and such names as Eli, Jeremiah, Joab, Abigail and Ruth are quite common. Elder Newcomb's wife is known as Aunt Phoebe . . . "

The end of this long letter shows a quite restored relationship with Mary who had offered Agnes financial assistance should she need it. Agnes replied:

> . . . dearest Mary you are not for a moment to think of sending me any of that money. Not one farthing. I wouldn't take it and James wouldn't let me even if I wanted to. I am glad you are getting a sealskin jacket. Long may you have health and strength to wear it. Nobody deserves it more than you do my darling.

In December James was away for most of a week conducting meetings in Woodstown, some twenty-three miles to the north-west. In a rushed and almost illegible hand he reported that "the meetings have been good and we hope for a good turn out tonight". The note is revealing though in that it is addressed to Agnes "c/o Mr John Cassidy, Sayer's Neck" — so Agnes was staying with a neighbour for that period, rather than being on her own. Secondly, James suggested "Would it not be well to have the eggs taken out of the nests should there be a hard frost". Even in the midst of a mission to another town, James was thinking of chickens on his incipient farm and had not dispensed with ingrained Irish attitudes born of the necessity of making the very most of any land available. He also bought two lamps for the house "and a tin pail to carry water to our room" sending them ahead by train with strict instructions about the opening of the package.

There was also a further, more minatory, reference to the fact that James had a cold, felt unwell and that he might have to return two days early. Illness, from our first acquaintance with James, seemed to be something he both suffered from and was fearful of.

Very cold weather continued and on New Year's Day, 1875, there was a hard frost, though not a flake of snow. Agnes, writing to her sister as the dusk was about to draw in, was in melancholic mood. She was alone as James was out visiting the sick among his flock. It could be a dangerous thing to do given the prevalence of contagious and infectious diseases. "I almost wish there wasn't such a thing as New Year," Agnes wrote. "One can't help recalling the past at such a time, and however happy the present may be, that always makes one a little sad, don't you think so?" It was two years to the day that she had taken that memorable walk with James on the banks of the canal in Edinburgh which was the start of her courtship, or perhaps her engagement. One year ago, she had been with the Mitchells, friends at Lauder, and now she was missing home. She thought of the "glee" she used to sing by Arthur Sullivan, "The Last Night of the Year". They were due to go out to dinner, but it had been postponed as their hostess was ill. Alone they had enjoyed their roast turkey, cranberry sauce and rice pudding. Christmas cards had arrived along with "The Review" and other magazines but Agnes had been unable to respond in kind as cards could not be had and newspapers, along with decorative leaves ("I waxed them for you") were the substitute.

Even so, she had little cause for complaint. That very night there would be music — Agnes would be singing at a fundraising event "of tableaux with music interspersed" for a second church held in a "nice new hall" in the town. She gives the names of the songs that she would sing; after all, a family of musicians would be interested: *O Charming May, The Braes of Balquhidder, My Mannie O,* and *Kitty Tyrell.* Great fun had been had in the rehearsals with Minnie Whittaker accompanying her on the piano. The tableaux were to be supplied "by one of our most stylish young ladies, Ida Bateman". This love of the limelight, of high fashion, music and social engagements is a far cry from the dour and starchy image that most of us entertain about Scots Presbyterians in the later Victorian period. When James went up to Philadelphia, Agnes used to love to go with him to:

> see the fashions in Chestnut Street, and buy my new summer bonnet and (perhaps) a new dress! I found last summer that I hadn't just the right sort of thin dress to go to church with. A white suit is hardly the thing for a married lady on Sundays. It is too school girl, too week day like, and on the hottest days silks are unbearable — so perhaps I will get a black and white striped thickish grenadine and have it made into a walking suit.

The fashions that other ladies followed, however, were not always to Agnes's taste and it may be that she did not like to be upstaged. At the start of March, a Miss Mary Wilson from Philadelphia, stayed with them for a fortnight. James had stayed with her father, Isaac Wilson in the city. With just a whiff of patronisation Agnes thought her "a kind goodnatured creature" but she,

> came down here with the most costly and elaborate toilettes, astonishing the Cedarvillians. Some of her dresses are absurdly rich and costly, but that is the American fashion. She said she enjoyed her visit very much and so did I.

Visits to Philadelphia were also useful for food shopping. Agnes listed a number of items much more cheaply bought in bulk in the city than locally in Cumberland County, including "crackers, rice, cornflour, meal and such things". Alcorn and Baker, General Commission Merchants and Dealers in Flour and Grain in North Delaware Avenue, were their suppliers. (On one occasion James sent home a barrel of apples by railroad. On another he sent crockery by steamer down the Delaware and then on via the "stage driver". In a letter of January 1878 Agnes wrote to Mary: "He buys all our provisions".[30]) In best Scotch fashion this housewife was also exact about prices:

> Butcher meat is very cheap here, steak and roasting pieces never more than 8d the lb. and sometimes I get a shin of beef or veal for soup (which gives us an excellent dinner for two days) weighing 3 or 4 pounds, the whole piece for 7d.

Of course, Agnes had her own views about how the food should be cooked and disliked the waste she saw (Scotland was far less bountiful):

> The people here waste meat awfully, almost always frying or roasting; soups and stews are almost unknown, so of course those pieces go very cheap. James would like to have broth every day he is so fond of it.

The Wilsons' letters throughout the period at Cedarville continue to shed light on the way of life of this self-sufficient close-knit New Jersey community of the 1870s, now otherwise closed to us. On one occasion when Agnes was writing to Mary, she was interrupted by two elderly widows, Aunt Martha and Aunt Ruth Ogden, "large and tall and straight, with a quick energetic manner and a black silk quilted hood on". Both were about seventy and had ten and twelve children respectively. Each lived alone but went about constantly together, "to church and prayer meetings and all". There were stories too about the Cassidys with whom they had enjoyed Christmas dinner at Sayer's Neck, a

---

30 James liked Agnes to have what she wanted. When at Synod he wrote to her: "If you want anything, get it and I will settle all bills when I get back".

tiny settlement a couple of miles off. Mr Cassidy was a farmer and "the only man of Irish extraction in our church". His wife, only two years older than Agnes, quickly became a good friend: "she has been exceedingly kind to me". Her maiden name was Ruth Howell. Agnes noted that she looked ten years older than she was — something she was to remark several times about other women. Life on a farm, even in the fairly benign Garden State, was physically very tough. We can hear the enjoyment felt as Agnes recounts Ruth's story:

> Her great grandmother was a Princess of Sweden, who had to be sent off from Sweden during some great war . . . and was wrecked on the New Jersey shore and married a Jersey farmer. All the Howells[31] are fine looking, and if you saw Mrs Cassidy walk into church, dressed in her best, you would never imagine she was a farmer's wife who did all her own housework. She reads Latin every day and has Tennyson, Dickens, all the best authors. She is as kind and sisterly to me as possible and never comes to see us empty-handed . . . she will bring us some pot plants, geraniums and fuchsias, or a bag of pop corn or peanuts and so on . . . she was married at eighteen but has no children.

Christmas dinner was shared not only with the Cassidys but the Osbornes. Both goose and chicken were on the table with two varieties of potato, cranberry sauce, tomatoes and onions, preserved plums and "no end of sauces". For dessert there was "plum pudding and mince and pumpkin pies, no wine of course but tea and coffee".

After dinner there was entertainment. They

> adjourned to the parlor where we had music (she has a small organ) till supper, after which we all got into the waggon and went down to our church, where a Sunday School festival was to be held. This consisted of some speeches and singing in the church followed by a 'sociable', i.e. 'soirée' in the lecture room. Of course I had to be

---

31   Jim Howell, still farming at eighty-four, is currently a senior member of the church who kindly took me out to lunch when I visited in April, 2017. In a letter of March 1877 Agnes mentions another Howell who was organist and an "enthusiastic musician" at Mr Maxwell's church in Bridgeton. Henry and Lydia were central to Agnes's letter of 15th January 1877.

very prominent then, and I assure you I did my duty, speaking to everyone I knew and getting them to introduce me to those I did not know. So passed Christmas Day. I often thought of this last one when Aunt and I dined with you. I had on the same dress too, the blue with silver buttons.

Agnes's unself-conscious style of writing, in which she uses such a conversational tone, allows her to slip easily from casual social exchanges to the very rationale for being in Cedarville: the growth of the church. Indeed, the two were opposite sides of the same coin: their work and their relationships in such a small community could not be prized apart. James had by this time visited almost everyone in his congregation and Agnes made three or four calls each fine afternoon that she was free. In turn, four or five visitors would frequently come to the manse and amuse Agnes with their views and gossip but also deeply impress her with their generosity and kindness. In the same letter, (now being continued on 4th January) Agnes mentioned that the prayer meetings for revival in the town would begin that night at seven p.m. They would continue every evening that week, and "perhaps for many weeks". James was also meeting with the young men to form a "Young Men's Association". Without pausing for breath, Agnes went on to describe the fundraising entertainment which had been a success, the hall being very crowded: "the tableaux were very good and I am told they enjoyed my singing very much". "The [numbers at] evening services are doubled and more since James came" she boasted to Mary. Perhaps her boost to the singing and music had helped with that. By New Year she had been made Secretary of the Home Missions Society and Vice-President of the Ladies Foreign Mission Society, largely honorary roles that she would enormously enjoy.

Later that year Agnes told her aunt about the fundraising which paid for the creation of improved facilities in the church building. She wrote to her of

The new room we got made by putting up a partition in our basement at the church . . . just a wooden frame, with window sashes all along which can be raised and lowered at pleasure, and it makes the nicest little room for our prayer meetings, the young men's meeting and the primary department of the Sunday Schl. now under my charge. But all this could not be done without money and to raise it we held a strawberry festival, early in June, in Bateman's Hall . . . it was a great success and we made more than enough to clear expenses and pay for the partition. To give eclat to it, the great majority of the ladies wore Mrs Washington caps and were in Centennial costume. I put on my quilted satin petticoat, and I had a neat little cap with a blue bow before and behind, and an apron to match. Some of our old ladies had real old things on. We had a quartet and I sang a solo, and about 20 little girls from the Sab. Schl. sang a piece which I had taught them.

There is further unique recording of social history in a letter from Agnes to Aunt Jane written in September/October 1875 (when she was given two hand-made quilts — rather quaintly from "North and South Cedarville"). It describes the process of making rugs out of rags — an activity that flourished widely in America and in miners' homes in the north of England, even continuing through the austerity of 1940's Britain. The process was, generally, to cut remnants of many different fabrics into narrow strips or tiny squares and then sew these into long coils which the weaver could put through a loom. In the Philadelphia area as late as the 1870s handloom production outpaced that of the power looms and produced better quality carpet. Agnes told Jane Crawford:

> One afternoon lately, being at leisure, I thought I would go into Mrs Gandy's and practise, as I often do. But when I reached their sitting room door, behold a scene! All round the room there sat a ring of ladies, sewing carpet rags! They were all members of our church, all elderly, and all widows but one, Aunt Rhoda Ogden, who was never married. In the clear space in the middle of the floor was an old quilt, and on this lay the carpet rags in many coloured heaps — all already torn into long narrow strips, and only waiting to be tacked together before being sent to the weaver. What a mixture they were. Old stuff, woollen, and cotton dresses, old trousers, coats and vests, old skirt braids, old cotton stockings cut round and round into a long long piece, in fact old rags of

every description, first washed clean of course, and then cut. They were the collection of nearly four years and Mrs Gandy had sent round and invited those of the ladies who had no great home duties and could easily spend a whole day away from home to help her to sew her carpet rags. Most of them had been there since 8 that morning, and there they sat with great big aprons on, plying their needles and tongues at once, and rolling up the strips as they got long enough, into large balls which little Alice carried out and put in a large barrel in the hall.

Agnes was quickly seated between Aunt Rhoda and Aunt Abbie Harris and "was soon sewing away like the rest" but possibly felt a little excluded by not knowing of the event:

> I remarked that I did not know of this party when I came in, and Aunt Abbie said 'you would have been invited if your husband had a' been dead.' Whereat we all laughed and I said I would tell him, when I went in, how much I had missed because he was alive yet.

They say, if you want to make God laugh, tell Him your long-term plans. Such irreverence might not have made Agnes laugh but the thought that all too soon she would have to come to terms with James's death must have been far from her mind. Their joint ministry was just beginning and proving a great success. Moreover, this occasion was not only sociable and public-spirited, but good humoured and witty:

> When Aunt Abbie went away she said, 'Now I want you all to come and see me.' 'Shall we come together?' asked Aunt Martha. 'No, indeed,' said she, 'for then I'd get no talkin' done myself'. A few went away before supper, myself included of course. (As I remarked, since my husband was not dead yet, I must go and get his supper ready), but the most of them stayed till late in the evening. Carpet rags and rag carpets are a great institution here — you see them in every home — some are quite pretty and they are certainly very economical as they last a tremendous time. Don't you think there is something very sweet and friendly and primitive

in this custom of going to each other's houses and helping each other with house-keeping emergencies? Somehow it savours to me of the early Christian Ch. when they had all things in common. They have quilting parties in just the same way.

If Agnes was somewhat dewy-eyed about her new neighbourhood and friends, it was with good reason. Everything seemed to be going well for the new couple and New Jersey was opening up exciting possibilities and ideas:

Letter from Agnes with
line drawing

How different from ways and customs at home — in Cedarville there is such perfect equality that it can be done quite easily, in fact it is the most natural thing in the world. But all places, even in America, are not like Cedarville.

What follows is a wonderful description of two ladies who were part of the cultural tradition Agnes was enjoying:

Aunt Martha Ogden and Aunt Ruth Ogden paid us a visit the other evening. They live in houses side by side, are both widows, and have both had very large families, who are all scattered away from them. I wish you could have seen them as they came up the walk, with their black dresses, black sunbonnets and fans. They looked something like this [a line drawing of the two, perhaps four inches high, is then provided]. Aunt Ruth tall large and stately, with a deep rich voice,

Aunt Martha small and sweet something like little Mrs Gray of Aberdeen, both of them great talkers. They are both over 70. They got talking that night about the time when they were young, and of the changes they had seen in this place, and of the Old Stone Church, and Father Osborne, just like old people anywhere. Aunt Martha has no children nearer than Bridgeton, but Aunt Ruth has most of hers here in Cedarville. Two of her sons Jeremiah and Benjamin being the handsomest men in the village. She says herself, and I can see it, that the Ogdens "are a good stock". About 200 years ago 7 brothers of that name came over from England to New England.

Their memories would have included the American war against England in 1812 when New Jersey supplied 6,000 troops and there were skirmishes with a British landing party. Rawer memories would have been of the horror of the Civil War, but everyone in Cedarville would remember that, save the young children. "The Old Stone Church" mentioned still exists nearby as a historic monument. Constructed in 1780 after fighting in the area came to an end, it is an adaptation of the Quaker meeting-house style but with an elaborate raised pulpit which defines the Presbyterian emphasis on the Word in worship. In a letter dating from that autumn, Agnes referred to a young "Quakeress", Mrs Ewing:

> She was brought up a Quakeress but married a Presbyterian. They invited us to tea the other evening and she had her sister visiting her, a young Quakeress who, as well as herself, has that indescribable aspect of peaceful serenity that all Quakers have. You would have smiled to hear them saying "Now I want thee to tell us all about Scotland". "Dost thou feel at home here?" and at tea, "Wilt thou pass thy husband the butter". Etc. It is exceedingly sweet to hear them . . . I have seen a great many since I came to America, in Philadelphia and on the cars and river steamers, but I have never spoken to any before. They all have that look of purity and peace which is lovely and winning.

Agnes enjoyed reporting on styles of speech, but one wonders what local people made of her Edinburgh accent. In the earlier letter about Aunt Ruth she wrote:

> Aunt Ruth speaks more like the folks in [illegible place-name] than any I have heard yet. She says 'jest so' and 'fur off', 'set up' etc. They are two dear old bodies and I enjoy hearing them talk above everything . . . as pious and godly, as serious and strict as any old Scotch Presbyterian could be. But of course they are descended from the brothers and co-patriots of the Scotch Covenanters, viz. the English Puritans, and that accounts for the resemblance.

This is an interesting comment because it reveals something of Agnes's stance towards the church of her childhood and is in keeping with her liberal opinions about dancing, music and entertainment.[32] She clearly admired and respected the old tradition of severe demeanour but also slightly distanced herself from it, as if she saw it as the hallmark of a previous generation and not of her own.

At this point in this long letter Agnes tells the sad story of Aunt Rhoda, one which, for the present-day reader who knows the outcome of this narrative, sends a certain *frisson* down the spine.

> She is one of the very few old maids we have here, and it seems when she was young, she was engaged to a young doctor. The wedding day was fixed, the bridesmaids chosen, her dress made, when the bridegroom sickened and died. The very day they were to have been married was his funeral day, and poor Miss Rhoda went to it dressed in her wedding dress and made all her young friends attend too, dressed as they were to have been for her marriage. Since that time she has been queer, eccentric, unlike other people, and I scarcely wonder at it. She lives alone in a little spotless white house next the church, and though she has nobody but herself to attend to, gets up at 5 every morning.

---

32   Blaise Pascal, from a quite different tradition, wrote in his *Pensées* (1670) that all the principal forms of amusement were a distraction and danger to Christians but the theatre especially so.

Such stories of sudden loss, of women jilted by death rather than a lover, as Dickens's Miss Havisham in *Bleak House* was on her wedding day, are reminders that the dramas of Victorian fiction were all too often drawn from life as much as from imagination.

Another social insight to the times was Agnes's enthusiasm for the spelling bee which was a fashionable pastime of the day in East Coast America:

> But the great feature of the evening was the Spelling Bee. I suppose you must have been seeing notices of these in the Scotch papers; they have been the rage in America lately as they are the revival of a very old fashioned amusement. A class of twenty 5 [sic] or so went up to the platform, old and young. Dr Robert gave the words, and James and Dr Harry Smith, with a huge "Webster" before them were the judges. Oh, how funny it was! I laughed till I cried with the fun and absurdity of it. I couldn't begin to describe it — it was indescribable. The schoolteacher, Mr Robertson, was very properly the best speller, and a young girl second best. Old Dr Eli and Dr Benny made a great deal of fun with their spelling. I think they are capital things and I wish you would get them up at home . . . I went to one in a private house with Dr and Mrs Patterson when I was in Philadelphia last, and do you know I was the best speller — better even than Dr Patterson who is quite a model of correctness . . . Three cheers for auld Scotland. Tell Walter to get one up if all is well this coming winter.

Like most of us, Agnes was enthusiastic in encouraging an activity at which she herself was able to shine but her helpless laughter at the absurdity of it all, at an essentially trivial parlour game, was delightful.

One further detail which might give the lie to any idea that Presbyterian couples in ministry had to conduct themselves with unsmiling severity is that when James had to go up to Synod on 18th October, Agnes would go with him for a particular reason: "We will stay at Mr Maxwell's father's house and visit New York". This allowed Agnes to pursue a long-cherished dream that she might place her "feet on the fanfared Broadway before this month is over".

"Won't it be delightful to see Central Park and the Hudson and to imagine I see Fleda at the street corners".[33]

One very wet evening in February, James told his wife that she should not come out that night to the church meeting, so she took the opportunity to tell Jane more about how their work was progressing. She was clearly missing Edinburgh, her mind "running so on all you dear ones at home, taking so many flights over the sea that tonight I feel I must have a chat with you". It transpires that James had been putting in enormous efforts to the growth of the church and seeing appreciable results. They were now in the eighth week of prayer meetings which took place seven days a week from 7:00 p.m. until 9:30 p.m. James had attended every meeting and Agnes all but two. For her husband's sake Agnes was glad they were coming to an end as a result of the approaching "Communion Sunday when all the new converts are received into the church". She told Jane:

> He has worked like a Hercules for those 8 weeks; preparing an address for every evening, and delivering it with exhausting energy, talking with enquirers after the meeting and visiting every day somewhere or other, hunting up stray people or trying to get hold of new ones, besides preparing his usual Sunday sermons.

That was by no means all however:

> And to crown all, he has started a Bible class, conducted by himself on Sundays, for the young converts. I protested, but in vain, against this. They all say here, that there never was a minister here worked so hard before. But, thank God, he is as strong as a lion, and doesn't seem a bit the worse.

James also started teaching Latin and Greek to Howard Bateman, one of the new converts, three times a week. Agnes wrote: "[Howard] seems so happy in the new life he has begun; you can see it in his eyes. Isn't that better than driving young men to Bridgeton and bringing them home drunk at night?"

---

33   Fleda was a character in *Queechy* (1852), by Susan Warner, a hugely popular American writer of religious fiction, a Presbyterian. She so influenced army cadets that she is buried in West Point cemetery.

— a reminder, if we needed one, that life outside the church continued much as it had always done and not even Cedarville was an earthly paradise.

She then continued the letter (now March 2nd) by elaborating on what happened at one of these historic services through which church membership was confirmed:

> Well, the Communion Sunday is over and a marvellous day it was. Mr Beadle came down on Saturday and conducted the preparatory services and then conducted the service on Sunday, James assisting him. He (Mr Beadle) preached . . . After the sermon James rose up and announced that 53 people had joined the church, 49 on profession of faith and 4 by certificate. He then read over their names and as he did so, one by one they left their seats and gathered on the platform which could not hold them so they overflowed into the aisles. Then James solemnly read over the vows they were now taking upon them, they bowing their assent to each one. Then he asked the congregation if they would give the hand of fellowship to these new members and sustain and assist them in their Xn course to which the whole crowded church responded by rising to their feet, and then all joined in singing "Praise God from whom all blessings flow". It was overpowering — I never saw a more affecting scene. Then Mr Beadle came down and baptised no less than 26 of them, after which all returned to their seats, and the Communion was dispensed as usual.

After the service there was much reflection on what had just taken place:

> On our way home we three agreed that this mode of introducing new members into the church is much more beautiful, more fraught with meaning and more deeply impresses the minds of both the new converts and the new members, than the way it is done in Scotland where new members merely sit down at the table and one scarcely knows who has joined the church. The people here are saying never was there such a sight in the Brick Ch. before and never was it so crowded.

Other news of this kind included an account of the illness of Ned Gandy, "one of the new Christians . . . a very fine-looking young man, well-educated but [he] has injured his health by dissipation" — suffering probably from consumption — and "so seriously ill that he is scarcely expected to recover". He had sent a message begging Agnes to sing for him as her singing had had great effect upon him when he was "under conviction" and being counselled by James. Naturally, Agnes agreed to go ("I don't think I ever felt such pure happiness in all my life") that afternoon and sang "The Prodigal Child" to him again and again to comfort him. She also left a copy of "The Service of Praise" with him, a book of 1866 her father had collaborated in producing a year before he died. "It was sad", she wrote, "to see the poor young man, with a handkerchief tied round his head to alleviate his constant headache, his chest heaving with laboured breathing". By April, however, the young man was "able to walk out again" and had much recovered.

Piano music was, unsurprisingly, an emotive experience for all three of the Hately children. Mary confessed to crying when she heard Walter playing and singing "My Mannie O" because it reminded her so much of absent Aggie. Agnes replied: "You mustn't cry when you think of me" but confessed to Mary that her "eyes were full of tears" when she played and hummed Beethoven's romantic setting of Matthisson's poem "Adelaide" to Abbie at the Gandy's house. The poem is an outpouring of yearning for a seemingly unattainable woman — in Aggie's mind, Mary, so far away in Whithorn, Scotland.

CHAPTER EIGHT

CEDARVILLE: A SAFE HAVEN?

IT WAS ON APRIL 7TH that Agnes wrote to Jane that James's appointment had been confirmed at the expected salary of $1,100. Agnes underlined the word "unanimous" on each of the two occasions in which she proudly mentioned the fact to her aunt: "they say the people were never so harmonious . . . the people just idolise him. This late revival has endeared him to them greatly". The Presbytery was to meet at Cape May, a prosperous fashionable resort at the southern tip of New Jersey, on 20th April, at which a date would be set for the "ordination". One immediate result of this is that James felt able to ask his father to see if Maggie Tait, "a good, sensible, strong girl of 17" would come over from Ireland to work for them as a servant. Perhaps James had in mind the hope that it would not be long before Agnes was pregnant.[34] In order to be ordained James had to pass a further exam, one for which he studied hard. After Princeton, Chicago, Auburn, and New College Edinburgh one might think he had done enough to be able to run a country church, but he was pleased to be "highly complimented" on the result. The congregation too took great pains to prepare the church for the service on the evening of Wednesday 28th April: "two days last week there were scores of them there, in old clothes sweeping and scrubbing, and shaking and dusting . . . That's the way they do things in this republican country, they co-operate". Agnes then glowingly describes the church building and the improvements to the furnishings: "It is a very pretty church, a thousand times superior to Whithorn

34   He had not long to wait. Anne Edina would be born in February, 1876.

or Greenlaw . . . or any country church that ever I saw in Scotland". This is probably true, given the plainness, even drab nature of much Presbyterian building in Scotland. The Cedarville church with its warm brick, slimly elegant white spire, large sunlit windows and brightly painted interior is inviting and distinctive, sited as it is among tall trees and grassland. There would be flowers and an anthem sung (by Agnes of course) at the service. In the event, it poured with rain all that day so many from Bridgeton and elsewhere were prevented from making the journey. Mr Maxwell, however, arrived from there to preach the sermon and Agnes was greatly impressed by the ceremony — James kneeling to have hands laid on his head as a sign of the charge he had been given. The Wilsons had two other ministers staying with them overnight, one of whom, Mr Campbell, Agnes was delighted to find, had studied at Edinburgh.

While James had been away for two nights taking his exam, Agnes had stayed with the Nixons, a local family that she would stay with again in 1880 under tragically different circumstances. Her comments about how hard such American women worked are a reminder or insight to a way of life long lost to the twenty-first century. Wishing that Mary could see the Nixons' house she wrote:

> It is just a specimen of American housekeeping and she is just a typical American woman. Her husband is Captain Nixon, owning his own oyster boat and she is a little woman with a pale clear-cut face, black hair, and the quickest sharpest black eyes. She has three children, the eldest 14, and her widowed mother lives with her, and like them all she does her own work, washing and ironing and sewing and making all the children's clothes. Her house is spotless. The large "living" room, where all the cooking is done is, if possible, the most spotless of all. She scrubs the lid of her rain barrel! And always after sweeping washes her brooms in a pail of water and drys [sic] them so that they are all like new ones. I felt ashamed when I thought of my own house, but of course I couldn't, and wouldn't, work as she does. At fifty she will be a

broken down woman, as many of the elderly women are here. She is 34 now and hasn't one bit of colour in her face and is thin and sharp looking. She bakes twice a week, not only bread but cakes and pies, and, as I said, makes all the children's clothes. How the women here do work . . . not only do they bake their own bread but they make the yeast for it, and they make all the bedclothing (for blankets are unknown here and they use quilts and "comforts" instead). And they make the carpets for their kitchens and dining rooms, of rags, all cut up and sewed in long strips and woven into breadths. And everything on their tables except meat is made by their own hands and all their clothes are made at home, except their best dresses, and they do all this and a hundred times more, and keep no servants! But, as I said, one rarely sees a fresh vigorous woman of fifty here. They wear themselves out, and at that age have rheumatism, paralysis, continual dyspepsia, weakness, and can't walk etc. They live to be old, many of them, but it is rarely a healthy old age.

It is apparent that Agnes was struggling with something here. She had always prided herself on her ethic of hard work and 'making do and mending' but in this community she found women whom she could not emulate, nor did she want to. This astonishing list of household tasks clarified for her that she had no intention of making her life a ceaseless grind and did not want to think of herself in twenty years' time as looking like her neighbours nor being in their situation. The idea of a servant was therefore very attractive; they could easily afford one. They proposed to pay Maggie £10 a year with bed and board all found — a wage that Aggie admitted was a low one for America, "but we think it enough".[35] Agnes laid plans for how she wanted the house to look after she had directed Maggie in her work but there is no evidence that Maggie Tait ever arrived. In August Agnes told her sister:

I forgot to say in recent letters that I have not yet got Maggie Tait from Ireland. You know we expected her by July at latest, but it

---

35 Live-in servants have never done well. In 1658 the diarist, Samuel Pepys, paid his maid £2 for a year's service.

seems that her mother is [sic] was very ill, and she could not make up her mind to leave the country at such a time. But we are hoping she still may come.

What finally transpired was that in failing to secure the services of an Irish maid, Agnes was very averse to having an American girl to live with them:

An American girl I will not have on any account. Imagine having a pert young woman in the house who would do just what she was pleased to consider her share of the work, would dress herself up in the afternoon, leaving you to finish what there was to do, would go out every evening, coming in at any hour of the night or morning etc. etc. Life would be misery at that rate.

The over-emphasis on such "misery" is, without intending to be, rather comical and suggests that Agnes had taken strongly against the attitudes of servant girls in other households and felt slightly threatened by their carefree nature and sense of entitlement which was quite the opposite of what she deemed the proper order of things. It is hard to avoid the irony of this. Having praised the "perfect equality" of Cedarville in an earlier letter, it seems she was not quite so keen on extending this to servants who were not deferential or who had a certain independence of spirit. By the end of the year, perhaps earlier, the Wilsons had engaged instead an African American girl, Sally, who "is becoming every day more useful". At a point soon after Christmas, early in 1876, Agnes unwittingly reveals that she was far more suited to a paternalistic relationship with an employee than an equal one. But her regard for the girl was high and her attitude was one of kindly responsibility:

I have had quite a time rigging up Sally, making up big aprons for her, and also a new wrapper. Red is her favourite color [sic] so I have indulged her with a brilliant red calico with a small yellow spot on it, in which she looks just like a picture. I sometimes feel as if I were living in a story book, for Sally is so absurd and amusing . . . I take great pains to teach her — she is a good reader but when she came had no knowledge of the Bible at all. I gave her an old one of mine and now she can turn up almost any chapter in any book and commits to memory several verses every week. Our meetings are going on just now and Sally repeats a verse every time she is there. She always sits with me, of course, and the moment I repeat a verse Sally comes out with hers. Certainly there is nothing so good for her as storing her mind with Scripture.

From April 1875 a period of settled development had begun for the Wilsons which Agnes hoped would last in Cedarville for "many happy and useful years". As it was, things would work out differently. Her letter to Mary at the end of the month highlighted the vulnerability of a community without vaccines, little scientific understanding of the causes of disease, local hospital care or even the guarantee of clean water: a "great many" local children died that winter and spring of scarlet fever and diphtheria. Both diseases, being highly contagious, were, along with tuberculosis and typhoid fever, among the leading causes of childhood death in America up until the 1870s.

Now that the Wilsons knew they could stay, James began work in earnest on the large plot that ran by the side of and behind the house. Besides Prince, the dog, which he had bought for Aggie from Philadelphia, and Comet, the cat, they had hens. As she wrote her letter on a warm late spring day, sitting in her rocking chair by the side of the house, she could see James in the plot overseeing the ploughing of part of the peach orchard by Mr Wollen, her "washerwoman's husband". James, however, did most of the heavy garden work. Overhead the apple and pear trees were coming into bud and further off she listened to the hens in the chicken coop "clucking and scraping"; nearer at hand roamed their black hen with "five little downy chicks just two weeks old". Sometimes they had three eggs a day from them. Country life in such a place was necessarily quiet so further down the village street she

> could hear the fish man blowing his horn and shouting 'Shad, Oh, fresh shad oh'. Shad is a fine fish, not as delicious as salmon, but something like it. These fish wagons pass three times a week so we get plenty of fresh fish — blue fish, rock fish, cat fish, herrings and shad.

Rather like salmon, the shad pour into Delaware Bay in spring to begin their three-hundred-mile trek upriver to spawn in the headwaters at Hancock. Halfway through their migration they are in perfect condition to be caught for the eight-week season when they may be netted. James was something of a fisherman himself and on a rare day off work he would go to Cedar Creek, a small stream that meanders gently down to Delaware Bay, where he would "likely bring home a bunch of fine fish". Agnes, too, had time to sit under the apple tree (with her sewing) by the house most evenings once the summer had arrived. Agnes sent a sketch of the house to Mary, detailing at length which room was which and the types of trees in the garden, not failing to mention the hitching posts for horses, on both sides of the maple-lined street.

By early May, the first of the pink blossom on the peach trees was bursting through, bunches of trailing arbutus with its scent of hyacinths was making the manse fragrant, they had fifteen chickens in the henhouse and Agnes was feeling that Cedarville was a "most desirable" place to be. "A large cherry tree by the front gate is one mass of white blossom". She sent her sister the last of the violets from the garden and was in expectation of grand crops of fruit and vegetables which she would preserve in the summer and autumn.

Those crops did come to fruition and gave Agnes opportunity to describe to her sister and preserve for us, in a long letter started on August 9th (and added to several times until it was completed on September 17th), the whole process of harvesting and bottling fruit as it was carried out in the Garden State at that time. On September 7th she announced:

> I wish you could just see our peach orchard. The trees are bending to the ground with their lovely fruit, for it is lovely, so rosy, soft and downy. The peach crop this year is something wonderful. The market is glutted and the peach farmers are making nothing. James has given away I don't know how many baskets . . . chiefly to the poorer folks in our church and still I fear a good deal will be wasted. We have them at every meal, 'sugared down' as they call it, that is, peeled, stoned, halved and sprinkled with sugar . . . I have

already 'spiced' 3 cans of them and 'canned' 10 cans and I expect to keep on canning, 2 or 3 at a time all this month. Then we have contracted with a neighbour to dry great quantities for us, on shares.

I wish you could see the 'cans' we use here. James has bought 8 dozen from a glass manufacturer at a great saving of cost. They are quart and pint glass jars with a neat tin lid, lined with porcelain, screwing tightly down on top of an elastic ring, which renders it perfectly airtight — no fuss and trouble with spirits, paper and string. It is all done in a trice. In canning, you merely boil the fruit with a little sugar and water, till it is soft, and then fasten it up. My cans of peaches look exactly like those you see in grand confectioners' shops in Edinburgh: glass jars with the fruit in a clear syrup, looking so luscious and tempting. Spicing is a different process. I am going to send you the receipt and you must try it . . . I have made 3 jars of spiced pears, 5 of strawberry jam, 8 cans of cherries, 1 of huckleberries,[36] 1 of canned pears, 3 little glasses of blackberry jelly and today 3 glasses of grape jelly which tastes like wine and is the loveliest colour . . . Canning is the great business of the hour in Cedarville.

Cedarville Manse today — with author

By the end of the season Agnes had canned 70 jars of peaches as well as a number of quinces. All this husbandry, along with the generous gifts they continued to receive from neighbours and members of the church, meant

---

36 The American name for the English 'whortleberry', sometimes also known as 'hurtleberries'. 'Spicing' involved adding cinnamon and/or ginger to the process.

that they had been able to save over half James's salary: £140 out of a total income of £220. That was a considerable sum; they clearly had aspirations for the use of this money, even if they had not fully formulated them, even to themselves: "We have kept a strict account of all expenses from day to day".

We also have a glimpse of a simple lunch recipe Agnes enjoyed:

> Fried beefsteak and potatoes, with fried tomatoes. The latter are delicious. I slice them, dredge with flour, pepper and salt, fry them a nice brown and then make a gravy with a little flour and milk boiled up in the pan and poured over them. How I wish you could taste them.

There is an example of breakfast for them both:

> This morning . . . we had fried ham and sweet potatoes, a dish of great fresh oysters (a present), and plenty of peaches, pears and grapes, besides coffee, bread and butter — a breakfast for a prince.[37]

This plenty, for someone such as James born into the years of the Irish potato famine, must have seemed heaven-sent.[38] The letter was completed a year to the very day after they arrived in Cedarville: "a very happy year it has been to me" Agnes told her sister.

At the end of this long letter, composed in episodes over a period of six weeks, one is left with the feeling that though Agnes was interested in so much and was appreciative of all the warm personalities and kindness around her, she was bound up very much with the good life she and James were leading and was inclined to be judgemental of those less virtuous. Having predicted that a certain Maggie Scott would turn, as she did, into the "most virtuous and respectable of matrons" when before she had been "deceitful, unprincipled and vain" she then continued by adding that another friend was "worth a dozen of Maggie . . . and, I think, much handsomer". But, in truth, perhaps we all do this to a degree and the Victorians were more forthright

37 In June 1877, Agnes included her recipe for Oysters in a letter: "The fried oysters were delicious; first dipped in beaten egg, then rolled in cracker dust, then fried in hot lard".
38 1875 was a bumper year for the Delaware fruit growers, especially for peaches.

than we anyway. Nevertheless, it is something of a relief to the reader when in conclusion she wrote, with some self-knowledge, "I doubt this is a very egotistical letter, and it has been too long on hand". Later in life Agnes felt this character weakness strongly and regretted it.[39]

The Wilsons' second Christmas at Cedarville was very much better than their first. James was assured of his position as minister; they had made many friends; their home included not only a spacious house but a garden which

was a place for delightful relaxation as well as a productive and money-saving enterprise — which played to James's business acumen. As the year ended, they were given a magnificent silver-gilt Britannia metal double-skinned jug for keeping liquids cool or hot at the table. It was engraved with flowers and the wording: "Presented to the Rev James Kinnier Wilson by the Congregation of Cedarville, New Jersey, U.S.A. 1875". It is a most handsome piece. They also received a wonderful package of smaller presents from

Classic double-skinned (originally silver-plated) jug presented to James by congregation

Mary and Walter in Whithorn and Edinburgh:

> That box! . . . James acted like a big laddie over it, capering all round it like I don't know what . . . all these little things that the dear hands at home brought together and wrapped up and packed

---

39 Writing in the mid-1920s she lamented that she had been too judgemental as a younger woman and had been allowed to indulge the attitude as a child: "We should have been checked for it. It is a very great fault — a grievous sin. It fosters pride, vanity and self-righteousness, it is the very reverse of Christ-like".

away for us have brought you nearer me than even letters can do. Thank you again and again . . .

Amongst the things they received were Agnes's part song music which she had left behind, and a number of books including a three volume *Life of Archibald Constable* inscribed by J Constable — the Scottish publisher for whom her father had worked — and sermons from Rev Arnot and C.H. Spurgeon who were variously admired by Agnes and James, and a copy of *The Family Treasury* for 1874 — a publication Agnes herself would write for when in Kansas. Also, in the parcel were tea, figs, shortbread, "two dear little china cups", a pair of ivory picture frames, an elegant handbag, and a tray. It was indeed a package to write home about.

In addition to all this, Agnes had a more profound gift. She had known since the summer that she was pregnant. As a result, she had been busy getting "all that sewing finished and put away all ready in a little box". She also had a pile of new books to read[40] and wanted to frame some oleographs[41] which James had bought her for five cents each. She would use "thin strips of walnut wood" which were given her by the Batemans for the "Oxford" frames, and white cardboard for the mounts. She also wanted to mount some steel engravings of Dalkeith Palace and "Roslin" (sic) chapel. Painting watercolours from the portraits of Mary's children, sewing gingham aprons and creating texts in "spatter work" were also on her list for when she could do no other work. Neighbours, meanwhile, were travelling to the city to hear Moody and Sankey: "The crowds here are much larger than they were at home because the buildings are so much larger".[42]

---

40   E.g. *Little Foxes* and *We and our Neighbours* by "Mrs Stowe . . . as racy and readable as her books always are".
41   Prints which used oil on canvas to imitate oil paintings.
42   The evangelists were in Philadelphia from mid-November till January 16th. In that time 700,000 people flocked to hear them. On the last evening, 13,000 attended the service in a packed-out abandoned railway depot, many thousands being turned away. http://www.proclaimanddefend.org/2014/07/25/moody-and-sankey. This is doubly interesting because it fixes the date of this undated letter to before January 16th. *Frank Leslie's Illustrated Newspaper* for 18th December 1875 carried a large picture of a meeting in full flow.

CHAPTER NINE

NEW ARRIVALS

WHEN IN JANUARY 1876 AGNES knew that there was only a month or so to go, she must have recalled what she wrote to Mary on the birth of her sister's third child: "I hope and pray that your recovery may be rapid and complete . . . How glad I am that you had Nurse . . . To think that you had three children before you were quite four years married!" In common with so many of their day, both women, despite their comfortable conditions, were aware that to bring a child into the world was to bring it into "this vale of tears". On more than one occasion Agnes intersperses her hopes and plans with expressions such as, "If I am spared" or the initials "D.V".[43] This is not mere piety but the acknowledgement that childbirth was dangerous and life always uncertain even in the best of times. Referring to the impending birth she says "If all goes well" she must try not to allow trifles of untidiness ("I cannot see a thread on the carpet without picking it up") to compel her into activity. There is, however, one thing she fears and that is the "shoals of ladies who are sure to come in, either from love or curiosity — but I needn't cry out before I'm hurt".

Agnes's brother-in-law's description of his wife Mary's sufferings with Helen, their new baby, was, according to Aggie, "graphic" so it is not surprising that when the time came the younger sister should reply in a similar vein. Her entire letter of March 10th is given over to a description of her labour, the birth, her recovery, and breast-feeding — a considerable insight to the whole fearful and lengthy process taking place at home in a middle-class Victorian

---

43   Deo volente, or, God willing.

household. She begins by announcing proudly that a fortnight after the birth she is already, though not yet able to leave her bedroom, sitting up in a chair and has been "allowed today to write a little" and chooses her sister, of course, as the recipient.

> First, I must tell you that I am getting on very well; I sat up last Sunday (the 10th day) for the first time, and I have sat up longer each day since. On next Sunday I hope to go downstairs. My appetite is excellent and though, of course, I feel weak, yet I can step about my room a good deal, without feeling very tired. One drawback I have had in which I know you can sympathise with me — cracked nipples. I took great pains with them for weeks before my confinement, bathing them with tincture of myrrh but still they cracked and I have suffered great agony with them. I used to shudder every time I saw nurse bringing the baby to me but now I am glad to say they are healing, and I trust will soon be quite well though the first pull always makes me grind my teeth and kick with pain yet.

The immediacy with which Agnes writes, her frankness and attention to detail, are illustrated so well in this letter and make the archive the historical resource that it is. She continues:

> I will just give you all the particulars of my illness as if you were here to hear it from my own lips, and you can burn this part of the letter afterwards if you don't care to keep it. On Wed. 23rd when I got up as usual in the morning I saw the "show" and knew at once what was coming on me. I had slight pains at intervals but went downstairs as usual and it was not till 5.30pm that they began to come on me in earnest. By that time I had sent for Mrs Nixon who had promised to be with me at that hour and by 7pm the nurse and Dr had come, and I was upstairs with everything in readiness — the bed all dressed and myself with clean underclothing pinned up all round me and only an old flannel petticoat round my waist. The first or grinding pains went on till 5 next morning when after a lull the down-bearing pains commenced, but so light and so far apart that the baby was not born till 5.30pm

on Thursday the 24th. Altogether I suffered fully 24 hours but Dr Eli says that is no uncommon time for a first labour. They all told me that my pains were "light" and with long intervals hence my labour was tedious but not exceedingly severe. To me it was "anguish" especially the first stage. The down-bearing pains I did not feel so much and even the last two great pangs that brought baby into the world were not so fearful as I expected. I had no chloroform as Dr Eli does not give it except in extraordinary cases and everything in my case was perfectly right and natural. Looking back on that long long night and day now it seems an unreal misty dream. I often fell half asleep between my pains and heard, in a confused way, the clock striking the hours, the voices of the three watchers gossiping about this and that or James' footsteps pacing the study floor below. But when it was all over and they drew me up on the bed, and arranged me all nicely and saw them washing and dressing my own living baby, I "remembered no more the anguish".[44]

What follows is a long description of the baby girl who was to be called Anne Edina Hately — the middle name being given by James in recognition of his time in Edinburgh, the others in memory of Agnes's parents, a longstanding Scottish tradition. She was very large, "so much so that the first thing I heard nurse say was, 'mercy sakes, aint it a big child'". Agnes was lucky in that, though the child cried for food a good deal, at night she woke only around about midnight and four o'clock demanding to be fed. By the time Edina was three days old Agnes was singing to her and reciting to her some lines from the American missionary poet, Emily Judson. A year later the baby was hearing a German *lied*, "Schlafe, schlafe mein kindlein" and other songs. Nor was Agnes forgetting to pray for the child: "Oh, how earnestly I have prayed for the child since she was born, and long long before that she might be blessed, and a blessing to others. I have not the shadow of a fear that but that all my prayers will be answered".

---

44   This is a quotation of Jesus's words in John's Gospel Ch.16, v.21.

It is difficult to read these words in the original manuscript without being moved by them. Agnes could not have known that the next few years would bring hardship and the greatest heartache, but nevertheless, her prayers for the child at this juncture would be fully answered in both respects despite everything. Anyway, her unshakeable confidence in the goodness of God and her deep sense that the child had been brought into the world for the profound purpose of being a blessing to others tugs at the heart strings unexpectedly. What a different world it would be if this was the unclouded faith and vision that parents invariably had, and sought to provide, for their children.

A week later the nurse left the manse and one week after that Agnes resumed her letter. At first, she felt as if half her support had been removed and she was "forlorn". Soon, however, the storeroom having been turned by James into a nursery with "towel screen" (presumably for breast-feeding), carpet, cradle, rocking chair, sofa and little stove, Agnes was getting on with things well: "Here baby and I are established".[45]

Nevertheless, even after a month, it was considered normal for Agnes to be circumspect about her movement round the house and she confined herself to the nursery: "I just come down the back staircase in the morning and go up again at night. I do not yet go into any other room or the kitchen, as the weather is cold. James does the cooking, and Sally the work, and I sit and give orders".

This humorous concision of how their roles panned out is followed by further details of how little Annie is growing and the confession that "I am growing so fond of her . . . I would sometimes like to wake her up just for the pleasure of having her in my arms". Maternal instincts were not lacking in Agnes, nor were sisterly ones. At the end as well as the beginning of the letter she longs for a letter in return immediately and then adds a postscript to the effect that her "nipples are quite healed". Emotionally, however, Aggie

---

45   In April Agnes was still breast-feeding but with difficulty, because of a 'gathered breast' — the details of which she discusses with Mary.

was still vulnerable to bouts of longing for home and in writing to Mary later broke down in tears "like a child" from her overwhelming desire "just to see your dear face and hear your voice again". Others are kind but they are not "'my ain folk'. But I am happy, dear, and thankful for all God's mercy to me, thankful for my dear good husband and my darling baby, and when I get stronger this mood will pass off".

By April Agnes was dreading the hot weather with all its complex problems of keeping milk and food fresh in the days before refrigeration and asking Mary for advice on feeds. As elsewhere her attitude to rural America at that time was ambivalent but she would have cause to be eternally grateful to her neighbours before long:

> I think more of a word of advice from you on this subject than of volumes from anybody here for the Americans in general, and here certainly, have no health and no constitution, and I dread lest my dear baby should be like them . . . Don't you wash your baby twice a day, and how soon did you begin to do so? Here they wash only once a day, and they are as afraid to take a young baby out as if the fresh air and sunshine would poison it. Last Wed. when baby was almost six weeks old she and I went out into the garden for a little as it was the first fine mild day since her birth, and several people thought it quite marvellous that I should take such a young baby out at all . . . Everybody thinks her very like myself . . .

As it turned out, the force of Agnes's personality, her intelligence and the strength of her opinions would all be handed on to Edina and their shared physical likeness was a measure of that. Nowhere is this better exhibited than in a letter of April 10th, as usual, to her sister. We have already seen that Agnes had an aversion to certain sorts of American women while enormously admiring others. The visit of Miss Pepper from Fairton as an applicant for the live-in job of "washing, ironing, baking and cooking" confirmed to Agnes, if not James, the "great difficulty we have of getting 'help' in America. Sally does well for a young girl . . . but of course I need to be always at her elbow, or things wouldn't be done at all . . . We have to give out the washing and once a fortnight a woman comes in to do a two weeks ironing and baking". Agnes objected to Miss Pepper's manners, her fashionable dress, her choosy approach as to which tasks she would condescend to do and the fact that she clearly considered herself "a great deal better" than her prospective employer. She was "insufferable . . . Just imagine giving $2 (8/-) a week to a woman who would do just as she pleased in your house . . . go out 'whenever she had a mind to'". This tirade leads Agnes to make a suggestion which in later life she must have been embarrassed to remember: would Aunt come out and live with them for $50 a year with her passage out also paid? "We would still keep Sally to do the rough work and all that we would ask of Aunt is that she would help me in what I do and do it for me when I was not able".

We need to remember at this point that Agnes had no mother from her infancy and that it was almost certainly Aunt Jane who had acted as house-keeper and helped her father bring the children up. But the thought that the older woman would risk such a voyage and leave all that she knew and loved in Scotland seems a serious misjudgment — unless of course Agnes knew that Aunt had no other close attachments beyond the children she had brought up. That is possible. She also had the good sense to say that if Mary thought either her aunt or Walter might be offended by the suggestion, she should not breathe a word of it to anyone. "We would try to make her happy and she need only try it for one year", she added. Seeming to overstate her case, Agnes underlined the sentence: "We are in absolute despair" but no subsequent letter suggests that Aunt Jane took up their offer. They surely cannot have been surprised. As it turned out, Sally became a success, for by July Aggie could tell her sister:

> Sally is staying with us and I think will probably stay for years, if she behaves well. Her parents are very poor and are very anxious she should stay with us, and she seems quite contented now and is doing very well, — she is very fond of baby and baby seems quite fond of her.

The following March Sally was still working for Agnes who was making clothes for her "including a white muslin basque made from one of my old dresses" as well as "two new wrappers" (morning dresses). Agnes was also altering various garments for her maid for summer wear and was looking out for a hat for her, as well as for herself. It was a matter of pride that she should have all the summer clothes ready made by the spring. One of the most contented of letters, from June 1877, describes the two women sitting together, Agnes in the rocking chair, outside the house in the shade of the apple tree with the baby, and of course, still the sewing.

It is slightly shocking to realise that Sally's parents were likely to have been born slaves and that just over a decade earlier the whole nation had been at war to decide the fate of millions of black Americans. Feelings on the issue still ran deep and were not far from the surface. For a few days the Wilsons had hosted Hannah Patterson who had brought with her a cousin, Miss Alice Kinnier from Lynchburg, Virginia — the youngest sister of Dr Patterson's first wife.[46] According to Agnes, she was, "I suppose, a specimen of a Southerner — dark, with a lovely smile, slow speech, and the most indolent manners". This, of course, did not appeal to Agnes one bit: "Before she left I could have boxed her ears for her laziness; she was always lying down, on the lounge or on her bed, and did nothing from morning till night". It was not, however, her indolence that is of account here, but rather her opinions: "She is full of venom, too, at the North, though only sixteen, and *wishes there could be another war that the South might whip the North yet*". How many other children and teenagers there must have been, too young to fight, who had seen their fathers and brothers humiliated, and not knowing anything of the horrors of the war first-hand, still longed for revenge. This single sentence from Agnes's pen speaks volumes.

---

46 The fact that Dr Patterson's sister married a Kinnier suggests that James initially knew him through his mother, Margaret Kinnier.

Part of the reason for Agnes's acute need for a "maid of all work" was the enervating heat ("some days I feel as if I had no backbone") and her continuing exhausting efforts at breast-feeding. At four months her milk had all but dried up despite her best efforts to continue to feed Anne Edina and trying "every means to produce a flow". It was a serious matter because as the heat increased cow's milk was

> so much less safe . . . than mother's milk. Hundreds of children under 18 months die annually in this country in the hot weather; the heat affects the bowels, and if not checked, produces cholera infantum, almost always fatal. Dr Patterson says the white race is not yet acclimated here. Annie . . . has had slight diarrhoea.[47]

Such is the relationship between Mary and Agnes that their letters contain much unself-conscious chatter which reveals the nature of everyday life in New Jersey which more formal exchanges would never stoop to mention. The process of keeping an infant healthy in the summer months was a laborious one:

> Twice a day Sally goes to Mr More's for a pint of milk from their cow (it is very good and rich) — this is boiled and I then add to it one third of limewater, which I make myself, and a little sugar. This is kept down in the cellar on the brick floor and every time baby needs it a little is brought up in a tin cup and heated on the stove, or the lamp if the fire is out. Then I keep two bottles for her, so that one is always perfectly sweet and clean and ready for use. Dr Patterson says the seeds of death lie in these nursing bottles, if not kept clean. I have been giving her oatmeal gruel for some while but it is too relaxing for her in this weather . . . The 'second summer' here is the most dangerous one for infants as then they are generally teething. I often tell our friends here that there is no talk of 'second summers' in Scotland, and they think it so strange. All this difficulty and danger in rearing children accounts, I

---

47 This was one of the major causes of childhood deaths in hot weather in the late nineteenth century. The symptoms were vomiting, diarrhoea and then collapse.

suppose, in some degree, for the smallness of American families. In spite of all these drawbacks baby is growing and thriving though not so well as she will in cooler weather.

The style of children's summer clothes cannot have made for much comfort either. Mrs Scott, Mrs Nixon, and Mrs Cassidy all sent materials for the first dresses for Edina. Agnes describes the style as "entirely gored, with no waist, and buttoned up the back, and with long sleeves and high necks".

Once Agnes had cut out the patterns, Mrs Cassidy

> soon 'rattled' them up on her machine and a basque and overskirt for me besides . . . I wear it with my black alpaca petticoat. I have plenty of print dresses which I brought with me . . . but one can't have too many thin dresses. James bought this in Bridgeton one day and brought it home as a surprise. I have also got a . . . new overskirt pinned back. The 'pull backs' as they call them are the fashion here just now and some of our girls' are pinned back so tight they actually can't sit down. Are they wearing them in Scotland?

Agnes also wanted to know the style of summer bonnets being worn in Scotland. She had just been given one in lieu of a fee for singing lessons: "it is of course the newest shape, . . . trimmed with cream coloured silk, with a handsome scarlet flower . . . the ladies here are extremely fashionable in their dress; they must spend a great deal of money on it".

In June, "baking in the sun, on this great sandy plain with the thermometer up among the nineties", Aggie contrasted her situation with Mary's who was enjoying the "caller"[48] sea breezes on holiday with her children at Garlieston Bay, close to the Galloway Hills in South-West Scotland. It had, however, been a delightful summer thus far in Cedarville: "I think I never saw such a lovely 'leafy' June before — everywhere, from all our windows the eye is filled with green, full, foliage. The walnut tree at the back door looks right in at the back nursery window . . . " The hot period having now started,

---

48 'Fresh' or 'cool'.

Aggie was writing in the study with the windows wide open, the mosquito nets in place and behind them the shutters almost entirely closed, darkening the room but creating the required draughts to sit or lie in which "would give you all colds in Scotland". To create further relief, she had

> got the palm leaf fans out again . . . two on the mantelpiece of
> every room that we use . . . We often have to fan in bed and I dare-
> say you would be amused to see the fans going in church — like
> the fluttering of leaves in a forest. And I think you would wonder
> at the minimum amount of underclothing I wear — stays I have
> utterly abolished. They are unbearable.

By mid-July the combined crisis of the heat and lack of help seems to have passed. Despite three weeks of "dreadfully hot weather . . . often at 100 and over"[49], with the baby sleeping well and half the day being spent outdoors under the apple tree "with baby and my sewing" Agnes found the routine more acceptable. She was lucky: Edina would go to sleep about 7:30 p.m. and not wake until about 4:00 a.m. "when of course we are thinking about getting up anyway. We keep very early hours here. I generally have the ironing all over and put away by 9am on ironing days, and by half past 2 or 3 there is usually no more work to be done except get supper".

During this summer an event of world-wide significance took place in Philadelphia: the Centennial International Exhibition, the first official World's Fair. Designed to celebrate the 100th anniversary of the signing of the Declaration of Independence and held in Fairmount Park on the banks of the Schuylkill River, the place so admired by Aggie on her arrival, it lasted from May 10th until November 10th and was visited by ten million people. Thirty-seven countries participated. We know James and Agnes visited it (it would be odd if they didn't) from their letter of October 10th to Walter and Jeannie Hately which spoke of "little trifles" they had bought for them from Machinery Hall at the Exhibition, such as a Japanese fan, post cards, "popcorn

---

49   Approximately 38 degrees Celsius.

balls ... from Annie" and a photograph frame — "little souvenirs from the great Centennial". In fact, Anne Edina probably never got taken there for in July Agnes told Mary she hoped to visit in the fall but could not take the baby as it would mean a change of milk for her which would be dangerous. She believed Mrs Nixon would look after Edina — she was "splendid" with babies.

It is worth pausing to describe this extraordinary event, not least because it almost certainly profoundly influenced the Wilsons' lives and indirectly led to James's early death. The idea of holding such an event was conceived straight after the Civil War in 1866 but the decision to go ahead with the ambitious plan was not taken till 1870. The costs were enormous. Four hundred and fifty acres of the Park were set aside for the building projects and seven departments were decided upon: agriculture, art, education and science, horticulture, machinery, "manufactures", metallurgy, and mining. More than 200 buildings were constructed in the Park including the five largest ones: the Main Exhibition building, Memorial Hall, Machinery Hall, Agricultural Hall and Horticultural Hall. Of these, only the Memorial Hall stands on the site today. It is an enormous and hugely impressive building, now a museum, which served in 1876 as the Art Gallery with 75,000 square feet of wall space and 20,000 square feet of floor space, underneath a dome which soars two hundred feet into the air. But it was dwarfed by the Main Building which was the largest building in the world, enclosing twenty-one acres and measuring 1,880 feet in length. Machinery Hall, visited by James and Agnes, was the second largest building and exhibited 8,000 operating machines dominated by the Centennial Steam Engine designed to show the power of technology which would transform the Union. This machine was seventy feet tall, weighed 650 tons and produced 1,400 horsepower. Twenty-six of the thirty-seven states exhibited in separate buildings. One of these would have especially interested James, but of that we shall speak later. It would be impossible to remain unimpressed by this unprecedented demonstration of both the nation's achievement and its potential as it expanded relentlessly west. Despite the heat wave through June and July the average *daily* attendance in the latter month was 35,000 and by October this had risen to 102,000. America's exports increased after the event as new inventions and technologies were drawn to the world's attention.

The fine summer and autumn gave way to a cold winter, even by standards that Agnes was used to. "We are passing through a very severe winter" she told Mary on January 15, 1877. "We have steady frost all the time, and have had two great snowstorms, the last beginning on New Year's Day". There was, however, a new opportunity offered by the heavy snowfalls:

> There has been plenty of sleighing, and I have had some delightful sleigh rides. We borrowed Dr Eli's sleigh one day, and had such a charming drive to Bridgeton, 8 miles and back, James in his fur cap, and I muffled up in shawls and . . . tucked up snugly in buffalo robes, and with the bells jingling round Gipsy's neck. Sleighing is very exhilarating; they go along so fast and smooth, and the bells ring so merrily the village has been quite gay with them lately.

The winter was severe in a more important sense as well. There had been a devastating storm off the sea one Sunday in September (Agnes had missed it as she was in Philadelphia) which blew straight up into Delaware Bay and "wrought great harm down here". It was so violent that

> [I]t blew several oyster boats clear out of the water, half a mile on to the marsh, damaging them greatly, and ruined nearly all this season's oysters, burying them in sand. Consequently many of our people are not making one dollar this winter, their oysters are buried and those they do get at are so inferior that they fetch no price in the market.

The vulnerability of this little agrarian, but also maritime, community was exposed to the Wilsons' understanding as it had not been before:

> So this is quite a hard winter in Cedarville, many of the people are quite poor, and all but the wealthiest need to live very economically. Yet, in ordinary seasons the oyster trade is quite money making.

A particular instance of hardship, and how the Church community resolved to help lessen it, is given by Agnes in recounting this episode concerning the Howells — Henry and Lydia — a farming family living on the edge of Delaware Bay:

> One of our elders, Mr Henry Howell, a very good man, is a farmer away down on the marsh, near the edge of Delaware Bay. His wife, Lydia, is a real lively little body, they have a family of 6 young children. They are not rich and cannot well afford to keep a "steady help" as it is called, and so this wonderful little woman, for to me she is a wonder, cooks and sews for, and looks after, all these children, and does all that a farmer's wife has to do besides. Her sister in law, Mrs Cassidy, told me in Novr. that Lydia is going to have another baby, and had fallen into low spirits, she had so much to do, and shortly after James paid them a pastoral visit, and came home to me, quite moved by poor Mrs Howell's condition. She was utterly discouraged, and had just "given up". Her sewing had accumulated on her hands so it was as high as a mountain, in fact, mind and body were quite worn out. James like a kind hearted boy that he is, set about getting up a surprise party for her, we told several of our ladies about it, and got it all nicely arranged. I made a big rice pudding to take and also a chicken. About 9 o'clock that morning, the other carriages met at our gate, and off we started, ours leading the way. We had a nice drive of 3 miles and had great fun, shouting and talking to each other from wagon to wagon. Just as we came in sight of the lonely farmhouse, "the old Howell homestead", we all started at full gallop and bore tumultuously down upon the astonished Mrs Howell, who, as we came crowding into her kitchen, could only gasp out, "Well, I never, well, I'm beat". In 10 minutes, we were all seated in the large parlor, needles in hand, sewing like bees, and the machine whirring away in the corner. Mrs Howell brought out piles and piles of sewing; my heart ached for her as I saw it, some had been cut out for a year but it began to melt away as we sat, and by the evening a goodly pile of made garments was to be seen. We had a splendid dinner for all had brought abundance, and altogether had a most enjoyable day.

As James said, this was practical Christianity. We went there and took up Mrs Howell's burden, and helped to make it lighter for her, and I know we have, for she is just like her old self again.

1877 was a year of great political instability in America. The secret and unhappy compromise by which the 1876 presidential election had been decided and President Hayes installed was only achieved by pulling the last troops out of the South. In due course this led to further abuses of the black population including discrimination and disenfranchisement which remained until the 1960s. This unrest was on top of the Long Depression during which, from 1873-1879, 18,000 American businesses went bankrupt, including eighty-nine railroads. Agnes's letter of March 12, (only eight days after the new president took office) makes reference to this among all the other domestic detail. She had apparently spoken of it at greater length in a letter to Walter and calls it "the great failure", adding, "The times are still hard, to use the current phrase. But now that the political fuss is over and the new President elected and installed it is hoped that things will improve". In New Jersey, in Cumberland County, it was not to be the case as far as the farming community was concerned — an outcome that changed the Wilsons' lives.

It was not just economics and politics that impacted this little community near the southern shores of New Jersey. Mothers and young babies were especially vulnerable to ill-health and early death. We have seen the high incidence of scarlet fever and diphtheria but uncertain water supplies and the difficulty of keeping food fresh in high temperatures meant that food poisoning and related digestive illnesses were hard to avoid. Agnes's care of Edina's diet contributed to the baby growing very fast. A staple part of this was "oatmeal porridge" ("poshie") which was always cooked for at least an hour — a dish that was "almost unknown here". At twelve months she was bigger and stronger than any other toddler Agnes had seen in the area (she calls Edina's legs "baumelein", or "little trees") and her neighbours called her "an uncommonly fine baby". She was starting to "creep" and pull herself upright on the sofa. Health was not something her mother took for granted: "I often feel thankful that we enjoy such excellent health" she told Mary in March. But by July, although James was "just robustness and vigour personified" their little girl was ill. The heat had been intense even for that time of the year, up in the nineties (Fahrenheit) again, and Edina was dangerously ill with diarrhoea which lasted for a week. At night James and Agnes had to "come downstairs and lie on the sitting-room floor" to get any sleep at all. "This is a very trying climate", she wrote,

> — trying to the constitution and to the temper also. How can one keep from fretting with the thermom. over 90, feeling utterly weak and debilitated, as if all the joints were relaxed, when rings on the fingers or earrings in the ears seem to make one hotter, and even to think is a burden, and with a dear little child made ill by the heat and fretting all day and tossing all night, and getting thin and pale — oh, it has been awful . . .

> You can imagine what it is to have a child in that state, to be running and wiping up after, and changing clothes a dozen times a day, in such heat as I have described to you. I fairly lost heart, partly from physical causes, and partly from worry about her, I felt so afraid . . .

The lurking fear was always that it would turn into dysentery or *cholera infantum* and the task of keeping the little girl hydrated was ceaseless. Agnes confessed that she was afraid the child would die and became ill herself as a result.

Children cutting their first teeth was also considered hazardous. In June, the baby was going through this process:

> Anne has cut all her 1st teeth but 4; she has now 16; eye and stomach teeth, the most dangerous ones all through. I feel thankful and relieved, for it is the teeth that make the dreaded 'second summer' so dangerous here.

This vulnerability must have contributed to Aggie's sense of isolation. "How intensely I long to see you sometimes" she told Mary, while at the same time complaining to her that other family members had not written for two months or acknowledged her Christmas letters.

Despite this vulnerability Agnes did not understand her neighbours' attitude to their children, or what she understood it to be:

> Children are not regarded here as (what they really are) a precious gift from God, but as burdens and nuisances, and a woman who is expecting to be a mother is commiserated and pitied as a most unfortunate creature. My friend Mrs Nixon who was so kind to me when Annie was born, is now going to have a baby in July. She does not say much to me, knowing my sentiments on the subject, but she has told others that she is "just as mad as she can be", and her mother actually said to me, that she could not understand how it had happened. Oh I feel so angry at this dreadful way of talking of children. Mrs Nixon was married at eighteen, about twenty years ago I should say, and has had only four children, three living, and so far apart in their ages that they have no sympathy with each other as a family should have.

This failure to empathise with a woman who had been so kind to Agnes, and who had lost a child and who was now nearer forty than thirty seems extraordinary. Mrs Nixon was admired by Agnes for her spotless house and ceaseless industry in an earlier letter quoted. The prospect of another child might well have been, understandably, not entirely welcome to her. Agnes may have rued her words when she stayed with Captain and Mrs Nixon just two years later in very different circumstances, but she had cause to re-think them much earlier — within a couple of months — when she heard sad news from home.

Mary had lost her fourth child — a miscarriage as the result of an accident — and Agnes commiserated with her in "the dear little life cut off in so untimely a fashion . . . and your great sufferings". The younger sister then went on to describe not only the ill-health around her in Cedarville (in contrast to her own) but to conclude her account of Mrs Nixon's trials:

... how many poor devining deein' creatures there are around us who scarcely ever enjoy one day's sound health. And I wish you could see just some of the children, little pygmy creatures, with no weight or solidity about them. Mrs Nixon's baby (you remember what I wrote to you formerly) was born on 5th of July, a very small boy, sick from its birth, who dragged out a wretched existence for about 3 weeks, and died at last under the influence of ether administered to soothe its agony and hush its crying which was driving its mother nearly frantic. It had consumption of the bowels for one thing and I don't know what all else, but how could it be otherwise with a poor sickly mother.

The almost Dickensian pathos of this situation must surely have been felt by Agnes who only a little earlier had wondered how Mrs Nixon could possibly think that another child was a "nuisance". She certainly felt for her sister: "how little I knew on the 2nd of July what was going on away over in Whithorn; I should have been nearly crazy if I had known; and I have often shuddered to think what might have been if Georgina had not caught Dr White just in time. What a mercy he was not gone. Well, it is all over now ... "

Whether Agnes's next sentences were deeply insensitive or not I will leave the reader to judge. So much depends on the precise relationship of the sisters:

Would you have called this baby Anne? If my expected baby comes all right and lives, if a son, we will call it plain Samuel, after James' good old father, if a daughter, Margaret Kinnier, after his mother who died when he was nine years old and for whom he cherishes the same love and veneration that we have for mother or your Alec for his mother.

Whatever the case, it is clear that Agnes was taking nothing for granted: she had known she was pregnant since March or April and that no mother or baby was safe during pregnancy; even after that everything was *Deo Volente*. Those who suffered the loss of a parent early in life have often felt this.

The Wilsons did not consider that they could afford to go away for a week together over the summer. To rent a lodging was almost unheard of and the "enormous hotels and boarding-houses with *table d'hotes*, where one has to pay enormous prices, and dress in the height of fashion" were out of the question. But the Cassidys at Sayer's Neck invited them to stay for a week, "and I think that did us both good". By the fall, with its "lovely, cool, bracing days" Agnes had her energy back, Annie Edina was well again, and her mother was preparing clothes for when she would have to be "laid aside" in her second pregnancy. James was able to enjoy his first break from work since arriving and went to Sandy Hill, near Saratoga, New York where he stayed with friends having first attended Presbytery at Swedesboro. He also attended Synod at Newark before coming home, much refreshed, via New York and Philadelphia. But there were further difficulties on the horizon, not least for their congregation.

THE BIRTH OF SAMUEL ALEXANDER KINNIER WILSON

As autumn slipped towards winter and all the summer clothes were folded away, Agnes became more and more visibly pregnant despite the more concealing garments required by the colder weather. She was not a tall or large woman, but she was carrying a very large baby which was due in December: the signs would have been unmistakeable. Today such matters do not excite particular interest, but it was not so in 1877. Tongues had wagged and Aggie was in no mood to be dictated to.

We have seen that in her courtship with James, in her friendship with her sister, in her views of neighbours and in her opinions generally, Aggie could be, on occasion, not only direct and abrupt but quite formidable: a difficult opponent. She had views that did not sit easily with the more conservative in her church. In matters of theatre and music, in dancing and perhaps in fashion there would have been some who disapproved her stance — especially as a minister's wife. When therefore (eight months pregnant) she wrote to Mary on November 4th she was already feeling combative: she was writing the letter on a Sunday and in one tiny part of her mind she felt guilty.[50] Mary too had written on a Sunday:

> I, too, am writing this on Sunday, I confess quite a frequent practice with me, especially just now when I cannot go out and cannot spend all the day in reading. I don't think there is the slightest wrong in writing to you to-day, wouldn't I talk to you if you were here — and where is the difference?

The instinctive underlining (used so much by Agnes to express the force of her opinions) of the little word "I" and the rhetorical question give away that she is asserting herself over and against the views of others around her. Indeed, this becomes clearer as she continues about a larger issue:

> No, I cannot go out; American etiquette is very particular in this respect — a person in my condition must not be seen anywhere, oh dear no, — "this people" being extremely sensitive and delicate in such matters, and in my opinion extremely indelicate in others of far greater importance. But I must do in Rome as the Romans do, and so, though this is a lovely, calm bright Sabbath I must not go to church, and on week days must not go out to call, though I feel quite able to walk a moderate distance, in fact have a longing to take a good walk sometimes. I believe, tomorrow, if the weather is fine, I will just go out and take a walk, without calling anywhere. I don't care for them and their abominable, spurious, pretended, delicacy.

This outpouring to Mary is clearly the result of prolonged frustration and Agnes's enforced inactivity. Her household organisation and sewing were complete a month ahead of the birth and the final wintry month of her confinement she was finding intolerable. Nevertheless, the strength of her expression is surprising as conveyed in the three carefully chosen epithets for "delicacy".

---

50 The Westminster Confession stipulates that there should be "no recreation" on the Sabbath and in 2009 *The Confessional Presbyterian* ran a long article on the Biblical basis for this and what it means for today. Agnes was probably struggling with whether her letter was 'recreational' or not and comes up with a common sense answer. N. Dickson recounts that any reading save sacred texts was prohibited as well. See *The Kirk and its Worthies* (T. N. Foulis, 1912), p.15.

What follows immediately gives us a glimpse of James's mild but ironic sense of humour which must have been a useful and balanced response to his wife's explosive feelings:

> Last Sunday morning, I said to James, "Oh, I wish I could go out and hear you to-day" . . . "Well," he said, "You may, if you will go one hour before the time, wait one hour after, and sit in the corner of the gallery with an umbrella up". Isn't that just like him?

James was also good at playing with and placating his daughter who longed for his return, greeting him with the new-found words "Papa, Papa". He bought her a doll from the city which they named Robbie. The little girl would follow him up to his study after breakfast:

> up she trots after him, kicks and cries at the door till he lets her in and then she will often spend the whole forenoon looking at some old books he lets her have, and solaced occasionally with a bit of candy from his desk, which is the candy emporium for the household. She is growing very tall and changing rapidly . . .

This mutual affection and closeness is both touching and informative to read. Not all Victorian households, evangelical or otherwise, were like this. Famously, father and child relationships in such times could be cool and distant. James, however, signed his warm brief letters with multiple crosses and the words "Ever, ever, Papa". When away at synod in September 1877 he wrote that he thought of "Kidd and wee Pete" (his nicknames for Agnes and Edina) a thousand times a day, made funny remarks to amuse his little girl and in separate letters repeated that there was "no place like home". Sometimes as many as twenty kisses would litter the bottom of the final page of a letter. It should also be said at this point that Aggie's affection for Annie also knew no bounds. A long, proud and detailed description of the child's appearance and beauty[51] is

---

51   It is this letter that gives us the date at which Edina sorted through the letters when she was thirty-nine — so in all likelihood, 1915. When the archive came into her possession is not known..

followed by accounts of how her words are beginning to form. To Mary she continued:

> She calls you "May" and Walter "Wa", and every morning when I dust the sittingroom and take his portrait down from the mantelpiece, she cries "Wa, kiss, kiss", and takes it and makes the glass all dim and sticky with her slobbery little mouth. I made a rag doll for her last summer and we called it "Scotia" — she calls it "Co" and goes to sleep with it every night.

On the night of Wednesday 5th December Agnes went into labour with her second child which was born at 4:30 a.m. the following day. The date is important to state because the Dictionary of National Biography in which Samuel Alexander Kinnier Wilson's extraordinary and brilliant career is briefly summarised gets it wrong, giving 1874 instead of 1877 as his birth date. On December 6th James wrote:

> Dear Friends,
>
> I drop you a few lines informing you that Mrs Wilson has a very fine boy this morning at half past 4 am. He is a great big boy 12lbs. weight. She is in excellent health and spirits. She was only a few hours sick . . . The name of the boy will be Samuel Alexander Kinnier Wilson.

Agnes's last letter to Mary from Cedarville was written a month after Samuel was born. She had received portrait photographs of the family which made her overwhelmed with desire to see them all again — especially Mary, "the dear dear sister of my youth (I am crying again as I write). Oh, that I could see you once more". But her main topic was a description of her baby son's arrival. They had been entertaining friends to dinner on Thanksgiving Day, 29th November, and even at that stage she "felt surprised at myself, at my own strength and activity". When her labour pains started, James was out, speaking at the Methodist church, so on his return he fetched the nurse, the doctor then arriving about midnight:

Dr Eli was much impressed with the baby's size . . . He said, 'We don't see a boy like that once in a year.' . . . He is so strong that he held his head up before he was a week old, and often now stands on his feet on our knees. He has an unmistakeably masculine look and strikes out with his arms and legs in the most vigorous fashion . . . Baby is now a month old and I feel just as well and strong as possible.

Edina reacted well to the baby, was stringing words together and singing "in perfect tune" songs that were being sung to the new baby. Agnes would not afford a nurse but would make the downstairs nursery her bedroom for the winter. But of course, she still had Sally (who was at Sunday school as she wrote) and James, "the most thoughtful man you can imagine" (and who did all the shopping) to help her. When she had time to read, while the children slept in the afternoons, it was Homer's *Iliad* — the result of recently reading about "Schliemann's wonderful discoveries at Troy and Mycenae".

When James wrote to friends announcing the birth of his son, he told them, "Our church is prospering very well". It is to that church that we must now turn our attention.

CHAPTER TEN

THE CHURCH AND CHURCH POLITICS AT CEDARVILLE

IT IS HARD TO DESCRIBE the peculiar excitement of searching for and discovering documents which reveal an aspect of the past which has lain hidden for generations; documents which, until opened and read, might no longer exist, or if they do, might never be found. Unearthing the oldest ledgers of a country church deep in the south of New Jersey may not seem out of the ordinary but, in fact, it is, and was for me, the experience of finding an ancient treasure chest detailing the affairs of the church in this uncomplicated, largely God-fearing society.

But session notes, minutes, and reports are a world apart from private letters; indeed, stylistically and in terms of intention they are opposites. They are written in accordance with rules, for the public eye, and for posterity, never for the moment, never to convey emotion, only the facts. But the facts, too, tell a story, one that might surprise or appal a modern reader; one that has to be gleaned, sometimes distilled from seemingly unpromising material.

Christianity had arrived in New Jersey some two hundred years before the Wilsons, but it was only in 1838, less than forty years before James's arrival that the First Presbyterian church was organized in Cedarville. The members of nearby Fairfield church in Fairton, an ecclesiastical centre for the New England crossroads, under their pastor, Rev Osborn, supported the idea that a new church should be started for their Cedarvillian neighbours. They began with sixty members — though there was already a Sunday School there as early as 1818. It averaged 147 students weekly and was led by Rev Burt — a name that will reappear less gloriously later. In 1838 the list of elders and trustees included names such as Whittaker,[52] Newcomb, Nixon, and Bateman: families that would be important to the Wilsons forty years on. Farming families had no reason to move unless crops failed. Mr Bateman was superintendent of the ten Sunday School teachers and fifty-two scholars.

1838 was a time of controversy: there were Old School and New School Presbyterians, the latter embracing a more aggressive attitude towards abolition — the issue that would set the whole nation at war until the Confederate army surrendered under General Lee in 1865 at Appomattox. The local church was also to suffer division: Osborn (New School) had appointed an assistant who turned out to be Old School so a Second Presbyterian church was formed under Father Osborn as he was often known — the founding father who Agnes had heard remembered by 'Aunts' Ruth and Martha. But by the 1870s the differences between the churches were largely historical and it was to the First that James was appointed. Only thirteen years before, the church had built an attractive new parsonage with a large garden plot for the huge sum of 1,868 dollars at 102 North Main Street.

In 1874, Rev James H. Clark, after four years, was moving on to a new post in Pennsylvania. From July 19th his pastoral relation with Cedarville was "dissolved" as the terminology would have it and Rev J M Wood was to "supply the pulpit" for three weeks in August. Clark's report for the year on April 1st had stated: "The church was revived and four, we trust, were hopefully converted". There were no "arrearages" on the Pastor's salary, and he declared the church free from debt. This is significant historically because times were hard: "The Envelope Plan of Systematic Beneficence has been continued", he went on, " . . . But owing to business prostration, the amount collected has been slightly less than last year". In July "nearly all" the Pastor's salary for

---

52   Mr R J Whittaker was the leader of the church's music throughout the Wilsons' time at Cedarville.

that quarter had not yet been found, "owing to peculiar stringency in business matters" as Dr Bateman expressed it in the church meeting. The Long Depression, begun in 1873, was gathering momentum. Even so, the Presbytery of New Jersey had decided at the end of April to "keep up" the two churches in Cedarville — they were, anyway, having a joint week of prayer in the year.

At the start of September, the *Minutes of Session* book for the church recorded: "Session do invite Rev James K Wilson to supply the pulpits for one year with a view to call and settlement as Pastor if the way be clear in six months or any time during the year at a salary of eleven hundred dollars". By September 23rd James had made his first entry in the book to record that Session[53] met at the parsonage.

Cedarville First Presb. Church today

It seems that from the early days of his ministry James was able to attract increasing numbers to the church. This was not done, however, by conducting a lax regime. Within a month, when the Batemans applied for membership, Mr Bateman was admitted but the application of his wife was "indefinitely postponed". Nevertheless, on February 16th the following year twenty-five souls were presented and admitted — including Mrs Lizzie Bateman. Three days later nine more were admitted to membership and by March there were "53 persons united with the church: 49 on profession and 4 by letter". This latter group would have moved from another church but the 49 were converts and the fruit of the eight weeks of prayer meetings which,

---

53   The term is used to describe the formal meeting of the Elders of the church.

we have seen, Agnes referred to in her letter.[54] The total membership recorded on March 31, 1875 was 227. One family who had moved away to Bridgeton were the Cassidys: Charles, Mary, Sarah Jane and James — no doubt related to the John and Ruth Cassidy who had been so kind. Sabbath School membership was 180 and there were in the year twenty-six adult baptisms; twelve infants were also baptised.

After this impressive start to his ministry it is not surprising that on March 27th a meeting was held in the lecture room to elect the pastor formally, "if the way be clear". We have seen that Agnes had boasted that the vote was unanimous but in fact this was window-dressing by the elders. In a later election (one that came to nothing) the vote for a certain Mr McGifford was split right down the middle but rendered "unanimous"; for James ("there being no other candidate") the voting was 84 in favour, 3 "blanks", and 6 against: again "a motion was carried to make the vote unanimous". The $1,100 would be paid quarterly, there would be three weeks' vacation and the use of the parsonage would be free. It was a generous arrangement. The salary would be found out of "pew rents and incidentals to be made up of collections or subscriptions as the Trustees may see proper". The minute was signed by Wm. B. Nixon — perhaps the Captain Nixon who owned the oyster boat — or a relative. James was duly installed as pastor on April 28, 1875. Within about two weeks the glass partition dividing the lecture room had been built and dedicated. The receipts for the fund-raising Festival were shown as $113.32. A November minute shows that further money was raised that year: "To money received by concert given in Bateman's Hall under the care of Mrs Agnes L K Wilson: $44.75".

A further five members joined the church in May — Mrs Agnes K Wilson included; she had had to get Mary to send her certificate from her home church, The Free High, for this purpose. In August the church grew again

---

54   It was on March 2nd that Agnes described the impact that this admission of so many at once had upon her.

as four more were admitted.[55] But not everyone was happy for during the autumn three left to join the 2nd Presbyterian Church — though at the same time it was 'minuted' that the second church was "cordially invited to unite with us in observing the week of prayer".

When a church grows, it is almost invariable that there are concomitant problems. Cedarville was no exception. The year 1876, while continuing to see significant numbers admitted, was a year of heartache for a few. It is lost to history as to why in February Mary Jane Layton was cited to appear before session "to answer to the truth or falsity of charges against her character" but whatever the cause she failed to appear and in such a society it must have been the occasion of much gossip. By the end of March, she had still refused to attend in order to defend herself so her name "was ordered to be stricken off the roll of church members for contumacy". The use of such a word indicates the power of the church, or at least its assumption of power, as it implies disobedience to some sort of court order.[56] Nevertheless, in February a further twenty-one joined the church and six were baptised — figures that in United Kingdom today (save perhaps in the Pentecostal churches) would be sensational. James's report for the year compiled figures at the end of March which show the membership to be 251 with 231 boys and girls in the Sabbath School. (The statistical report for exactly two years earlier showed communicants to be 217; five persons were added to the church and five "dismissed"). Church members' giving had also increased with $116.23 being raised for Home Missions and $184.25 being raised for Foreign Missions. There is an interesting further line to the charity of the church for they gave $12.14 to the 'Freedmen'. For years churches in northern states used their networks to raise monies for the education of freed slaves, and Cedarville, the church

---

55   It was also at this point that "it was resolved to procure unfermented wine for next communion".

56   The "Rules for Sessions" book, dated 1906, for the Presbytery of West Jersey, states that sessions are "charged with maintaining the spiritual government of the congregation" and defines the minimum number and age of the elders that must constitute a legitimate body as well as their financial commitment to the church.

ledgers reveal, was part of this programme. Southern states had prohibited the education of slaves but immediately after the Civil War, between 1865 and 1872, the Freedmen's Bureau had been teaching slaves to read and write and encouraged plantation owners to re-employ their slaves as wage earners.

While small numbers continued to join the church through the summer and autumn of 1876, matters of church discipline were still an issue. On July 6th three church members were cited to appear as a result of "complaints being made and general rumors in circulation in the community" which affected their Christian character. On July 18th the three failed to turn up and by August 18th this continued recalcitrance meant that "it was unanimously resolved to suspend them from the church for their contumacy till they repent".[57] Was this something we would consider important today or was it a matter of unfair allegations, village gossip, misunderstanding? The mists of time are unlikely to let us know, but in the case of a Miss Burt, (perhaps the granddaughter of the Sabbath School leader of sixty years earlier?) we know a little more. "Rumors [were] being noised abroad in reference to the Christian character of Miss Emily Burt" (she had been baptised only in February that year); so in late November she was summoned. By the end of January 1877 she had still not presented herself but on February 9th the session note tells us:

> Emily Burt appearing before session and having expressed the deepest sorrow for her sin, but yet in view of all the circumstances in connection with her case, it was resolved to postpone a decision three months.

In line with the decision, three months later, on May 26th the matter was reviewed and it was noted:

> Miss Emily Burt was suspended till she give satisfactory evidence of repentance.

---

57   Such terms were standard in the "auld kirk" in Scotland: "*Repentance* or regret on the part of the offender invariably told in his or her favour; but *contumacy* was at once proceeded against, and the party handed over to the beadle for punishment on the stool of *repentance* . . ." (My italics). N. Dickson, Op. Cit. p.244.

Then, in a paler ink, above the word 'suspended' were written the words — clearly at a later date — *"for the sin of fornication"*. Perhaps her behaviour had been initially merely unseemly with the village lads but had now become illicit and resulted in an unwanted pregnancy but the circumstances remain obscure. Had James been embarrassed at first to include this? Had he been urged to add this to the record against the day when a full account of such an action might need to be justified? On January 15, 1878 there was an exactly similar insertion in the same ink and almost certainly made at the same time for the same reason. The girl this time was Emily Dallas and she *had* presented herself before session. It is hard to imagine how these meetings were conducted: presumably a young girl confronted by a panel of middle-aged men but perhaps she had an advocate with her, or even her mother; we cannot know.

It is commonplace today to assume that it was always the woman brought to the dock and that the man in such cases was excused or spirited away. James's church, however, was not averse to disciplining men, too. In February, Mr Mark Caisen was suspended for refusing a summons issued at the end of the previous year. Summonses were not issued lightly or cruelly. There are several instances, including this one, where elders would (rather quaintly) "wait upon" a fellow member to ask him or her privately about the cause of the misdemeanour in the hope of resolving the issue. In May 1874, George Gandy had been sent to wait upon Dr Robert Bateman who had "absented himself from the sacrament for more than two years". The visit revealed that "his practice interfered somewhat with his attending morning service" and that "he made it a point to be always present at Sunday School; but was sorry that his absence had excited unfavourable comments and would endeavour to be present hereafter". The incident happened in the time of James's predecessor, but it seems extraordinary that a doctor, whose responsibilities would be well known, should be subject to such investigation. His answer was remarkably gracious, and the matter was allowed to rest. At any rate, it seems that it was only when failing to appear before session for a *third* time that suspension would follow. The suspension would usually be lifted as soon as the sin was evidently repented and a welcome back into the church was swift.

That welcome was not forthcoming from society at large in their usual treatment of "fallen women" or adulteresses — as opposed to adulterers. The Church is often the focus of this hypocritical double-standard, most famously expressed in Thomas Hardy's novel *Tess of the d'Urbervilles* written in the 1870s. However, the double-standard was enshrined in law for which parliament, not the Church, was responsible. The Matrimonial Causes Act of 1857 stated that while a woman could be divorced merely on the grounds of her adultery, for a man the grounds against him would have to include other offences as well as adultery. In other words, it was harder for a woman to pursue the action of divorce successfully than it was for a man. The Contagious Diseases Acts of the 1860s were similarly unequal. The "kept woman" of mid-Victorian society was seen as "ruined" by more or less everyone, not just the established Church, as Hardy's poem *The Ruined Maid* (1866) implies.

It was during this period of dealing with disciplinary matters that James, on the evening of Sunday, July 2, 1876 took as his text Psalm 48 verses 12 and 13: "Walk about Zion and go round about her: tell the towers thereof. Mark ye well her bulwarks, consider her palaces, that ye may tell it to the generation following". It was, of course, the week-end marking the centenary of Independence Day so it was fitting that he chose as theme the history of the church. The sermon is the only one of his that is extant and is held in the offices of The Presbyterian Historical Society in Philadelphia. Written out longhand with the odd pencilled note as reminders of asides he wished to make, the preaching is plain and unemotive but clearly purposeful. The pastor was concerned to show that the vicissitudes of the church had not defeated it and the recent influx of new members had been one of the largest in its history. At the end of the address there is a scrawled note asking "Who will preach the second Centennial sermon and who will be in these pews?" The obvious inference is that his hearers were expected to realise their responsibility to those who came after, which takes the mind straight back to James's text: "consider her palaces, that ye may tell it to the generation following".

The source of the sermon must have been the session notes and minutes kept by pastors from the earliest days, as well as the recollections of local people and older members. The details are different from those in the document, *History of Cedarville First Presbyterian Church 1838-1978*, and I suspect the authors of that history did not know of James's Centennial address. The tone of it cannot have been his only *modus operandi* for he was an evangelist as well as something of a scholar. He reminded his congregation of the growth figures. The average incumbency of each pastor was "a little over seven years" and the "most ever taken in at one communion" was under Mr Curran, the church's first full-time pastor, when 58 joined "on certificate from Fairfield" — effectively, it was therefore a church 'plant', the moving of part of a pre-existent congregation. Under James, however, 53 were added at a single service as a result of profession of faith, the result of evangelism. In his first two years, James calculated, some 85 souls had been added to the church, which was remarkable. Agnes admired his preaching in several letters, not least when she wrote to her sister Mary in January 1876:

> I do wish you could hear him preach sometimes. Though I am his wife and know him so thoroughly, do you know that I listen to him every time as if I heard him for the first time, his manner and delivery are so fresh and attractive. My mind never wanders when he is preaching.

It seems that James was one of those unusual pastors who enjoyed not only preaching of different kinds — evangelism and exposition — but also administration and leadership. In one of his few longer letters (undated like all of them) but dateable by its content to the week ending Saturday September 22, 1877, James described how much he enjoyed being moderator of the presbytery for the whole session, jokingly telling Agnes and Edina: "Papa is getting to be very important among the brethren". Sometimes an issue was debated for up to seven hours at the meetings with the result that he would be away longer than expected, but, he said, "I feel my health in every way improved". Some issues raised a lot of "excitement" and he was stimulated by the addresses, one of which, Mr Muller's, "left a lasting impression on our minds". Evangelism was, however, a different sort of joy. When at Woodstown for a week in December 1875 he wrote to Agnes: "I am very much needed here and it is glorious work". He explained: "I speak every night. I suppose there were 15 or so enquirers last night and many in tears. This is a very interesting field for Revival work". He warned Agnes that he might not get back when expected but added: "I will only remain because of the great urgency of case in these meetings".

The first signs that the church at Cedarville was in renewed financial difficulty came early in 1877. The Long Depression was biting hard and many in the State had lost investments or jobs.

Unable to pay the Pastor's full salary at the start of January, the church paid him $196.25 at the end of the month to make up the deficit. In March there was a deficiency of $50 in the first salary payment and in July and September payments of $227 and $115 were made suggesting that it was now difficult for the people of Cedarville to reach the normal quarterly payment of $275 on time. Irregular payments followed in October and November (as well as in January and March of the following year). At the Annual General Meeting of the church on November 10th, William Nixon, Church Secretary, recorded that "the Treasurer reported that the income of the church was not sufficient to meet the expenses". The matter was no longer something that the eldership could keep to themselves but one of which the entire congregation should be informed. On December 1st, therefore, a meeting was convened for everyone at which it was made plain that the "church was two hundred and twenty five dollars behind". In time-honoured fashion a committee was inevitably formed and tasked with the job of canvassing the congregation and soliciting subscriptions. Good work must have been done in this regard because by November of the year 1878, the church debt had been reduced to $100.

In the meantime, James and Agnes Wilson, and their two children, had left Cedarville. On April 16th his pastoral relation to the church was dissolved by the West Jersey Presbytery and on 28th April the pulpit was declared vacant; that month James received his final salary payment of $247.50.

What had happened to this faithful pastor and evangelist who had suggested in July 1876 that the church had survived through the lean years and could do so again? Was he abandoning the sinking ship, and, to change the metaphor, leaving his flock when they most needed him, and what reasons might be found for his departure after only four years?[58]

Psychologists tell us it is the human condition to think more frequently of the negative than the positive and to be judgemental, but to be an impartial historian requires a more rounded and objective approach. The first reason that presents itself for the Wilsons' departure is financial. For over a year the church had been struggling to pay James's salary. It was not just that the income of the congregation had dropped in the Depression but that the expenses of the church had increased. In particular, a terrible storm of 1878 damaged the roof of the church and it was found necessary to replace it at the cost of nearly $350. In the previous October the Parsonage roof had to be repaired and there were other development costs for that building, too — the roofing of an outhouse; netting for the doors one hot fly-ridden June; the construction of an arbour and a fence. Every detail of church expenditure is listed in the accounts which provide insight both to the trades and economics of the time. A heavy summer hailstorm broke some lights that had to be replaced; a street lamp outside the church needed fixing; blinds had to be repaired. Materials and labour cited for the roof included shingles, carpentry, lumber, carting, day work, and "machinery work". Tacks and nails were inventoried at a cost of 28 cents. Heating too was needed. Three tons of coal cost $20.25; six barrels of charcoal at 50 cents a barrel cost $3; Oil was needed

---

58 Four years was not an unusual length of stay for a pastor at the church in Cedarville. It was the average shared by the five men who occupied the post in the eighteen-seventies and eighties.

for the lamps in church. The sexton was paid $25 a year for his heavy work; Mr S Conover was paid $12.50 for five days working as a carpenter. Doors had to be "grained", floors laid, walls and fitments painted, chandeliers hung. All these tasks are enumerated and 'minuted' in the church records.

The result of this financial downturn was that when Mr McGifford was elected to replace James, his salary was to be $600 — hardly more than half what James was paid. Interestingly however, it seems that the new minister was never employed. Did he decide that the remuneration of less than two dollars a day was not viable? When Rev G L Smith came in his stead, in July 1879 he was paid his quarterly $176 — an annual salary of $704: effectively, two dollars a day.

There is nothing especially surprising in these church accounts, but they are a reminder that such societies are fragile and rest on the continuance of prosperity and order. Without those there has to be change, or a new vision, which will find a different way of negotiating reduced circumstances. Had James's concern been predominantly about his salary he would hardly have been planning to move to the tiny fellowship in Wakeeney, Kansas, where there was no Presbyterian church at all and where everything, not least income, was more uncertain than in New Jersey. Indeed, there were many reasons *not* to move: good and supportive friends had been made; the church had grown substantially; the eldership was steady and reliable; the manse was unusually spacious and the garden very productive. The two small children, Edina and Sam, were happily settled there and Agnes had the help she needed in the community where she could enjoy a variety of music-making. Anyway, moving the family would be an enormous upheaval. With such a young family, if a change were desired, it would have made more sense to move to a larger congregation, easily found in the not-too-distant cities of New Jersey and Pennsylvania. Instead, the Wilsons moved to the very edge of civilisation with all its risks. We need to examine what might have induced them to make such a move.

CHAPTER ELEVEN

REASONS TO MOVE WEST

THE FIRST THING THAT NEEDS to be said is that James was an adventurer. Though countless others had also left Ireland behind, he had made the journey alone, in 1863, at the tender age of seventeen merely, as we have seen, to stay with friends in Philadelphia. But he had also visited Canada in 1865 and New York, as well as Pennsylvania. Moreover, his journey across the Atlantic was even more uncertain than when Agnes boarded ship over a decade later. Breaking with family tradition, he had then studied at Princeton and in Chicago, in Edinburgh and at Auburn: he clearly liked new places and meeting new people.

The second point to note is that James came from farming stock and knew what it meant both to own land and to be deprived of it. Ireland in the mid-nineteenth century was a place of all but indescribable poverty which was overwhelmingly evident before, during, and after the Great Famine into which he was born. His delight in the large garden or plot at the parsonage and his care for both the crops and the livestock in it, come through very strongly in both his own and Agnes's letters. Fencing it off, getting help in it, harvesting the produce, buying and husbanding the animals was all a source of great pleasure to him. Twice he mentions that he hopes Sally is taking "good care of the cow, pig and chickens" and adds once that if she does so he will buy her a "nice present". When writing from Sandy Hill, New York, he says to Agnes: "tell Mr Cassidy that beef cattle can be bought here for 3 cents per pound". In another place he says he is looking at "cattle etc." In a letter of January 3, 1878, Agnes told Mary that they had sold their cow and bought another and that in the mornings James would bring in the warm milk for them all. A steer was also kept at the parsonage for beef, as well as the pig for bacon. James also notices landscape and the farming quality of the land. Of Woodstown he says it is "much like Cedarville, only better land and richer people".

At some point, James's general interest in farming began to find its focus in Kansas. This is likely to have been as early as 1876 when, as we know, the Wilsons, in common with most of New Jersey, visited the Centennial Exhibition where the Kansas and Colorado building was a centre of attention. In two (as ever) undated letters, one from Bridgeton and the other from Sandy Hill, he variously wrote to Agnes "I like Kansas", and "I saw Mr [?]Bernard here. He says my chances are good about Kn—". Since it is inconceivable that he had been that far west without it being alluded to in letters from both the Wilsons, he must be referring to discussions he held about what he had discovered — and what more likely to fire his interest than the Centennial Exhibition?

During and after the Exhibition interest in moving west to Kansas was widespread. The Kansas Pacific Railroad produced a fifty-two-page booklet designed to attract as many settlers as possible to a seemingly limitless area. Though it is pure advertisement, the 1879 booklet draws on factual information to make its appeal. The long account that it gives of the developing state was what James and other migrants would have been hearing from multiple sources in the mid-eighteen-seventies. Others had written less sanguinely, including Rev Thomas Ambrose Butler, an Irish priest, whose advice, in his 1871 pamphlet[59] to would-be Kansas immigrants, was to stay in Ireland unless life there had become impossible or future prospects were very dark. To those, however, who were victims of eviction and crushing English law there was the incentive that they would have "no master over you but the Great Lord of Heaven and Earth". After five years of ministry at Leavenworth, to those who came he recommended a continuance of the farming life as a means of prosperity, beginning again as a farm labourer if

---

59   *The State of Kansas and Irish Immigration*: http://www.kansasmemory.org/item/220006.

necessary, rather than coming to grief in the eastern cities as so many had — as dockers, canal builders and railroad workers. Their plight, wrote the priest, was often more deplorable than "beggars in the ruins of old Ireland".

To all Europeans, Kansas was an astonishingly new country. Geographically in the centre of the Union it covered 81,000 square miles from the Missouri to the Rockies — roughly the size of England, Wales and Ireland combined — and was 'empty': only the wild Indians roamed its plains, leaving little trace of their passing. It is easy to forget that only twenty years before the Wilsons arrived in New Jersey, Kansas was practically unknown to anyone save the Indians, Jesuit missionaries and the few soldiers who lived on its vast prairies, broken only by the Indian trails and those of trappers. Prior to this Kansas was considered unsuitable for white settlement. Its native peoples, the Arapaho, Cheyenne, Comanche, Osage, and Pawnee, while having preferred areas had often moved where the seasons and hunting took them and did not regard the land as something to own. It was only in 1854 after the land opened for settlement that the first small stream of immigrants made their way up the Missouri from St. Louis heading for the protective walls of Fort Leavenworth to trade with the soldiers and freighters. Thereafter the town, like all subsequent settlements was built through land surveys, mapping, and the selling of cheap rectangular 'lots'. Within fifteen years stone and brick buildings, churches, schools, banks, theatres, shops, store-houses and tradesmen's workshops all supported a population which grew to 25,000. Thousands of these were Irish, mainly industrial labourers. Their pay in 1870 was $1.50 a day from which it was impossible for a married man with children to save anything. The emancipation of the slaves had meant the labour market was glutted and rates of pay had dropped. But those who had bought land early when it was cheap and skilled labour was rare had already paid off their debts[60] and 'lots' bought in the town quickly

---

60 Carpenters and blacksmiths could earn $3-4 a day, bricklayers $4-5 a day — but the latter only from spring to the start of November.

quadrupled in price. From that eastern edge of the territory development rapidly spread westwards.

Those who worked on the farms, however, could earn good wages in Kansas. A single man earning twenty dollars a month, and board, could save $200 a year and in four years buy a small farm or rent some land with a view to buy. Rev Butler in his advice to his fellow Irishman wrote: "The money thus acquired was sufficient to purchase a fine farm within a few miles of the city". It is entirely possible that James, in considering the move to Kansas, had either read this pamphlet or was familiar with the good advice it gave — for he was to act in accordance with it, but instead of saving while out there he had done so beforehand.

The economics of such immigration are interesting for they gave rise to the pervasive 'American Dream', the rags to riches fairy tale. The landless immigrant could acquire land in two ways. 'Pre-emption' allowed the squatter on public land to purchase up to one hundred and sixty acres in preference over other claimants when the land came up for sale. In the early 1870s, at $1.25 an acre such a farm would cost $200 or about £36. A farmhouse could be built for $100; horses or mules, several milk cows, a plough and other implements might cost a further $400 so four years' savings could cover the costs of owning and working the land — land without rent or landlord or the threat of eviction: a seeming Garden of Eden to an evicted Irishman. As Butler in a sublime but unwittingly ironic moment (he was not prone to exaggeration) said: "You can soon possess land as fertile as the green fields of sorrowing Erin, where the voice of famine can never reach you, nor the threats of tyranny strike the ear".

The other means of owning property was through the Homestead Law which permitted any person over twenty-one (or head of a family) to acquire, by occupation and payment of eighteen dollars, one hundred and sixty acres which would only become his after five years of sustained improvement. 'Landmarks' or stakes would be driven into the boundaries to demarcate the property from a neighbour's and thereafter the process of 'grubbing' the 'claim' to prepare it for planting or stock would take place.

In one important respect, however, Butler was wrong in that he extrapolated from his own experience to comment on the freedom from disease in Kansas (He made only three 'sick-calls' in a year). "Chills and fevers" arising from newly turned soil and in the depressions of creeks he dismissed as little more than the equivalent of sea-sickness and prescribed the liberal use of quinine as a remedy. Interestingly, the Kansas Pacific propaganda claimed that typhus fever was absent from the state and it may be that this too was an incentive for the Wilsons since we have seen that James was subject to a number of times of illness. If so, then their move west was a terrible further irony in their story.

One further possible but controversial motive arises from the reading of Butler's pamphlet. He was a Catholic priest and passionate in supporting the faith of his widespread flock whom he travelled long distances to visit on horseback. The growth of Catholicism in the state had been a considerable success. In 1854 there were three Catholic churches but by 1871 there were forty-five. Nevertheless, huge distances had to be travelled by some congregations to attend mass, so Butler called for "zealous young priests" to join him in serving the "noble-hearted peasantry . . . in want of the consolations of our holy religion". If we fail to see why this might incentivise couples like the Wilsons it is a mark of how far we have moved away from such times.

It was only in 1870 that the First Vatican Council had closed its proceedings. During them the doctrine of Papal Infallibility had been defined dogmatically and the nature of the 'true Church' confirmed. The Council determined that any deviation from Catholic truth and the acceptance that the Roman Pontiff possessed "the primacy over the whole world" was impossible "without loss of faith and of salvation".[61] The Church rather than Christ had now become the Mediator between God and man — the absolute reverse of Reformation theology. For a Presbyterian, or indeed any Christian of any sort other than Roman Catholic, such a proclamation was not only disturbing but

---

61   See Prof. F J Paul's *Romanism and Evangelical Christianity*, (Hodder and Stoughton, 1940), p.321.

an affront.[62] No other mainstream churches were exclusive to this degree and, of course, everyone other than Catholics not only deemed it to be entirely false but, to those who cared, a dangerous heresy leading individuals *away from* rather than towards a direct personal faith and experience of the living God. For the virgin territory of Kansas to be hearing that falsehood rather than the true Gospel would motivate people like James to go out and spread the evangelical faith in this new frontier country. In a single year during the period of James's ministry, Presbyterians founded one hundred and forty-six churches across the Union, eight of them in New Jersey and twelve in Kansas. One thing, however, Wilson and Butler could agree on, as the latter put it: "The one great fault here, as at home, is love of intoxicating drinks".

As for James himself though, it is hard for us to escape the feeling that he wanted to farm — at least as a sideline to his ministry. He clearly had great energies and organisational ability which would allow him to do both, given the support and strength of purpose which Agnes brought to the partnership.

The 1879 Kansas Pacific Railroad (KPR) booklet referred to earlier had a confidently assertive title: "*Kansas Illustrated. An Accurate and Reliable Description of This Marvellous State for the Information of Persons Seeking Homes in the Great West*" by L T Bodine.

After helping his readers locate Kansas on the map, Bodine opens his eulogy of the state with the announcement that "Owing to its greater altitude Kansas enjoys immunity from malarial diseases" and continues, "The Climate of Western Kansas is particularly inductive to health" citing the increasing altitude as the KPR snaked over the "undulating plateaux" westwards from 778 feet at the capital, Topeka, through to Wallace (3,300 feet) up to 4990 feet at Hugo (in Colorado). Some of the finest wheat in the state, Bodine assured the reader, was growing high up at Grainfield, thirty-six miles west of Wakeeney and two hundred and ten miles west of the line at which, fifteen years before,

---

62   It is by no means certain of course that all Catholics or even priests believed this dogma.

agriculture was deemed impracticable. By the late 1870s that view had changed, partly through better knowledge of the area and partly through improved technology. A dozen major rivers, some fed by the meltwater of the Rockies, threaded through western and central Kansas forming "one of the grandest systems of water courses in the whole country". This supply of clean water was complemented by a beautiful dark, rich, loamy soil of extraordinary depth. The ravines and 'bottom lands', as they were known, were full of tall trees: cottonwoods, oak, elm, maple, black walnut and hickory. The stone outcrops were suitable to use for masonry. There were, therefore, the natural materials for building as well as ground that was immensely fertile, either as grassland for raising stock or for the cultivation of corn and cereal crops.

1854 saw the erection of the area into a territory and in 1861 it joined the Union as a 'free' state, but only after it had earned its reputation as 'Bleeding Kansas'. The epithet was a result of the widespread violence following the Kansas-Nebraska Act which contained the stipulation that settlers would vote on whether to allow slavery within the Territory. Pro and anti-slavery settlers from neighbouring Missouri and from the North ("Free-Staters"), respectively, poured in to gain the Territory for their cause either as a slave state or a free one — presaging the Civil War and the infamous Quantrill Raid of 1863 which largely destroyed the town of Lawrence. At that point almost the whole population lived in the eastern half. The western half was the domain of the "wild buffalo and the still wilder savage" as Bodine calls them, inhabitants of the "American Desert".

No railroads existed in the territory until work started in 1855 on the eastern border at Kansas City. By 1864 forty miles of the line were in operation as far as Lawrence. By 1867 the line had reached Salina and in 1869 its name had become the Kansas Pacific Railway. In August 1870, the construction running east from Denver, Colorado, met the rails running west from Kansas at Comanche Crossing and the first coast-to-coast line was completed. The pace of change which the KPR allowed was sensational. In order to provide the passengers who would finance the line, and so expand the economic capacity of the Union by turning prairie into farmland, the Pacific Railway Act authorised large land grants to the railroad along the "Golden Belt" twenty miles either side of the main line, thereby encouraging new towns and economic growth. Wakeeney, dubbed "Queen City of the High Plains" by its founders, where James and Agnes would end up, was one such town. By 1878, the year they moved, Kansas was raising more wheat than any other state in the Union. The corn was promising well too. Barley, oats, buckwheat, sorghum, beans, cotton, flax, hemp, and tobacco were all being grown successfully. Livestock products were also doing well, fed by "the finest and most reliable grazing land in the world". It also had the smallest outstanding debt of any state in the Union. Forty-six million acres of the state were up for sale for between two and six dollars per acre by 1879 and land prices were expected to rise sharply. For those willing to work, and whose prospects back east were bleak or unpromising, this young state seemed to offer an earthly paradise, "a home where every honest, thrifty man is the equal of his neighbour". Of those who emigrated in 1878, as the Wilsons did, forty-three percent settled somewhere along the line of the KPR, following as it did, the fertile Kaw or Kansas river valley for one hundred and fifty miles and the Smoky Hill for two hundred and fifty. Within this Golden Belt the corn and wheat fields would soon stretch illimitably from horizon to horizon. How odd then that this State of Kansas, full of hard working farmers, during the decade when the Wilson family set out towards the setting sun, was the location, as we shall see, for so many adventurers whose names have become legendary either for lawlessness or for the taming of the "Wild West": two contrasting worlds alongside each other. Where they touched, they sparked wildfire. After all, what Bodine in 1879 called "The Wild Lands" still amounted to upward of 40,000,000 acres. In Trego and Graham counties alone, Kansas Pacific had nearly 350,000 acres to sell at that date. The attraction to so many was that "any man with a little money and a good stock of energy can readily make himself master of a noble landed estate, and secure independence in a few years" as Bodine put it. Reduced or free rail fares accompanied trips to inspect land, and free accommodation for immigrants on the journey — sometimes in elaborate hotels — at certain points capped the propaganda. The sentiment and phrasing ("landed estate", "independence") seem precisely calculated to appeal to the Irish poor and the provisos that Rev Butler prudently included are nowhere to be seen.

There were, of course, negatives. Typhus and malaria were certainly not absent as we shall see; the winters on the high plains were bitingly cold with hard frosts for two months while July could be scorching hot; not every harvest was better than the one before and drought or locusts (as in 1874) could devastate a year's crop; with the advent of steam-powered machinery it was harder for tradesmen to get jobs. The Native American problem few thought of but with hindsight it can hardly be ignored and would rapidly impact, if briefly, the Wilson family. It was only in the extreme north of the state that any "wild" Indians continued in their traditional ways. Since the Civil War any small bands found by army or settlers were liable to be shot or removed to the Indian Territory further south. Rev Butler was sympathetic to their plight, calling them "generally good citizens, and as kind and gentle as the majority of the Caucasian race" — happily accepting the fact of their interbreeding with whites. Nevertheless, he concluded, eventually "the noble red-man will be exterminated, if the teachings of civilisation fail to reach his heart and curb his inclinations". Butler might have added that since he knew "the teachings of civilisation" enabled land speculators to buy a plot from an Indian woman for $400 one day and sell it for $900 the next, the Indians might well feel their own culture was more honest. He also knew that numbers of them, intolerably removed from their homelands and traditions, were leaving the alien land they were expected to farm and returning north to hunt buffalo (bison) and antelope. But Kansas was no longer a place where they could survive — even as peaceful nomads — without fear of attack from the invading myriads. James would not have thought he needed to consider them a threat, but he was entirely wrong.

The facts and figures about crop yields and livestock would have been graphically illustrated for James when he and Agnes visited the Centennial Exhibition. We know from newspaper pictures what the interior of the Kansas and Colorado building looked like: elaborately decorated with grasses and cereal crops in sheaves and other elegant architectural shapes, it was also full of the best vegetable products that could survive the journey east. On one wall there was a map of the state with the counties demarcated and on its left a tableau of stuffed animals representing the range of both farming and hunting that was available. The Kansas exhibition was a natural focus for him when so many were already heading out there. But in fact, James's attention might have been drawn to Kansas seven years earlier, as early as 1869, for in that year there was the National Exhibition of Fruits in Philadelphia and the show's Great Gold Medal was awarded to Kansas over all the other states in the Union — an achievement worth the notice of the newspapers.

There was, however, a catalyst which may have been also the foundation of his thinking about the move, a motive more essential and urgent than any of the propaganda or popular feeling which undoubtedly swayed the majority. We know of this event from only one source: James's obituary. In that document the writer tells us: "Moved by the wants of the West, as presented by Dr Sheldon Jackson, the heroic Bishop of the Mountains, he came to Kansas ... "

Nowhere does this event appear in the surviving letters, but Sheldon Jackson's ministry is remembered today by local communities. He was an extraordinary man. A Presbyterian minister and missionary, just five feet tall but with a full beard and a piercingly direct gaze, he travelled more than a million miles, mostly across the Western United States, founding a hundred churches. He had been at Princeton about ten years before James. From 1872 he published a denominational newspaper, *Rocky Mountain Presbyterian*, which included pictures of the West and which James and Agnes may well have read. Like Butler, he was an advocate for his cause, and unquenchable, insatiable, in his desire to see remote districts brought under the influence of the Gospel.[63] That combination of vigorous adventure and earnest preaching — two of James's own attributes — would have been irresistible and inspirational to him.

Before describing James's final journey, it is worth reflecting on this young man's life thus far. Leaving a settled home life in County Monaghan he had boarded ship for America at seventeen, travelled through Canada and several East Coast states, become a successful businessman (though it seems he never went out with that intention) and had been accepted for study by no less than four theological institutions in succession. By the time he was in Edinburgh he had somehow saved enough money to visit the cultural capitals of Europe and enjoy much of the best of the "Grand Tour" usually affected by the wealthy. Once married, he took over a struggling rural church, built up its spiritual life and greatly enlarged its congregation while experimenting with farming livestock and crops, albeit on a very small scale. Within four years he felt the need to move again. A divine discontent complemented by his innate wanderlust and reinforced by the circumstances we have listed, ensured that he would move. Like David Livingstone setting out for Lake Ngami exactly thirty years before, his motives were varied: taking the Gospel to a frontier area, a desire to explore the unknown, and the need for a challenge beyond his current situation.

Why, however, was Wakeeney the Wilsons' choice? There is no doubt that both of them would be involved in the decision. Some women are overwhelmed by husbands of extraordinary energy and commitment, but Agnes was clearly not one of those. She would have discussed with her husband both the difficulties of the journey there with an infant aged six months and a toddler of nearly two and a half as well as the rigours of setting up a new home in an area completely without hospital facilities and without, initially,

---

63 He became famous for his endeavours (which ended in Alaska) and also for his political stance.

any of the social life or other amenities to which she had become accustomed in New Jersey.[64]

The origins of the settlement in that part of County Trego lie with the purchase in October 1877 of land alongside the railroad by James Keeney, a land speculator in Chicago, a city in which James had lived and studied. With his business partner, Albert Warren, Keeney formed *Warren, Keeney and Co.* and surveyed and plotted the land early the following year. Naming the town with a hyphenated portmanteau of their surnames they billed it "The Queen City of the High Plains". A small tributary of Big Creek River (two miles south) flowed through the centre of the plot and this in turn was a tributary of the grander Smoky Hill River which rises in Eastern Colorado. The Saline is also close, a few miles north. Soil, climate, water supply and rainfall all suggested to them that the area would sustain development. It was about two hundred and eighty miles west of Kansas City, the same from Denver, capital of Colorado, and expected to become the equal of those cities. The rapidity with which the speculators were proved wrong is shocking. The 1879 Kansas brochure, however, confirms that it was seen as a "new town, which from its rapid growth and future prospects deserves especial mention". Bodine explains that in March 1878 there were only four buildings — the first two being the Warren and Keeney Hotel and its ice house. The hotel manager was also the sheriff and in January of that year the train made its first stop at Wakeeney (one mile west of today's "incorporated city") to let his wife and family off. Just five months later it would stop to let off Rev Wilson's wife and family. At this point supplies for the hotel were hauled up from Hays (thirty-four miles away) by men operating a hand-car on the railroad. By the time of the publication of Bodine's text (summer or fall in 1879) there were six hundred inhabitants and over one hundred houses as well as hotels. Supplies would come up by train. There were

---

64   Livingstone's wife Mary would not hear of being left behind and brought their three young children with her as he set off "to plant the seed of the gospel where others have not planted". See O. Ransford, *David Livingstone, The Dark Interior* (John Murray, 1978), p.54-5. Livingstone's lonely death in 1873 and the arrival of his body at Southampton, 15th April 1874, just as the Wilsons were about to emigrate, may well have impacted on James's thinking. It was an event "unequalled since Nelson was brought back from Trafalgar". Op. Cit. p.309.

also a "laundry, brass band, two newspapers, furniture, millinery, five dry goods and groceries, two drug stores, three hardware stores, meat market, four harness and shoemaker stores, three livery stables, three housepainters, three blacksmiths, a bank, five land-agents, tinsmiths, lumber dealers, etc. etc."

It certainly looked as if the Wilsons had chosen well and that their new home would be at the centre of a thriving community with rapidly expanding churches. However, within two years many new settlers were leaving as rapidly as they arrived and by 1882 all that was left commercially of Wakeeney were five poorly patronized retail stores.[65] Its population today is less than two thousand, and on the decline.

The other things that would have attracted any energetic migrants were the abundance of possibilities: wells could be dug as shallow as twenty feet; soft magnesian limestone could be easily quarried, cut with a common saw and dressed with a jack-plane. As a result, the stone was as cheap as lumber. There was also plentiful sand and lime. The rich nutritious grasses made Western Kansas unexcelled as stock country; the claim was that summer or winter there was no need to feed cattle a single "pound of hay or grain". Letters to the *Chicago Tribune* (September 11, 1875) referred to the Smoky Hill and Saline river areas as "a veritable land of Goshen — a paradise" so fertile were they — an interesting reflection on how well they expected their readers to know their Old Testament. Another correspondent wrote that out of a single twelve-hundred-acre field of wheat in one year he made a net profit of over $18,000, an utterly astonishing sum. As so much about this story, there is, however, a deep unrealised irony here. The writer moves from Goshen to mention "the new town of Keim . . . designated as the county seat of the new county of Trego". But today Keim is not even a ghost town: no one has yet been able to establish where it once was. Like Shelley's *Ozymandias* it was abandoned and "Round the decay / . . . boundless and bare / The lone and level sands stretch far away". Wakeeney came close to the same fate. It was after all on the one hundredth meridian, the official frontier, beyond which the land was in

---

65   https://en.wikipedia.org/wiki/WaKeeney,_Kansas.

the rain-shadow of the Rockies where annual precipitation falls below twenty-four inches a year, a hostile environment for homesteaders, even today. The propaganda of the time, however, stated that year on year the rains were spreading west, seemingly following the new cultivation and fences.

All the propaganda and advertising may have whetted James's appetite, but he needed a call to a church before he could ever consider also buying land to farm.

The Presbyterian church in Kansas in the 1870s was in its infancy. The presbyteries (administrative bodies representing all the congregations of the area) were far too large and had to stretch from the Missouri to the western border. In 1873 a church was organised at Hays (with eight members) in Ellis County to the east of Trego and the next year churches arose in Smith and Norton Counties to the north. In 1876 there were only ten ministers in the whole of Kansas and the need to establish churches among the ever-increasing tide of immigrants was pressing. The Presbyterians responded to that need and were the first denomination to organise churches successfully in Trego.

By chance, one of the earliest immigrants in Wakeeney, Mr A H Blair, was son-in-law to the Chairman of the Home Missions committee of the Presbytery of Solomon, Rev George Pierson, who was instrumental in seeing the need for a church there. Pierson was a cousin of the Cassidys of Sayer's Neck who had so warmly befriended Agnes. And so it was that Wakeeney obtained the services of a highly educated minister from a church in Cedarville. Accordingly, Rev James Mitchell from the Presbytery of Solomon, a "city"[66] some one hundred and forty miles away to the east, called a meeting at three p.m. on March 31, 1878 at which James's application was read out. A ballot was taken to establish the preferred method of government and the Presbyterian vote was carried and Presbytery was asked to send James 1,500 miles west to the new church.[67]

---

66 Early settlers liked to designate their villages and towns as 'cities' irrespective of their size if they were an administrative hub. Solomon, founded twelve years earlier, had a population of some 500 at the time.

67 In fact votes were cast for six different denominations — surely a foreshadowing of the current state of North American Christianity where, by some estimates, there are 1500 sects.

CHAPTER TWELVE

THE JOURNEY OUT WEST

THERE WAS CERTAINLY NO DELAY in James's movements once his mind was made up and his resignation made public. It was in mid-April that his relation to Cedarville church was dissolved and by April 25th Agnes, Edina, and Sam were in Vernon, Indiana, already some 700 miles into their long journey west. James had gone ahead of them to prospect their accommodation, arrange for passes and try to ensure some sort of readiness at their destination. Unlike their Atlantic crossing, letters are extant from this period so we can catch tantalising glimpses of the nature of the journey. One, dated April 20th, is on the headed notepaper of Warren, Keeney and Co., Dealers in Real Estate. From their office at 106, Dearborn St., Chicago, they wrote (to their land office in Wakeeney) a letter of introduction for James:

> Who goes to Trego Co. to make a permanent settlement. A large circle of acquaintance at the East will be governed by his judgment and follow him if his report is favourable. Please aid him in selecting a location and in any other way it may be in your power to do so and oblige.

While the second sentence is obviously the result of James pulling strings, the third reveals that at this date, although he had a job to go to James knew he had no house to live in on the frontier meridian. He would have to arrive well ahead of his family if they were to be safe. There was then a P.S.:

> Mr Wilson aside from securing a house for himself and family also proposes to devote his time mainly to Home Missionary work

in establishing churches and developing the religious instincts of the community.

Warren and Keeney were obviously concerned to make the best impression in the hope that the Wilsons' migration would encourage others who would also buy the land in which the partners had invested $27,000. The note also reveals (using Warren and Keeney terminology) that the young Mr Wilson was ambitious for the Gospel: his aim, like Sheldon Jackson's, was not just to establish one church but many.

Crossing the continent in the 1870s was not at all the simple thing that it became several decades later. There was a complex variety of possible routes to take as the Rand McNally map of 1870 railroads makes clear. Different track gauges were prolific, rolling stock often could not be transferred between different companies each running their own stretch of track and each interline connection required travel by alternative means to another, sometimes distant, depot. On top of this there were fifty different time standards across the Union for it was not until 1883 that four standard time zones were agreed from East to West. Because of this the differing local times made the accurate following of a timetable highly complicated, as well as making connections between trains and the creation of convenient schedules very difficult.

Having embarked at Philadelphia, the Wilsons travelled (probably via Pittsburg) to Cincinnati, Ohio, where Agnes had some unspecified trouble with a "little trunk" she had with her. By that point James had left their company and they paused to stay at Vernon, Indiana, from where they almost certainly travelled on to St. Louis, Missouri — without James while he attempted to secure a property and obtain "passes" or further tickets for the family. At St. Louis they would cross the mighty Mississippi and for the first time Agnes might have felt it was the Rubicon, for in crossing the border into Missouri she knew that the next border would be Kansas itself. At Sedalia the line would cross the Missouri Kansas and Texas Railroad, fork north-west to Kansas City and so climb westwards into the great unpopulated high plains and prairies towards Hays and the lonely little halt at Trego water tank where her home was to be. If the journey was continued without a break it would take four days and three nights by train; as it was, Agnes and the two children took about eight weeks to complete it.

Despite the obvious difficulties of travelling so far with a baby and a toddler the journey would not be without its comforts. In fact, Agnes, never a sentimentalist, describes the children as being "very good" all that Friday when they eventually arrived at sunset in Vernon to stay with the Burt family — presumably relatives of the Burts, who were church members in Cedarville. Agnes had been "nursing" the baby when James left the train and he had thought she was asleep. They must, therefore, have had a reasonably private area to themselves in that train and, depending on the class of fare one afforded, some carriages were luxurious. In 1872 Sarah Chauncy Woolsey[68] travelled by rail from the East Coast to California and left an account of her journey in which she describes both the comforts of a Pullman Palace Car and the inconvenience of lesser carriages:

> No one can realize until he has travelled in the delightful quiet and privacy of these small drawing-rooms on the Pullman cars how much of the wear and tear of railroad travel is the result of contact with people . . . Their faces attract or repel; you like, you dislike, you wonder, you pity, you resent, you loathe . . . But how is the body to steel itself against unwashed and diseased people with whom it is crowded, and knee to knee, for hours?[69]

This candid and rather unattractive depiction of how the privileged perceived the less so is balanced by a realistic and humorous account of the sleeping arrangements, in a "cupboard" on board, when *not* in a Pullman:

> A heavy and poisonous air fills your cupboard . . . snores rise in hideous chorus about you . . . and most of the ventilators are shut . . . you try to open the window at the foot of your bed . . . You take the skin off your fingers; you bruise your knuckles; you wrench your shoulder and back with superhuman strains, — all the time

---

68 Better known as Susan Coolidge, author of *What Katy Did* (1872) and many other books.

69 http://history.hanover.edu/courses/excerpts/336RR.html.

sitting cross-legged . . . A fierce and icy blast blows in and your mouth is filled with cinders in a second.

Woolsey documented her account in revealing detail about the rigours and exhaustion of such travel and its lack of privacy between the sexes. There was help to be had however. "Chambermen", (often freed slaves), in grey caps and uniforms with rows of bright brass buttons travelled aboard the train to assist passengers with the nightly routine of transforming the armchairs into beds, releasing privacy curtains from the carriage ceilings and with packing away luggage that needed moving as a consequence. They also reversed the process in the morning which, according to a railroad brochure for 1884, allowed for "comfortable sitting room for four persons . . . Emigrant passengers are accorded the same privileges at the eating stations along the line as the other passengers, but those travelling in this way, particularly families, preferring to carry their own provisions, may make tea and coffee on the stoves in the cars in the winter months". Such ease in travelling was unheard of, though to our sensibilities the beds would have been hard: "The Emigrant Sleeping Cars are not upholstered, but are furnished on the interior in hard wood and after each trip are thoroughly washed . . . No bedding is provided by the railroad company as passengers usually prefer to supply their own mattresses and blankets. Wooden partitions separate the berths and curtains ready to hang may be purchased at the Depot at a cost of fifty cents".[70]

But there was no getting around the numerous complex transfers between the trains of different operating companies. These transfers were what Woolsey described as "the distinctive expression of American overland travel" — queues four or five columns deep waiting outside enormous sheds where all luggage was weighed yet again and rechecked amid a babble of different languages, a confusion of tickets and passes, indifferent officials, anxious passengers, forbidden zones and non-matching schedules.[71]

---

70   http://www.kansasmemory.org/item/1441/page/3.
71   Willie Arnot failed to "re-check" his luggage at Kansas City when he went out to Wakeeney in May '79, with the result that it arrived two weeks late.

By the time Agnes wrote to James from Vernon she had been there a week for she had been waiting for letters from him that had failed to arrive. They had mistakenly been delivered to North Vernon (two miles off) but Mr Burt had asked the "hackman" (carriage driver) to enquire there and three were found. After that week Agnes considered herself duly "quite rested and refreshed". Breast-feeding Samuel on the journey, who at six months was much heavier than his birth weight of twelve pounds, as well as keeping the two-year-old Edina from being fractious must have been a considerable effort.

At this point in the letter there is a surprise: the Wilsons did not leave for the frontier from Cedarville *on their own*. Agnes mentions at this point that Mrs Cassidy is with them, and like her, has also been rested. Later in the letter she tells James:

> Mrs Cassidy seems anxious to leave here, and though I have been telling her that in your first letter from Solomon City you will tell us whether there are quarters there for us and when to come on etc. still she wants to leave here next week and wants me to ask you to tell us what route to take, and also to get us a pass and send it to us if you can as she does not think Clark Burt can help us in this matter.

If it were needed, further confirmation that this is the Mrs Cassidy of Sayer's Neck is provided by the mention of Annie Howell being at the house in Vernon (Mrs Cassidy was born Ruth Howell) and the fact that once in Wakeeney, Agnes will refer to Ruth being with her there as a close friend. Privately Agnes told James in her reply that she thought her friend was

> of a very restless and changeable nature . . . When I say to her that we must wait till you have a place to put us in she says we can go straight to Mr Pierson's anyway as they are expecting us there. But of course you will tell us all about the best and most direct road to take, and indeed all that is necessary for us to know — and I am not going to stir till you give us the word to do so. But of course I would like it to be as soon as possible. When we ask Edina where papa is she says "Gone to Kansas".

The final confirmation that the Wilsons and Cassidys left together for Kansas is provided in those lines, for the Cassidys were, as we have seen, cousins of Rev Pierson of Solomon City whom we have met already — he being instrumental in finding James for the Wakeeney church. But it is only in the history of Wakeeney church (held in The National Archives of the PC(USA) in Philadelphia), that it is mentioned that John and Ruth Cassidy were received into membership there on 14th July at the same time as Rev and Mrs J K Wilson, and a Mr Alfred Davis, all of Cedarville. The circle of acquaintance that Warren and Keeney and Co. were hoping would follow James's move was already starting to take shape. James and John had not only a common Irish background, but Cassidy was a farmer. Ruth was hard working, cultured, and two years older than Agnes but without children. As companions on this new adventure they would be ideal.

From Vernon westwards Agnes's travel arrangements were complicated by the separate movements of James back and forth across the continent. A month after the Vernon letter Agnes was in Solomon City, just west of Abilene in Dickinson County, Kansas, but had received letters from James who had been in Chicago, Illinois, Hays, Kansas, Mansfield, Ohio, and back in Bridgeton where he had to attend a Presbytery meeting. Chicago was the headquarters of Warren and Keeney; Mansfield was a railroad hub just north of Vernon where many lines met. There was clearly a lot of work to be done in preparation both for the job and in providing a home for the family.

While her husband travelled hastily through three points of the compass, Agnes had been pressing slowly westwards. There were many miles before she could rest up again. At St. Louis, the largest city west of Pittsburgh, she would have marvelled at the river as she crossed into Missouri over the new Eads Bridge[72] which boasted longer arches than any other in the world. It was high enough to allow the steam paddle boats with their shallow draught, distinctive wooden hulls and tall funnels issuing plumes of black smoke, to pass

---

72 Construction did not begin on The Forth Bridge, just west of Edinburgh, till 1882. It then had the longest single cantilever bridge span in the world.

underneath unhindered on their way downstream towards Memphis and New Orleans. The railroads soon took the place of the steamers commercially but the romance of *The Adventures of Tom Sawyer* (1876) had already made Mark Twain and the Mississippi (himself a pilot on the river) famous by the time Agnes crossed it. Paddle boats still ply its complex currents today.

Passing Sedalia, a railhead terminus for cattle drives and cowboys, but famous in the 1870s mainly for its prostitution (one newspaper of the time calling it "the Sodom and Gomorrah of the nineteenth century"), Agnes and the children would soon be in Kansas City, the border town of the state, incorporated only in 1872, on the confluence of the Missouri and Kansas Rivers. The Missouri, at 2,714 miles, the longest river in the Union, rises among the Rockies in Montana, then drains the Great Plains before pouring its waters into the Mississippi. At Kansas City its steamboats took a sweeping turn downstream, following the current east rather than south.

Twelve rail lines converged on the city from every direction and by 1878 even more lines reached out towards it. The old Oregon, California and Santa Fe covered waggon trails passed nearby and in 1868 there were already 5,000 inhabitants — including those who decided they had travelled far enough to find a homestead and settled instead for a house in town. The building of a swing bridge across the Missouri which allowed passage to both steam train and paddle boat brought a further flood of emigrants and within ten years the population had risen to over 60,000 despite the difficulties of building on the steep bluffs above the river. When Agnes's train heaved itself towards the city boundary and she peered out with nervous expectation she would see hardly a street that was not stacked with building materials — timber, brick and limestone — and busy with the frenetic activity of new lives being established. On reaching the Union Depot of the Kansas Pacific Railway she must have been impressed. Its long imposing façade was completed only a year earlier; in Gothic Revival style, its steeply pitched roofs, intricate towers, arched windows and rows of dormers were the equal of anything she had seen in Philadelphia. All trains to and from the city arrived and departed from the Union Depot. It was the launching pad for the one hundredth meridian: the frontier.

Between the two were some three hundred miles of fertile valleys and the Great Plains, a distance which today, in Europe, we would travel overland in a day without undue reflection or fatigue. In 1878 it was closer to the three hundred miles between civilised Londinium and the empty landscape around Hadrian's Wall in second century Britain. The travel time between the two paired locations was, of course, incomparable but the wildly different worlds they looked out on do bear comparison. For, in the 1870s, America was two nations and the separation between the urban east and the most rural west was almost as complete as that between the northern border and the south-east in Roman Britain. It was not just a matter of empty space and lack of facilities, but of law. Dodge City, perhaps the most famous of all the "cowboy" towns was on the same meridian as Wakeeney and less than one hundred miles south. In the very year that Agnes and James were settling into their new home, Wyatt Earp was an assistant city marshal in Dodge and in the same year met John "Doc" Holliday. Bat Masterson was a county sheriff. Dodge was "Queen of the Cow Towns" with its huge stock yards, the annual destination of thousands of heads of cattle coming up the Chisolm and Great Western cattle trails. When cowboys shot up the town and terrorized town folk it was Earp, Holliday and others who took them on. Outside the city, where the law hardly reached, it was truly a world apart from Kansas City with its opera houses, board of trade building, excellent hotels, churches, and schools.

Agnes, however, would see the West through her carriage window but not, perhaps, exclusively that way. Some companies attached observation cars to the rear of the train to which passengers would crowd for a better sight of the wonders they passed through. Sarah Woolsey recorded her observations:

> Twice too many passengers crowded in; everybody opened his umbrella in somebody else's eye and unfolded his map of the road on other knees than his own; but after a few miles the indifferent

people and those who dreaded cinders, smoke and the burning of skin, drifted back again into the other cars . . . [73]

It was only in 1870 that the first passenger train had left the city for Denver, over six hundred miles distant across the "Great American Desert" which had been thought of, "as a vast sand plain fit to be roamed over by savage beasts and more savage men. But now, as we are whirled across it, the whole country becomes a vision of beauty".[74] In reality, Wyandotte and Leavenworth Counties, opening up as Agnes left the city and crossed the iron bridge spanning the Kaw River were both picturesque and fruitful. Passenger trains left Kansas City on the westward route every morning at eleven o'clock. Had Agnes been able to continue her journey unbroken, she could have expected to arrive at Trego Tank for Wakeeney at 1:55 a.m. the following day — about fifteen hours' travel, averaging twenty-one miles per hour: an extraordinary speed when compared with the weeks the covered wagons would take on the old trails. A ticket for those 321 miles of track cost sixteen dollars.[75]

The stately pace of the trains allowed passengers to catch glimpses of the river as well as enjoy the orchards, wheat and corn fields and the stock farms. Thirty-six miles from Kansas City the tracks passed Bismarck Grove, a beauty spot famed for its fifty acres of imposing oaks and elms surrounding a lake. In August that year it was the site of the First National Temperance Camp Meeting which was attended by no less than 50,000 people. This would certainly have interested the Wilsons; Kansans were proud to be the inaugurators of such conventions. One mile past the Grove lay Lawrence, with its bloody Civil War history, but now the seat of the State University. After this the engine would pick up speed over the undulating prairie dotted with farmhouses, stopping only momentarily at Perryville, Medina, Newman and Grantville before slowing down for Topeka, the capital, a "meal station" where the Palace Hotel was connected with the railway. Once past Wamego, one of the largest grain

73 http://history.hanover.edu/courses/excerpts/336RR.html.
74 *Handbook for the Kansas Pacific Railway, 1870.*
75 From the KPR Timetable: "In effect May 1877".

shipping points in the state, there would be a stop at St. George, the last station in Pottawatomie County, after which the line followed up the east bank of the Big Blue River to Big Rapids and then on to Junction City where passengers could see a branch line was being built up towards Clyde and Concordia.

It was, however, Abilene, 162 miles out on the line, which was the first place-name Agnes saw that now resonates with the myth of the cowboys and the Wild West. Abilene was the first of the major railhead cattle towns and set the pattern for those that followed. In 1867 the railroad reached the town and it became the terminus for the Chisolm Trail, shipping 1,500,000 Texas Longhorns to the East in five years. Saloon keepers, gamblers and brothels were attracted by the trail-parched cowboys wanting to spend their earnings and it became a byword for lawlessness — so much so that Wild Bill Hickok was employed there for a time to keep the peace. There were eleven saloons in 1871, for up to 5,000 cow hands who would arrive in the summer and fall. By 1872, however, the town had grown so much that the cattlemen were asked to drive their herds elsewhere and order was restored.

The next station was Solomon, and from there Agnes wrote her letter of May 27th. The town was located on the north bank of the meandering Solomon River where it joins the Smoky Hill. The train was scheduled to arrive there at 7:14 p.m. and in the evening light the prosperous little community, supported by the export of salt from nearby mines as well as its well-watered farms, appeared an attractive stopover. It was to prove to be so for Agnes and the children enjoyed the warm hospitality of the Pierson family. Agnes told James: "The Piersons are extremely kind. I think Mrs Pierson one of the best women I have ever met". This is high praise indeed from Agnes whose standards we are familiar with, but the letter also suggests a certain vulnerability about her as she undertakes this daunting journey towards a very uncertain future. There is just a hint of whistling in the dark, or perhaps of biting the lip as she writes:

> I thank you very much, dear Jim, for writing to me so frequently.
> The sight of your handwriting just rejoices my heart . . . you are

a dear good husband, dear Jim, and your courage and energy and hopefulness keep my heart up and do me good. But I think I am hopeful too and I may say have never been anything but cheerful and happy all along.

Ruth Cassidy, Agnes's travelling companion who had also been on the train without her husband, had found the experience more trying still, but was recovering in the care of her Pierson cousins:

Mrs Cassidy is getting stronger and certainly looks better. I think when she gets her husband here she will be all right . . . She is anxiously awaiting your return.

One of Agnes's main concerns was of course the children — susceptible enough to illness in any age, but then, as we have seen from statistics earlier, most prone to life threatening diseases. The lack of prophylaxis then, and particularly in a frontier state, was a serious issue, especially when travelling in the constantly changing company of a wide variety of strangers for long periods:

One reason why I have written just now, though I feel half afraid you may not get this letter, is to ask you to try to get vaccine for Samuel from Dr Patterson. If you can get it without much trouble, get it, but if it is going to make you take a long car ride and worry and hinder you, don't — for I am sure the Dr would send it to us by post.

There is another concern about Samuel too:

I also think it would be nice if you could bring a baby carriage of some kind it would be a great thing — for baby is so heavy I can't carry him any distance and the dear little thing gets no air at all except on the doorstep. I don't see how I am going to get along without a carriage. I don't care how plain it is. My arms and back often ache with lifting and carrying him so much.

For the first time there is a slight air of muted panic here: the boy was simply too big now for Agnes to take around with her.

Edina was less of a worry and often a cause for some fun. Agnes had told her not to laugh when she was saying her prayers to which the little girl replied:

"I want to see God". It was also Edina who told everybody, "Papa has gone to bring Uncle John here", meaning John Cassidy, Ruth's husband, who presumably had his New Jersey farm and livestock to hand over. James, the inveterate traveller, was clearly the lynch pin of this whole enterprise: "I needn't tell you other things to bring", Agnes told him, "because you think of everything" but she confessed, "I am as anxious as you are to get into our own home", adding, "I think with God's blessing it will be a happy one. I'll do my part to make it so".

As it was, Agnes had to wait a further three weeks before her journey there was complete. She gathered the luggage that had not been sent ahead and, with the children, boarded the afternoon train for the last leg of her odyssey on Tuesday 18th of June. There were 149 miles remaining between Solomon City and Trego Tank. The journey took nearly seven hours for there were twenty small halts at which the train would pause. Forty minutes would see them at Salina, a town of 2,500 on a great south-west bend of the Smoky Hill; it had a self-catering "emigration house" where those without other accommodation could stay free till they were settled. There was an impressive public school building and the exploitation of salt springs and sandstone quarries added to the prosperity of the farms. Only a few years earlier the whole area had been dismissed as mere buffalo grassland unfit for agriculture, but the steel plough and wire fences had revolutionised its potential. Agnes was about to enter the country where just ten years earlier a certain William F. Cody was hired to supply buffalo meat for the railroad workers and deplorably (to us) shot over 4,000 in just eighteen months, earning his famous sobriquet Buffalo Bill. By the end of the year when Agnes's train steamed through it, Saline County produced, in that year alone, over one and a half million bushels of wheat and not much less than a million bushels of corn.[76] On either side of the fertile wide valley bottoms were rolling uplands of now productive prairie stretching on towards Brookville and Ellsworth, the next stops. The latter was a major shipping point for the end

---

76   http://www.kansasmemory.org/item/209737/page/38.

of the cattle trails but the farmers with plough and harrow had forced the cowboys further west still and so another great strand of the Western myth was woven: the conflict between the "free grazers" and the ranchers; the one believing in their customary right to move stock over the open prairies, the other in their right as homesteaders to buy and fence off lands to farm.[77] In the very month that Agnes was travelling, May 1878, a group of homesteaders at Collyer, just twelve miles west of Wakeeney, wrote to the State Governor:

May 3rd 1878

Honorable Sir,

We, the Chicago Soldiers Colony, at Collyer, Kansas, have been informed that Texas cattle are now enroute [sic] east, and that it has always been the custom to camp and graze along the course of Big Creek in Trego and Gove Counties, and on the land now occupied by the Colony as homesteads, and as the damage caused by the run of thousands of cattle upon it would be a very serious matter to us, utterly ruining us financially, as we have our all involved in the endeavour to obtain a home for ourselves and families, and as it is well known that those herders are composed of the outcasts of Society, unprincipled and lawless men, who disregard the rights or life of any person, we would most respectfully request that a detachment of military be sent to prevent the cattle entering the lands of Trego and Gove counties as we are not provided with arms to protect ourselves and families from such lawless men.[78]

There could hardly be a clearer 'primary source' statement of the fear that the cowboys (Agnes would call them "herd boys" in her descriptions) inspired in the local populace, if this group of ex-soldiers felt so in need of protection. In this case, the myth was based on reality — and it was not only the men who were frightening. The Texas Longhorns were wild, fierce, and raw-boned. Their horn spread could be up to five feet and a typical herd might be as many as three

---

77 Patents for barbed wire were first taken out in Kansas in 1873.
78 http://www.kansasmemory.org/item/218972.

thousand head. The damage they would inflict on agricultural land would be catastrophic and in the case of a stampede human fatalities were always possible. For those living at Wakeeney the safety and comforts of Salina were a full six hours away, but the danger felt at Collyer could be upon them in a matter of minutes. A further danger was that the Texan cows were immune to cattle tick but spread it to other breeds which could be decimated by disease the tick carried.

As the locomotive pulled its passenger cars ever upward through the prairies it would pass through the small stations of Black Wolf and Bunker Hill before reaching Russell, capital of Russell County, a growing town of about 800 people. Then in a few miles Ellis County was entered and a stop made at Victoria, a colony founded by a wealthy Scot, George Grant, who had bought no less than 30,000 acres to sell in parcels at a profit. Its station building was made of limestone, a statement of power. The county seat of Ellis was Hays, the next stop, near where a garrisoned fort was kept, originally to protect stage-coaches on the Smoky Hill Trail. The Wilson family would have cause to be grateful for its proximity before the year was out. The town itself had been a cow town to rival Dodge and in the late 1860s one employee in the foremost saloon, who slept in a room above the bar, installed sheet iron beneath his bunk to protect him from stray bullets.[79] At Ellis itself the laid tracks had reached just over three hundred miles from Kansas City. Soon after the railroad arrived, it became, in 1875, a cow town, shipping herds from the south: another place where the cowboys with cash and Colt revolvers could terrify the populace. Agnes would be glad not to have to alight there for her journey was nearly done and her heart rate must have risen faster than the altitude, both in anticipation and more than a little trepidation, for herself and the children. Within the hour she would be in Wakeeney as the train continued to climb to an elevation of nearly 2,500 feet above sea level: the High Plains awaited her.

---

79   Keith Wheeler, *The Townsmen*, (Time-Life Books, 1975), p.103.

CHAPTER THIRTEEN

ARRIVAL IN WAKEENEY

IN TRACING THE LAST PART of this long journey, we are fortunate to have, in addition to the myriad contemporary documents curated at the Kansas Museum of History in Topeka, four other sources. As well as Agnes's continuing astonishing output of letters there is her writing for a wider audience back home: three articles for *The Family Treasury*. We also have important information from the Minute Book of the Presbytery of Solomon 1876-1884,[80] and a locally published history of the church in Wakeeney which draws on early documents.

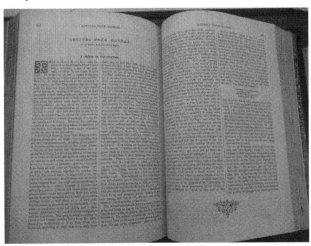

Agnes's article for The Family Treasury *1879 —*
held in British Library

Perhaps more than anything else, it was the High Plains which, on alighting from the train, first drew Agnes's attention on that bright moonlit June night. She had to walk over "quite an expanse" of rolling open ground to reach the house.

---

80 Held in Philadelphia at The National Archives of the PC(USA), 425, Lombard Street.

The gently undulating prairie was compelling simply because it was empty. The overwhelming impression was a sense of space; a sense only made more powerful by the very few buildings which interrupted it in the same way that silence is emphasised by a distant cock crow or the bark of a dog. For magazine readers at home Agnes described the buffalo grass prairies as "a land-ocean . . . The long, rounded, swelling 'rolls' look like great waves suddenly arrested in their onward sweep". To her sister she wrote: "In all directions lie the smooth gently rolling prairies like a green ocean, with not a single tree to break the lines, overarched by the vast expanse of sky". The smell of the cool, bracing air, Agnes felt, reminded her of the pure and invigorating atmosphere of the moors at Greenlaw in the Borders.

After trying to take in the immensity of her surroundings at the little halt at the Trego water tank, Agnes would have turned her attention to the few signs of habitation that she could see. The newest building she noticed would have been the home she was about to enter. It was still being completed and very visible, for the ground to the north rose from the railroad towards it. The house's land, on its southern edge, bordered the tracks. She told Mary: "To the right of the house lies what there is of the town; two dwelling houses quite near us, one that of a Mr Barclay, a wealthy man from Chicago — and beyond on a sort of crest the hotel, railway station, Warren and Keeney's office, blacksmith's shop, store etc. — very little else". Her initial reaction to their isolation in such a vast wilderness was that it was "terribly forlorn and desolate" but within a week she was able to write: "There is a silent majestic grandeur in these vast green plains and a delightful feeling of freedom . . . takes possession of me". In the first of her "Letters from Kansas" written for *The Family Treasury* readership back in Scotland towards the end of the year she explained that, "in the beginning of this year there was simply nothing at all here but the prairie, the sky, and the railroad!" By the time she wrote, however, the town had 150 inhabitants and thirty to forty buildings had been erected. The speed at which these small settlements grew was extraordinary. Garland City, in neighbouring Colorado, for instance, saw the building of one hundred and five houses in its first twelve days.[81]

It was just as well James was there to meet the three of them for it had been a long journey without him and there was much to be done. Many trunks and cases needed to be brought up to the house and in a building that as yet had no interior plastering but merely the timber-clad wooden frame it would be difficult to make settled arrangements. But the house had a parlour or sitting-room and "shed kitchen", a cellar below and three bedrooms upstairs: ample for a family of four. Its land amounted to five acres comprising twenty-two "city" lots which "clever and sagacious" James had clearly bought as an investment. The deeds to the whole property, however, were in Agnes's name and the property was to be paid for in instalments — the "universal way here"[82], Agnes hastened to add, as it allowed money to be spent on developing the new properties. All the improvements which Agnes envisaged were expected to cost another $200 or £40. She was very excited to be in "our own" home for the very first time.

For a week John and Ruth Cassidy lodged with them while their own house was being made ready to live in and the two women became the closest of friends. Agnes wrote, "She is like a sister to me" and called her "very kind". Moreover, any loneliness she might have felt was overcome by the neighbourliness typical of isolated rural communities where there has to be real interdependence if people are to survive. Sitting one day soon after arriving, with Samuel in her lap, Agnes was paid a visit: "two lady callers approached the house and in an instant I felt transported back to civilisation . . . one was young Mrs Warren, a stylish young lady from Chicago, the other Mrs Pratt, and both looked as if they had stepped out of fashion books. They are members of our church".

---

81 Keith Wheeler, *The Townsmen* (Time-Life Books, 1975), p.17.
82 The Union Pacific required only a tenth of the asking price as a deposit, and eleven years to pay the balance.

This Mrs Warren is most probably the wife of the wealthy Chicago entrepreneur and speculator, Albert Warren, who gave his name (or rather part of
it) to the township. It was not without importance that Agnes befriended her
for in the earliest days of Wakeeney, James's church was fortunate to use the
Warren and Keeney office building in which to meet. But equally, it is easy to
imagine that these young ladies would be all agog to meet the new minister
and his wife and keen to make the right first impression with their outfits.
Frontier or not, standards had to be maintained.

The other source of company, besides casual callers and the curious, was
of course the church James and Agnes had come to pastor and develop. Of this
much more will be said later but Mary is told about Agnes's first visit to it.
Predictably, her first comments are about the appearance of those who attended:

> I was out at church last Sunday for the first time, and was quite
> impressed with the appearance of the people; you no doubt have
> imagined that they must be a rough and rude-looking set; quite
> the reverse my dear, they looked very much like a city congrega-
> tion, the ladies appearing in their knife pleated silks, gold chains
> and fashionable bonnets, and the gentlemen to correspond . . .
> There were about 30 present that day.

It is easy to sense that Agnes's spirits are perking up as she contemplates
getting to know all these new people. She says nothing about the service, the
music or the preaching, but later she will.

Perhaps it is unfair to be too critical of the new minister's wife at this
stage by reflecting that her comments are to do with superficial things. In
a sense, because everything was so new and strange, everything had to be a
matter of surface impressions. Not only were the embryonic town, their new
home and the virgin territory around them entirely without precedent, so
was the fact that she was now not only a minister's wife, but a farmer's. She
coolly reveals to her sister (perhaps Mary had seen this coming) that they had

> also taken a large farm about 8 miles out, of 800 acres. We took a
> drive there yesterday, children and all, and I can truly say that I

have seldom seen more beautiful land. In the first place the prairies always remind me of the moors at home, and that gives me pleasure, but besides . . . James . . . knows what he is about. He rode about a great deal, spying out the land, on his first coming here, and has fixed upon a most beautiful region of country, admirably adapted for the raising of stock, which is what he principally intends doing. It is beautiful undulating land, breaking up here and there into ravines and dells, with a stream of clear running water winding through it. It is also adorned by 5 cottonwood trees, the first I had seen in Trego County.

The family had a picnic on the "farm" sitting on a high bluff overlooking the stream, where afterwards James "in his broad hat, bronzed face and black beard" rapidly caught four fish — perch, sunfish, and catfish which were plentiful locally. In her letter Agnes continued, "Everywhere is the short green buffalo grass, full of nutriment, and in the lower places by the water longer, ranker grasses, and flowers everywhere, most beautiful flowers, handsomer than many garden ones". The farm had cost them $1,000 (paid again in instalments) which is $1.25 an acre. The property was about a mile and a quarter square and included the rights to the stream which meandered for some two miles within the boundary markers. They thought of calling the farm, "Maple Brook". The cellar for a small house on the property was already being dug, a place where James's man or men could live while they tended the cattle, a job which James also intended to have a hand in.

The combined excitement and industry of the first week ensured that Agnes had no time to be homesick — for Cedarville or for Scotland. The children alone kept her busy enough — Edina (not any more called Annie) Agnes wrote, "speaks very plainly now, and is a very intelligent child. Samuel is . . . cutting his first teeth . . . a big, fat, good-natured laddie, very like his uncle Walter, dimple, fair hair and all, and is several times larger than most children of the same age". Agnes was lucky that such a large boy needed feeding only once a day, "and yet he is fat, and I am fat, fatter than ever in my life before".

It was Mary who needed reassurance that the family would survive on this distant edge of the world, so the younger sister wrote of the "present advantages and future prospects" of being where they were. The propaganda, as well as their experience so far all reinforced such an opinion. To further assure Mary of the wisdom of their move Agnes told her of the difficulties in Cedarville where "Mr Gandy has failed, involving still more of the people in poverty; they are completely discouraged and the whole place is just wrapped in gloom . . . We think it extremely probable that a good many of our old members will come out here beside us". (Warren and Keeney would doubtless be delighted to hear that.) She goes on to mention the halving of the pastor's salary as a result of the downturn. It does not seem to occur to her that it might sound a trifle complacent or uncaring that the minister's wife was effectively saying "we got out just in time" when her neighbours and friends were suffering appreciable economic hardship. James, however, was not the only minister to want to escape the impact of the Long Depression. There were so many applicants for each vacancy that James felt he had to accept the post without ever having visited it. To have done so would have risked a delay that might have lost him the job. With hindsight, Agnes might later think, humanly speaking, perhaps he should have waited and been less urgent. Still, for the moment she felt "It was really the best thing to do, I am fully convinced". She had "a nice boy of 13 years old" in place of Sally to help her with the housework and children. Despite saying that none of the "elegancies" of life were yet available out west Agnes had already enjoyed a game of croquet with Professor Bagley, of Abilene, "a very nice man, born of English parents on the Island of St. Helena". There were, clearly, some curious and interesting figures visiting or settling in North-West Kansas. Her first week in Wakeeney seemed to have been propitious.

By September, the house was plastered inside and painted white on the outside. Green shutters had been fitted too — just as they were in Cedarville — so that Agnes could tell her aunt it was "quite a superior little house" for

Wakeeney. Though smaller than the New Jersey parsonage it was "an untold blessing after 'living in trunks' since last April". They had the upstairs adapted by creating two large rooms in place of the three smaller ones, and by using further space over the stairs for a large cupboard and making "Jim's 'den' where he holds undisputed sway. He has shelves with his books, a large writing table, maps, pictures, straps, strings, I don't know all what, hung round the walls, his gun in a corner, and newspapers etc. everywhere". This sounds like a workshop as much as a study and the casual mention of the gun is a reminder that the wilderness around them was not tame and might contain unnamed threats.

Agnes's own work would be enhanced by the imminent arrival of a sewing machine bought from Rev Mitchell, their nearest ministerial neighbour, who was leaving Hays. They both had great plans for the house including a stone kitchen, further building at the front for a larger parlour (also in stone), more bedrooms, and outside "piazzas, fences, gates, flower garden, croquet ground etc. Of course," Agnes continued, "all this will take time but there is no harm in laying our plans and talking about them, and (D.V.) we will carry them out".

As it was, time was the one thing they did not have. Although the plans sound rather grandiose, we have to remember that besides the simple, square, timber-framed building, there was *nothing* there on the plot other than dirt, weeds, wild flowers in season and the ubiquitous prairie grasses blown by the ceaseless wind.

This letter to her aunt also lets the family back home know that the company the Wilsons will keep is by no means the "roughs" that polite Edinburgh society expected to be present in a frontier town: "in fact we have no 'roughs' here at all". Agnes added: "The Keeneys and Warrens are wealthy and 'stylish'. Most of the others, however, are not wealthy but have come here to better themselves, and are mostly intelligent, well-bred people". When the "herd boys" came in it would be a different matter. Dated September 29th, the letter not only tells us of how quickly the town was developing ("new buildings are going up all the time") but is also the earliest description of the young life of "Hammie" — Samuel Alexander Kinnier Wilson — who was to become one of the world's leading neurologists and, in the medical world, a name to conjure with. His monumental work *Neurology*[83] has been described as perhaps the greatest single-authorship medical textbook ever written. Agnes describes both children:

> Edina is getting so much sense, and is so sweet and companionable that she is a great comfort . . . Samuel . . . begins to need watching and correcting. He is of a much stiller nature than his sister, and has a wise, considering, look, but is also full of life and spirit; he is very large and strong, and I think will walk sooner than she did. She is so full of energy and vitality, so restless, noisy, ready for frolic at any time that James calls her his "wild little Irish girl" while Hammie[84] is the "sober little Scotchman".

The mother had been repeatedly complimented on the fine skins and good looks of both children as she met all sorts on her journey westwards. Edina was now singing a good many nursery rhymes and being taught hymns line by line — much as her father Thomas, the precentor, would have taught Mary, Walter, and Agnes. And, of course, Edina was also learning the basic elements of the Gospel:

> [she] tells with a sorrowful look how Jesus, the little baby, had no pretty cradle to lie in, and how his mother laid him in a manger, in the ' 'table'. After some naughty fit, when the outburst is over, she will say, 'Jesus doesn't like little girls to do so.'

During their first three months the family made occasional visits to the farm all together to inspect the cattle. The summer was a good time to go for in winter the eight miles of track out there might become treacherous and the rudimentary dwelling for the cattle men hardly hospitable. In the warm

---

83   S. A. Kinnier Wilson, *Neurology,* Ed. A. Ninian Bruce (Edward Arnold, 1940).
84   We have already seen James's fondness for nicknames.

September weather, however, she told her aunt that the drive gave them excellent appetites and that they would cook their meal with "'Al', our herd boy, and have dinner in the 'dug out' cooking our dinner on the hearth, and eating and drinking from tin plates and cups, in regular Kansas camp fashion".

It was a picture Agnes would elaborate on when she came to write *The Prairies* for a Scottish audience.[85]

How much Agnes knew about the recent history of the prairies it is impossible to know, but she was now living in a place whose recent history had been an equal mix of extreme hardship and heroism. Before the Civil War the pioneering spirit of the earlier settlers who crossed half a continent, seeking adventure or freedom or prosperity, had forged the overland wagon trails through "The Great American Desert" of Kansas and of this little needs to be said here. As we have seen, during the War, in 1863, construction on the KPR began and the railroad began to slice its way through barren Indian territory, but this was of little benefit to large households needing to transport several wagon-loads of goods. For them the old trails remained the only option where the dangers of a broken limb, wagon breakdown, snakebite or cholera were as real as ever. Those using the railroad for their initial transportation would have to transfer to a wagon for any journey away from towns on its tracks. In the month that the Wilsons travelled, June 1878, another mother and two little girls arrived at Fort Hays. They set out the next day with the father who had driven in from his 'claim' only to become lost in the darkness listening to a chorus of coyotes and unable to locate their new home.[86] Other travellers in the 1870s were beset by wolves or failed to find water for days on end. Locating a "dug-out" was notoriously difficult even in daytime, for the roof was level with the prairie grass. To those travelling by wagon or by train such places were invisible making the desolation seem even worse than it was. These homes, the easiest and quickest to build, took the place of log

---

85 Not published in *The Family Treasury* (issued monthly) till December 1879.
86 Joanna L. Stratton, *Pioneer Women, Voices from the Kansas Frontier* (Touchstone, 1982), p.44.

cabins in the western regions of the state where there was no timber or stone readily available. They were cramped and primitive, dark, damp and inevitably dirty but afforded some insulation from the cold and protection from the wind. In the winter rains they were invariably wet.

In that third "Letter from Kansas" Agnes, inviting her readers to accompany her across the prairie, describes their construction and use in much more positive terms:

> But what is this strange-looking place we are nearing now, which seems part cave, part sod-house? This is a "dug-out", a kind of dwelling which is quite fashionable in Kansas. You see that first a cellar has been dug out of this bank, just above the 'draw', leaving spaces for the door and window; then it has been roofed over with poles; these, again, overlaid with brush; and lastly, finished off with sods. This makes a rough but warm and cosy dwelling, in which one can feel secure when the fiercest tornadoes are sweeping over the prairie.

She is undoubtedly describing the home of 'Al' and the "cattle-men" on James's farm. Others like them would also live in sod-houses. These were certainly better than the dug-outs and constructed from strips of sod sliced off the prairie by an ox plough, cut with a spade into blocks and the turf then laid upside down to form walls up to two feet thick. The brushwood roof would be finished with strips of sod making a cabin which was fireproof as well as well as cool. But it took an acre of turf to construct the average one-room 'soddy'.

Agnes also romanticises the cowboys on this occasion, though perhaps that is unjust since the 'hands' that they employed on the 800 acres would not be the rootless figures on the Chisolm and other cattle trails:

We can see their herds feeding over there among the rich grasses, besides those pools of water. And here comes one of the herd boys, on his little Texas pony, looking very picturesque indeed in his broad hat and blue shirt, top boots, spurs, and revolver.

The tone of this (realistic or not) is close to the presentation of the cowboys in the early Hollywood Westerns. Of the cattle owners Agnes writes:

> Many of these . . . are gentlemen of good birth and education whom loss of health or fortune, or mere caprice or restlessness, have induced to enter upon this free, unconventional life.

It was a mark of the immigrants that they were determined to see the hand of Providence in both good fortune and in setbacks. James and Agnes were no exception but could hardly have known how tough life had been, and continued to be, for those in remote areas away from all other habitation. There was no one season of the year when the elements might not undo a year or more's work: drought, prairie fire, flood, hailstorm and snow blizzards of catastrophic proportions might strike after only the briefest of warnings. In 1874, on August 1st, huge swathes of Kansas were enveloped in countless millions of locusts darkening the sun and reaching a depth of four inches or more on the ground. When they moved on nothing was left: all crops, all tree branches, all green plants save the buffalo grass, had been stripped bare within hours. Clothing was eaten off the backs of those wearing certain colours. Melons, even turnips, simply disappeared. Desperate farmers placed shawls, dresses and quilts over the most precious crops, all to no avail. Wells were poisoned with locust excrement and livestock which bloated themselves on the locusts became inedible themselves. Though many settlers became discouraged and left, many stayed, still believing in "The Promised Land" and insisting life out there was still worthwhile.[87]

Agnes accepted both the desolation and the beauty. Finding the latter in the former she contrasted the landscape with the familiar sights around Edinburgh:

> No smooth, well-kept highroad with thrifty smiling villages every few miles, no stretches of forest or bits of woodland, no pretty winding lanes or by-paths, are here to attract the eye: no

---

87   Stratton, Op. Cit. p.106.

rocky hill or distant mountain, no woody dell or flowery hedge-
rows vary the scene. One can travel for days together and see
nothing in the way of scenery but the same unvarying rise and
fall of green, rolling prairie in every direction.

She is describing, of course, County Trego, the landscape around her
for a radius of thirty or forty miles. Elsewhere there were bluffs, hills and
woods but around their new little town "we have no bluffs and the timber
along our two rivers is very scanty". Despite the monotony there was the
grandeur of the sea about this landscape and "the observant eye and intelligent mind can find much to admire and much to interest". In summer
great splashes of colour would adorn the plains as the "lovely crimson
stars of the cactus" burst out and "asters with petals of mingled scarlet
and gold, beds of purple verbena" and the poppy shaped, maize-yellow,
double bloomed flowers of the "great prickly pear" punctuated the monotony with vibrant displays. There was the sunflower too, "which springs
up with the greatest profusion wherever the ground is broken — as on
railway embankments".

The prairies were not bereft entirely of wild life either, despite the depre-
dation of them by the tide of immigration. Pointing out to her readers "those
little circular hollows all over the prairie" Agnes explains that they are "buffalo stamps and show where in former days many a tired and tormented buffalo has rolled and stamped and wallowed to rid himself of the flies". Would
that these wonderful animals had only the flies to deal with. Their complete
extinction from the landscape was only narrowly averted and their whole-
sale slaughter was one of the most disgusting of all atrocities on animals
perpetrated by man. Agnes believed it was "about ten years . . . since the buf-
faloes were here and one has to travel about a hundred miles west of this to
find them". In the middle of the century some herds were estimated to contain up to half a million animals. Travellers might have to wait several days
while a herd slowly worked its way across their route and on the Missouri the

steamers could not get through when a herd was swimming the river. In 1872 hunting them began on an industrial scale such that by 1885 the herds had been wiped out.

Other wildlife besides the grey wolves and coyotes were the herds of antelope: "Their sleek fawn and white bodies and dark ears and hoofs, contrasting with the bright green of the prairie, their lustrous eyes and graceful movements make up a pleasing picture. But they also", Agnes adds, "are gradually disappearing, being more rarely met with than they were even a year ago". Prairie-dogs' or marmots' "towns" also caught Agnes's keen eye, each one looking

> very much like a collection of large mole-hills, each having a hole at one side, the entrance to the dwelling within . . . See, there are one or two sitting on the top of their hills, as if on the look-out, and in an attitude suggestive of a kangaroo. You can hear their shrill short bark, like that of a very young puppy. Owls are frequently seen in company with prairie dogs and it is believed that they live in the same holes. I have also heard that rattlesnakes are found in these holes . . .

In winter, however, Agnes had to concede that the prairies

> look dreary enough; when the flowers are all dead, the laughing verdure replaced by a robe of ashy-brown. The azure heavens by heavy leaden clouds, or when all is shrouded in a mantle of snow, I know nothing so dismal, so desolate in aspect as the prairies then.

But as with the other settlers, it was often faith that sustained the spirits in times of depression or weariness. This *Family Treasury* letter concludes with this paragraph:

> Yes, in winter our outlook here is far from cheerful and the sensitive nature must be influenced thereby more or less. But what of that? The sunshine of the heart can gild and gladden the dreariest landscape and a strong heaven-sanctioned motive can sustain the heart in cloud as in sunshine. "I will bless the Lord at all times: His praise shall continually be in my mouth".

These are brave words, and much earlier than she could have imagined at this point, Agnes would have to live them out.

Before leaving the topic of the prairies, Agnes had one further area of interest to raise for her audience back home: the Indians. Earlier in the letter she had written:

> Like the buffalo, the Indian is driven further and further west by the advancing tide of civilization. Fifteen years ago the Cheyennes frequented this region, but they have left scarcely any trace, as they merely crossed these prairies from river to river in search of game. Up north-west, on the Saline, a mound or cairn is pointed out as the grave of an Indian chief.

In describing the plentiful tumbleweed, she continued:

> In winter, when withered and dead, these weeds, loosened from their place, are blown by the winds, tumbling over and over as they go, hence their names. In a wind storm hundreds of them may be seen in motion at once and the impression they make is indescribably eerie and sad; they look almost like living creatures out in the storm, houseless, homeless, hurried along by the relentless blast, which sweeps them with savage fury before it. To one in a fanciful mood, they might be the ghosts of departed Indians who used to frequent these regions and who, in re-visiting their ancient haunts, are caught and scornfully scattered by the winds.

This is a fine piece of writing showing that the author was aware to some degree of the plight of the Native Americans. It also shows her to be imaginative as well as practical. What Agnes did not know was that before the year was out it was not the ghosts of Indians she would have to fear "like living creatures" but the Northern Cheyenne themselves.[88]

---

88 *The Encyclopaedia Britannica* (1910 edition) described the Cheyenne thus: "Their whole history has been one of war with their red and white neighbours. They are a powerful athletic race, mentally superior to the average American Indian".

CHAPTER FOURTEEN

THE INDIAN RAID

Mr Gandie's

Russell

Monday, about noon

My Dear Jim,

Mr Gandie has returned from the post office, and has brought nothing from you. I am very anxious to hear from you . . . I want to hear from yourself and know what I am to do. Please write to me at once. Russell is in a ferment today. All night long they have been coming into town from the farms and camps. There are now about 25 families in town, the court house is full. They are cooking in there.

The start of this letter, undated, strikes a note of fear not heard in Agnes's voice since her earliest anxieties for Jim's safety when he was ill in Europe and she, stuck in Edinburgh, longed to be with him.

Clearly, something has gone very wrong. Without warning, we find Agnes in retreat sixty miles east of Wakeeney, in Russell, and the town of 800 is in alarm and commotion as perhaps 100 refugees flood in during a single night. The letter continues:

Also, at Walker,[89] a number have taken refuge in a stone building and have sent for arms. The reason for all this is not on

---

89   The next settlement, a few miles west of Russell.

account of the Indians out at Wakeeney, but because it is said that another body of them, 1000 strong, have broken away from the Reservation and are heading northwards. They are expected to pass between here and Hays. Mr Gandie says he never saw Russell in such a state of excitement before and so crowded. I fear from this that I ought not to return west yet, and feel anxious to know what I ought to do. I have a P.C. from Mrs Cassidy. She reached Solomon city in safety, but is quite knocked up, she is very anxious about her husband and begs me to write now, do write at once. I suppose you have written but it has not reached me, and never will, I think. The children and I are well, but I don't care to stay here longer than I can possibly help.

There is then a postscript:

Tell Mr Cassidy to write to his wife at once.

Baby Edina shortly before the "Indian Raid"

So many things about this letter are indicative of its urgency and the agitation that Agnes was feeling: the lack of date, the imperative tone, the thrice repeated "anxious" and "at once", the doubt of letters getting through, and her fears for Ruth Cassidy who had fled in fear to her cousins even further east.

"The Indians out at Wakeeney" was probably a concept that the Wilsons had never entertained, let alone a phrase to describe an event then use in a letter. What then had happened to bring this about and to what was Agnes referring? To understand their experience we need to set it in context for what Agnes illustrates for us first-hand is the panic felt in what became known as "The Last Indian Raid in Kansas" or "Dull Knife's Raid". It was an event of some significance at the time which continued to be referred to in newspapers — some of them savagely racist — as late as 1920.[90]

The history of the fate of the Native American peoples in the nineteenth century is too well known to need much elaboration here. For two centuries their homelands and hunting-grounds had been usurped by the white settlers and their nomadic ways curtailed by white settlers. Herded into reservations, some tribes acquiesced, others decided to fight to a very bitter end. Until the mid-nineteenth century separate tribes had been regarded by the federal government as independent nations and the land concessions of these tribes were ratified by treaty. However, land ownership was not something the Indians fully understood, and they therefore did not expect to be entirely excluded from the homelands they once occupied and controlled. Neither side kept to its promises. On the one hand a constitutional republic was not familiar to the warrior braves who traditionally had the right to make their own decisions and act on them; on the other, land-hungry settlers did not adhere to the terms of the treaties and the government was too frequently unwilling to give back to the Indians what the settlers had claimed.

By 1825 the federal government had decided that the whites needed all the land east of the Mississippi and by 1830 Indians were being forcibly relocated to lands west of the river. The Great Plains were not considered suitable for settlement anyway, so this effective 'apartheid' was thought to be a solution.

It was nothing of the sort for those relocated. Not only did they have to abandon the forests and rivers that were fundamental to their religion and culture and make forced journeys to alien landscapes, but because of the influx of the Eastern tribes into Kansas, the peoples of the Central and High Plains — the Pawnee, Cheyenne, Arapaho, Kiowa, and Comanche — suddenly had to accommodate others on their historic game reserves. This, combined with the inroads made by explorers, miners, homesteaders, and hunters, made

---

90   See *The Western Star* for July 4th 1885 and January 23rd 1920.

for increased tensions between the settlers and Native Americans. By 1854 settlement in Kansas was legal and in the 1860s the unprecedented rapidity of growth by railroad companies and the near-extermination of the buffalo forced the Kansas tribes to accept, once more, relocation, this time to Indian Territory (now Oklahoma) immediately to the south of the state.

Prior to these relocations there had been peaceful co-existence between some of the races for many of the tribes. Difficulties had frequently been a matter of misunderstanding rather than threatened or actual violence. Native American culture was utterly alien to the settlers and the static, apparently luxurious lifestyle of the homesteaders, surrounded as they were in their cabins by seemingly superfluous objects was a fascination to the Indians. Concepts of personal space and property were different for them so their silent intrusion, without warning, upon camps and cabins was often extremely alarming. Some settlers became anxious when Native Americans were seen near settlements or thought to be on the move. In 1876 there was much uneasiness at Hays, a mere twenty miles from Wakeeney, such that Brigadier General John Pope ordered the commander at Fort Hays to "send out as soon as possible one company of cavalry fully equipped for field service to scout slowly by the way of the Saline or Solomon rivers . . . for the purpose of observing the movement of the Indians".[91]

Also, in 1876, only two years before the Wilsons reached Kansas, one of the most famous of all Native American battles took place between the legendary Seventh Cavalry and the Cheyenne and Lakota Sioux tribes at Little Bighorn ('Custer's Last Stand') in south-eastern Montana Territory. It is important for our story for two reasons. First, the two tribes, previously at enmity, had joined forces to defend the Black Hills, discovered to be rich in gold, from the illegal incursions of miners who could not be kept out despite a treaty and attempts by the military to do so. It was, therefore, without question,

---

91   See Professor Socolovsky's article, *Kansas in 1876*, at http://www.kancoll.org/khq/1977/77_1_socolofsky.htm.

the greed of white settlers which caused the catastrophe of the battle fought to defend land given to the tribes by statute. Second, the punitive result of the cavalry's defeat was that Congress enacted the 'sell or starve' rider to the Indian Appropriations Act which cut off all rations for the Sioux until they stopped fighting and ceded the Black Hills to the United States. Faced with starvation the Indians had no choice but to bring the Great Sioux War, sometimes known as the Great Cheyenne War, to an end. The Great Plains and other hunting-grounds could no longer be the Indians' home. They were taken again to Indian Territory, land which was not only useless to them for hunting but unhealthy and malarial. In 1877 remaining bands of Cheyenne surrendered or fled to Canada.

Popular reconstruction of what happened in this "last raid" among a party of Northern Cheyenne in Western Kansas in September and October 1878 has been a mixture of hesitant guesswork, gross exaggeration, journalistic sensationalism, and personal reminiscence, as well as serious history. Agnes gave her own account of how it impacted on the Wilson family on one unforgettable foggy night. It significantly adds to the extant available sources in several ways.

Her letter, dated November 3rd, is ten pages long and only part of it deals with what became known as 'The Indian Scare'. Agnes had doubts about telling the story to her sister but she (needless to say perhaps) decided to and told it well. It is best to let her relate it in her own words:

> Just south of Kansas is the Indian Reservation where various tribes are located on lands given to them by government. This fall, a body of them, several hundred strong, broke away from there, and set out for the Black Hills, their former home, north-west of us — they were Cheyennes. For weeks various rumours were afloat as to their being dangerous, and at last a regiment or two of militia were sent on to Wallace about 40 miles west of us. They had one or two skirmishes with the Indians and from that time reports and rumors came fast and thick, as to the white settlers being in danger and I confess that many a time my heart was full

of fear and anxiety, tho' James always declared there was no danger. Some here were like me, others pooh poohed at it all and it was really difficult to find out anything definite on the subject. At last, one night when James was away at Hays, 20 miles east, on church business, I was awoke from my first sleep by a knocking at the front door, and thinking it was James (who was to come by the first train he cd. find and not come by the regular passenger train, which passes through about 2 a.m.) I went down and opened the door. There stood Jim Curtis, one of the men here, with a gun, and he asked to see Charlie Morcom, a young carpenter who is making his home with us this winter, and working for us. I awoke Charlie and sent him to the door, and went up stairs again, when hearing them whispering, it came over me all in a moment "the Indians". I turned dizzy and sick and faint for a moment, and then went down, when the man was gone, and made Charlie tell me. It seemed that a party of Indians had attacked a cattle camp, 3 miles out, the cattle had stampeded, and the men had come running into town, all in a fright, only escaping with their lives. Parties had been sent round to warn the people of the danger, and so we had been warned. Charlie's face was white, and his eyes dilated with terror, as he told me. I came quietly upstairs, and dressed, though my heart was beating thick and fast, and began to put my jewellery etc. into a satchel. Just imagine what a situation — and James gone, and my two little unconscious darlings fast asleep on the bed. Charlie meantime, was getting his revolver into order, also a rifle which we had in the house, and then he and I sat and waited for the train. We knew that the Indians could not attack the house or get near it, as there were men on the watch all around the town. By and by the train came tearing along the track (you know it passes near our home), and in an incredibly short time James arrived. His first words were "get ready to go". That made me feel worse than ever, as I had not dreamt of such a thing as our going, but he had heard the news at Ellis, and was not going to let us his dear ones run the slightest risk. The train east was due in about an hour and before that time we had packed a trunk, awoke and dressed the children, and were on our way to the depot, calling for Mrs Cassidy on the way, as she was leaving too. I felt utterly miserable, I assure you, flying from our new home, on that dark, foggy night, with two helpless infants, and a heart full of fear and anxiety. The station was full of men, looking mostly pale and uneasy, nearly all around, and enrolling themselves under Mr John Keeney into a company, to attack the Indians at daybreak.

In short time we were in the train, and on our way to Russell, 60 miles east, where James preaches occasionally, and has made a number of friends. Ruth went on to Solomon City. James merely waited to see me and the children comfortably settled in the home of one of his friends and then took the next train back. How I hated to have him go! He soon wrote to me however, to the effect that the Wa-Keeney corps had been out hunting for Indians all the next day and had not seen one, but had found a number of Indian ponies.

Agnes goes on to tell Mary that by the time of writing the whole episode was being referred to as the "Indian Scare" rather than the "Indian Raid" and that James had written to her (still in Russell) reassuringly that "none had been near Wa-Keeney[92] and, at any rate, they were now clear out of Kansas" so she could return as soon as she cared to do so. In fact, there is good reason to think a scouting party, at any rate, had been *very* near Wakeeney. One account (held in Trego County Historical Society) related that a cook and his dog had left a campsite "several miles" east of town in order to hunt. The dog returned with an arrow in its stomach; the cook's body was not found until weeks later. Agnes's concluding note on the affair was: "I would not have mentioned it at all to you, but I thought I would let you know some of our frontier experiences".

Other correspondence about the incident dating from September/ October 1878 and digitized by the Kansas Historical Society (KHS) includes detailed reminiscences of fire fights with this Cheyenne group; casualties, both

---

92   In its earliest days the name was spelt that way.

Indian and white; accounts and maps of the route they were thought to have taken; telegrams to the authorities appealing urgently for help, especially for arms; a letter referring to the perceived crisis at Wakeeney and the sighting of Indians on Big Creek River just south of the town (along with doubts whether this was true and the tendency of the newer settlers to take alarm in a way that others did not); requests for arms to be returned, countered by requests that they be kept for future protection, and finally the allowing of this precaution. Some of the later letters date from 1906 when firmer details about routes, casualties and results were being further established. The reading of the whole collection gives one a vivid sense of the fear the newest settlers harboured close to the surface about the Indians and provides a magnificent insight to the history of Kansas at this time.

It was, certainly, a scare: many were terrified. The larger question is, was it a raid or odyssey? Did the Cheyenne intend to make war, or were they simply attempting, after the displacements of war, to return to their homelands? *The Encyclopaedia Britannica* in 1910 described the event as a 'revolt'. And still, a century on from it, Joanna L. Stratton had no doubt:

> "In the fall of 1878 . . . the prospect for a permanent peace in western Kansas was suddenly shattered. On the night of September 9, one final war whoop was sounded . . . Throughout September they swept northward across the state, murdering homesteaders, plundering property, and spreading terror".[93]

Stratton does accept that the "restless warriors" were returning to their homelands but her language throughout suggests that it was the Indians who were on the wrong side of the law from the start.

In 2010 *California Law Review* published a long and superbly documented article[94] on this very event, "The Last Indian Raid in Kansas", by Sarah Krakoff, Professor of Law at the University of Colorado. Krakoff begins by considering

---

93   Joanna L. Stratton, *Pioneer Women, Voices from the Kansas Frontier* (Touchstone,1982) p.126.

94   http://scholarship.law.berkeley.edu/cgi/viewcontent.cgi?article=1077&context=californialawreview Volume 98, Issue 4, Article 7, (p.1265 ff.).

the accounts, held by the KHS, in local papers of the day: late September to early October 1878. Casualty lists vary from nineteen up to one hundred settlers killed, but one of the fullest recollections was published in the *Lawrence Standard* just one year later on October 9, 1879.[95] It draws on the narrative told by Wild Hog, one of the Cheyenne leaders, who took part in the events. In prison, in Douglas County jail, on trial for murder, the warrior told his story: of how, in inter-tribal warfare, the Cheyenne had been defeated by the Sioux; of how many of them moved south and how the remaining Northern Cheyenne were tricked into joining them and exchanged the Black Hills of Dakota for the Indian Territory rather than face extermination. Wild Hog, along with Dull Knife and Little Wolf, went south with their faction. They were assured there would be plenty of game, abundant rations, and a healthy climate. Moreover, if they did not like the reservation, they would be allowed to return. They would have to give up their arms for the journey but these would be returned upon arrival. Not one of these assurances proved true.

One thousand Indians were packed into the government camp where disease was rife. Fifty Northern Cheyenne children died of measles; only one doctor was assigned to the whole camp so "ague, bilious and malarious fevers" carried off scores of Indians.[96] They were fed rations on only two days a week. In an emaciated state after a camp fire council meeting the Cheyenne requested permission to return home and were refused. If they left, they would be killed they were told but this death, they knew, would be better than awaiting it in the camp. Supplied with arms and ponies from an unknown source, over three hundred men, women and children left the Darlington Agency in September. In the moving words of Wild Hog:

> The trail was long . . . In the North our warriors and squaws would have lived and our children grown into strong men. In a strange, sickly, country without medicine or food they died. We were told that the Great Father, at Washington, promised that we might return

---

95 http://www.kansasmemory.org/item/210684.
96 Quinine did not arrive until after Dull Knife's group had fled. (Krakoff, Ibid.).

to the hills in the North if there was no game in the Indian Territory, and its swamps killed our children. The promise was broken.

Krakoff does not quote this passage but says that historians have largely corroborated Wild Hog's version of events and that rather than being a "raid" the exodus was part of the Northern Cheyenne's long struggle to return home. Their alliance with the Sioux against the Seventh Cavalry had embittered subsequent commanders against them and determined them to eradicate the Cheyenne from the Plains. Thus, when 353 left the Agency on September 9th and the cavalry caught up with them, despite the Indians' wish to negotiate and claim their right to return, the soldiers fired on them. Only ninety-two of Dull Knife's band were men. The incompetence of the soldiery in containing this outbreak by a starving and exhausted group (predominantly women and children) led to the deaths that followed on both sides.

The details of the exodus show that Agnes was wrong to dismiss it afterwards merely as "a scare" for the Cheyenne were to pass not so far from her house and their route would, anyway, have been unpredictable as they cleverly evaded the patrols in search of them. On September 17th and 18th they crossed into Kansas and two battles took place in the state that month. On the 27th the Indian pony herd was destroyed but doubtless some escaped and these may have been those referred to by Agnes in her letter and seen just south of Wakeeney. However, without their herd and food more scavenging was inevitable, and the scouts would have had to range more widely and indiscriminately from the main body to sustain their progress. This probably explains Agnes's hearing about the attack on the cattle camp three miles from town in which the men escaped only with their lives. Dull Knife and Little Wolf had instructed the braves that settlers should not be attacked, and Wild Hog's account confirms this, but the Cheyenne had to eat and where they met armed opposition there would naturally be a fight. On the 29th there was a skirmish at Prairie Dog Creek some fifty miles north-west of Wakeeney where some eighty cattle were lost. By this stage the Indians had killed twelve people, according to Krakoff's research, wounded five others, and destroyed 640 head of livestock. The situation was now deadly serious. No more deaths are mentioned by Krakoff until the disaster in Decatur and Rawlins Counties, north-west of County Trego when from September 30th to October 1st young scouts of the Northern Cheyenne killed a total of thirty-one settlers. Outrages happened on both sides: settlers scalped a wounded young brave and clubbed to death the older abandoned Cheyenne who were too weak to continue the route; Indians killed settlers after bargaining for their property in pretended exchange for their lives. The *Lawrence Standard* quoted earlier, confirms that "the Indians did their worst in North-West Kansas". The paper records that after a march of some 600 miles through Western Kansas, then Nebraska, the Cheyenne reached their old home in Western Dakota. In fact only half the band survived the exodus and when, in thick snow, soldiers and Cheyenne stumbled upon each other by accident on October 23rd and the Indians agreed to be led to Fort Robinson in North-Western Nebraska, they effectively surrendered. Adamant that they would not return to the South, after a long confinement, starvation and crippling cold, the Indians broke out of the fort after which most were recaptured or killed. Eventually, Dull Knife (who with his immediate family evaded capture) and remaining survivors were allowed to live out their remaining years at an agency in Montana Territory to which Little Wolf had earlier fled. Their descendants live there to this day.

The details of the 1878-1879 story make shocking reading — a shameful episode in the history of the United States government and its military. The *New York Times* labelled government action a disgrace.[97] The Wilsons, however, would never hear the final outcome. It was only in 1901 that the United States Supreme Court determined that, up until the time when the

---

97   http://scholarship.law.berkeley.edu/cgi/viewcontent.cgi?article=1077&cont
ext=californialawreview.

Chief Dull Knife of the Northern Cheyenne.
Drawing: courtesy of Daren Horton, from the
photograph held by First People of the US

pursuing cavalry fired upon Dull Knife's band in Indian Territory, the Indians had committed no wrong and were "in amity" with the United States.[98] In other words, it was the U.S. not the Indians who committed the first aggression and offence.[99]

---

98 https://en.wikipedia.org/wiki/Fort_Robinson_massacre.

99 Nevertheless, today some websites still merely speak one-sidedly of the Cheyenne "outrages in western Kansas". See http://genealogytrails.com/kan/trego/history1.html.

CHAPTER FIFTEEN

LITTLE TOWN ON THE PRAIRIE

EVACUATING YOUR NEW HOUSE IN fear of your life just three months after arriving in a wild and strange land must have been an unforgettable and worrying experience. However, Victorians were frequently made of sterner stuff than we, and anyway, the young couple had a great deal to occupy them. There was little time to reflect or for recrimination, "my mind is so much engrossed" Agnes wrote. Through the winter and spring, she found herself ceaselessly busy. The two young children were demanding; Edina was constantly curious, and Sam was crawling upstairs and liable to all sorts of unforeseen dangers. Agnes was equally proud of both children, but Sam's size drew the attention of others: "Everybody loves and pets him . . . he has such a wise, superior and lofty air too" Agnes told Mary, continuing, "'He's the finest boy in Kansas' is a speech very often addressed to Hammie, by all and sundry".

As with all of us, the process of looking back on life caused Agnes to be amazed. Reflecting on the fact that Sam seems more attached to her than Edina was at the same age, the young mother remembered that for seven or eight months, in Cedarville, she had to get up two or three times every night in order to feed her baby from the bottle with its associated problems of either heating the milk in the middle of the night or keeping it cool. She had had no such problems with breast-feeding Sam and concluded: "The nursing of them makes them love you more. I scarcely nursed Edina at all". By November the toddler was weaned, and Agnes felt a pang of regret: "I feel as if I had lost my baby". It would not be long before Sam was running everywhere and because he was out all day, "his cheeks are as firm and rosy as apples, his eyes large, dark and round, his hair a bright golden red . . . " Edina was a very pretty child, her eyes a "clear bright hazel" and her complexion "red and white and very fine skinned . . . and her figure as erect and straight as a dart".[100] Along with being very quick-witted and clever she was often very naughty so her mother feared: "I shall have trouble with her before I get through". She learned and remembered things very quickly and easily. Indeed, "the children are all that we could desire" but both parents were thinner with the strain of frontier living. They were content, indeed, very happy, but Agnes was prepared to admit to Mary: "there are many drawbacks and disadvantages in frontier life . . . which those . . . in the Old World cannot think of, or enter into at all".

If feeding the children had become a little easier as the year ended, there were increased tasks of other kinds. Clothes were being made for a new doll for Edina (there were few other toys) and Agnes liked to complete her immediate sewing projects before Christmas. Later she would have to be making the characteristic sturdy prairie "ginghams and calicos for the children" and two suits for herself along with mohair and alpaca items and "an overskirt of silk and lace". It was when she was sewing that Agnes most thought, sometimes plaintively, of childhood days in Scotland, gathering primroses at Dalmeny Park, holidays with the Gordons, "the Gogar days with father, can we forget them?" These were "golden summer days" and the times at Greenlaw, as well as later times at Queensferry and Largs were remembered with equal nostalgia. Even Cedarville joins the ranks of places now distant to Agnes and James in every respect. Reverting to her old perception that "ways of living in American books is exactly as they are" she told Mary that "the description of the Quaker kitchen in 'Uncle Tom's Cabin' even to the rushbottomed rocking chair with the patched cushion is exactly like almost any kitchen in

---

100 Such lengthy physical descriptions are a reminder that portrait photography (like Christmas cards) was not an option at that point in Wakeeney — something which Agnes explains to Mary.

Cedarville. One sees them in every house — I had one and did so like it". And, of course, she was missing friends from New Jersey:

> I have formed and broken one new set of friends and associations already, and am busy forming another; and my old life and even friendships and associations before marriage, begin to seem far off and almost unreal, like a dream . . . new names and new acquaintances are the rule here . . .

It was fortunate therefore, that before the unforeseen storm broke, Agnes could say that "the present days are even happier to me than they were, with my kind dear husband and my lovely children around me". It was as well that these short days were so richly enjoyed for there were not to be many left to her with James.

For the moment, however, the future seemed as limitless as the horizons around their timber frame house whose windows looked out over the green billows of the prairies. The couple were still making many changes to the original building. After the plastering was completed, they changed the kitchen into a sitting-room and the little parlour into a study for James. Agnes had a new good-sized kitchen built on the east side of the house where the early morning sun would stream in through the windows. Porches too were added to front and back making the house much easier to keep clean and dry. Proudly, Agnes told her sister that "the first papered walls in Wakeeney" were now to be seen in their sitting-room. She made the room look pretty with pictures, ornaments and books; the glass fronted corner cupboard added something which gave the room "a quaint, uncommon look".

In the spring they were planting trees, mostly cottonwoods "as they grow so fast" but also "some box elders and maples, as well as apple and cherry trees, grape vines, raspberries, strawberries, blackcurrants etc. as well as vegetables". Honeysuckles and the climbing rose "Prairie Queen" had been planted round the front porch: "They already give the place a different look", Agnes was pleased to write. As the new plants put down their roots so did the family. A hedge of osage orange, a dense, tough, thorny shrub, was planted to demarcate the property from the prairie around it. They had noticed how effective it was in Solomon, rather like a fast-growing holly, Agnes thought. No wonder, with all these developments, this letter was written on a Sunday, when no other work could be done. Even now though Agnes is still uncomfortable enough about that to feel the need to excuse herself: "I cannot help it . . . there is so little time for anything" she complained. Agnes did, however, have assistance. From March, a little girl aged ten, Louise Weber, "of German parentage" was helping with the children in just the way Agnes liked:

> She is so different from our old Sally, being mild, obedient, rather slow, but with not a particle of sauciness or impertinence. A little girl like that assists me much better at present than a young woman who would always be in my way, and with her beaux and late hours (which they always have) would be too much responsibility.

The Wilsons also had the services of "a little Irish fellow, 'Paddy from Cork' literally Jim Carrol by name, and a most faithful, good worker. Both James and I like him very much".

What the Wilsons were doing to their house in the winter and spring of 1879, soon dozens of other settlers were engaged in as the basic building blocks of the quickly erected houses were altered and enlarged. Before long it would be scores and then hundreds.[101]

The once silent prairie, visited only by the winds, herds of buffalo, and the nomadic tribes hunting them, was no longer subject merely to the hiss of steam on hot metal at Trego tank, the whistle and rhythmic shunting sounds of the KPR locomotive as it slowed or picked up speed at the little halt. The plains must, in those months, have echoed to the sound of constant building activity: the sawing of lumber, the thud of hammers on freshly cut timber, the ring of iron beaten on anvils at the smithy, the snort of horses pulling heavy wagons, and the creak of their axles drying out in the early summer heat. Only

---

101 According to the US Decennial Census for 1880, the population was then 418.

at night would the subtler, older, sounds of the high plains reassert themselves as a reminder that all this activity, so seemingly tireless, so irreversible, was subject to the unpredictable whim of daunting natural forces. The frontier town was vulnerable, and "often only a solitary cluster of ramshackle buildings jutting from a sea of prairie grass".[102] The law required just 320 acres of land to be reserved for the town site for it to be officially established.

Three times in her letters Agnes mentions the speed at which the town is growing, and three times she refers to the investment which they both believed they had presciently made by James's purchase of a block of twenty-two lots "in the centre of town on which our house is built". Each lot bought at $9 in April of 1878 was by December believed to be worth $50. The house, too, had quadrupled in value. By April the estimate was that each lot was worth $80. "Don't you think that was a pretty good investment?" Agnes boasted with an unwitting double irony, the first of many in these months which make her story's conclusion so like *Romeo and Juliet* and other tragedies. For Wakeeney was not to prove a good investment in any regard, and when she had written so confidently back in November that, "after all there is nothing like investing in land which can neither burn up, nor fly away, nor fail" she could hardly have been more wrong — as we shall see. The prairie fires did burn up the land of many homesteaders; in the Oklahoma dustbowl of the next century, the land did "fly away" in the winds and crops failed across Trego County in the early 1880s.[103] Land prices then dropped sharply as the settlers, after only a year or two, left in droves.

But this, in the winter and spring of 1878-18779 was unforeseeable. The letters detail for us some of the early ways this settlement grew. In November, "two new large stone buildings" had appeared and Agnes noted "Near the railroad the Warrens have built a handsome stone residence". In addition, "a

---

102 Joanna L. Stratton, *Pioneer Women, Voices from the Kansas Frontier* (Touchstone, 1982), p. 187.

103 16,000 acres yielded crops in the county in 1880 but by 1881 only 10,000 were under successful cultivation. 1882 was worse. Livestock farms suffered less. See http://genealogytrails.com/kan/trego/history1.html.

mill and a new stone depot (i.e. a railway station) are projected, and there are ever so many new houses and stores besides, of frame". By the end of April Agnes considered that it was "not like the same place that Mrs Cassidy and I, and the two sleepy babies stopped at" the night they arrived ten months before. Then they had had to walk across open prairie to get to their home "which stood quite detached and by itself"; and, as she remembered it, "there were only the hotel and the depot and a few scattered houses". Now they had close neighbours:

> We have houses all around us and the streets are becoming defined, stores have multiplied, trees are planted, changes are making con-tinually. We see a house today where yesterday there was none, and it will be the same tomorrow and so on for years to come.

As usual, some of Agnes's most interesting comments are reserved for people rather than buildings. Her feelings are ambivalent, especially towards the women. In contrast to changeless, sleepy Whithorn, her sister's village home in Galloway, "people are pouring by the hundred into this county, and Wakeeney gets her share . . . and the people who come in here are so nice and superior, you would be surprised to see them". "Superior" is not a term we would be comfortable using today but it must have been in frequent use for Agnes to employ it so freely. Expecting a rabble perhaps,[104] she was pleasantly surprised: "On Friday last, in my little sitting-room here, I entertained a suc-cession of lady callers who, for appearance, dress and manners, might have just stepped off George St. Edinburgh". Mrs Warren, wife of the entrepreneur who founded the town, again makes an appearance at this point. Having told Mary that "the women, generally speaking, are superior to the men; more cultivated and refined, better read, better talkers, more polished and stylish in appearance", Agnes continued:

---

104 When Rev Richard Cordley reached Lawrence some twenty years earlier he had expected to find the "traditional roughs of the frontier" and instead found "people of culture and character". "It was quite common to find cul-tured people and college graduates on the farms and in the cabins all about". (*Pioneer Days in Kansas*, 1903). See Dodo Press reprint, pp.25 and 39.

> Mrs Warren . . . is the acknowledged leader here, in general so-
> ciety, and in our church, which both she and her husband have
> joined. She is very stylish looking but not pretty, and rides on
> horseback or drives about in a little phaeton. They have no chil-
> dren and live in a handsome stone house on the edge of town.
> We were invited to dinner there some time ago and spent a very
> pleasant evening.

Such occasions must have tempted Agnes to think that the Wilsons could be the centre of a society which might eventually become a little like the genteel Edinburgh she knew of old. Hopes were, among many, that Wakeeney would become the largest city between Denver to the west and Kansas City to the east. A Literary Society had been started at which there were readings, recitations, and music — precisely the areas in which Agnes could shine. It met every two weeks and along with sewing circles and church activities was a place where friendships could flourish, and news and confidences be shared. Mrs Warren also lent Agnes a book which Mary had earlier recommended (*Macleod of Dare*)[105] which the younger sister found "very interesting, even fascinating". What is more revealing, however, is the passionate strength of feeling with which Agnes responded to this entirely fictional situation which suggests how formidable this minister's wife could be:

> It made such a strong and disagreeable impression on me that
> I could not shake it off for days. I think Gertrude White sim-
> ply abominable, I hate her out and out entirely, even to her very
> name, which I think the ugliest combination I ever saw or heard
> — but oh what a pity it was that poor Keith was so mean spirited,
> that he could not shake off his infatuation, and despise her as
> she deserved.

It is no surprise therefore, that Agnes continued to be over-critical (as she had been in Cedarville) of others around her. Later she would change her views but her initial reaction had been:

---

105 A romance by William Black (pub. 1878), set on the Isle of Mull.

I don't think I fancy the Western ladies much. Many of them here are from Chicago and so are real "Western", and they strike me as bold, and self-sufficient. There is nothing soft or retiring or what we call feminine about them. They give one the impression of glorying in the feeling that they are perfectly able to take care of themselves and want nobody's advice, care or protection.

Realising, I think, what this would look like to her reader, Agnes added, "All this, of course, is quite compatible with real goodheartedness and so on, but oh, how unlike they are to 'my ain folks'". This sounds as if Agnes has not come to terms here with the nature of those women who had the strength of character to survive the Old West, to emigrate, to start afresh or who had the acumen (or the husbands) to see the opportunities that Kansas seemed to provide. Moreover, if she had approached some with any degree of patronisation the reaction to her may have been sharp and this would have heightened her feelings further. Whatever the case, such judgemental attitudes were ones that much later in life Agnes severely blamed herself for and deeply regretted. Early acquaintances such as Mrs Beulah Ewing, a gentle "Quakeress", were much more to her liking and greatly admired. She also struck up a warm friendship with Nelly Simms, Ruth Cassidy's youngest sister, who arrived from Cedarville probably in early 1879[106], along with her husband and a young baby. The Simms built a house close to the Wilsons' which made Agnes "feel even more at home, as Nelly is as much of a sister to me as Ruth almost, and a very fine creature". By June Agnes had become more accepting of Kansan ways and was able to speak of "their direct speech, and simple, natural manner" as something of a tonic. Her own, sometimes brash, manner might have been indicative of her insecurity and isolation, her fears for her children and husband, and worries about how Edina and Sam might be best educated in a frontier town.

---

106 The exact date is uncertain.

Some sense of personal isolation is certainly the subtext in the first of the "Letters" from "A Home Missionary's Wife" published by *The Family Treasury* and entitled *A Town on the Frontier.* In that article, written no later than the fall of 1878, she begins by describing Kansas as "the centre of the most unprecedented immigration" ever since the Centennial Kansas and Colorado building "drew all eyes and was the theme on every tongue".[107] What follows is an evocative contrast between the Scotland she remembers and the town she now sees growing around her. As she first saw it, it was a few "houses scattered about on the bare green prairie, not a hedge or fence or bush or tree in sight — such is the little western town of Trego". The fact that she uses the name Trego, and the present tense, rather than Wakeeney, suggests a very early date for the article. The writer, revealing her soul, goes on:

> The long line of telegraph poles which skirt the railroad is quite a feature in the landscape, fading away in the distance east and west and seeming sometimes to wistful eyes like the links of a mighty chain, by which, even in this isolation, we still maintain our hold on the far-off world of men.

Curious details, seldom considered, mark the first impact of the planners at the new site:

> The town is all already planned and those ploughed lines in the grass, intersecting each other at right angles, indicate the different streets and avenues. Here is Franklin Street, where are located the hotel, the post-office, principal store, drug store, butcher's shop etc. This is the business street and some day the lots here will be very valuable. Strange, is it not, to see the main street of a town guiltless of sidewalk, causeway or footpath[108] of any kind: nothing but a grassy road, with three tracks worn in it by the wheels of vehicles and feet of horses. Occasionally in the very track of the

---

107 More than 100,000 registered as visiting the exhibit. See http://www.kancoll. org/khq/1977/77_1_socolofsky.htm.

108 Richard Cordley noted the same, along with two feet of mud in the streets of Quindaro, 40 miles east of Lawrence: Op. Cit. pp. 18 and 24.

Looking north on Franklin St., Wakeeney, 1880s. To the left is "Commercial House" where the church first met

East side of Main St., (looking south), Wakeeney

First school building (1878), Wakeeney, where JKW was superintendent

Union Pacific depot, 1879. The early hyphenated spelling of the town can be
made out on the notice

Historical Photos courtesy of Trego County Historical Society, used with permission

horses' feet, some sturdy prairie flower will still rear its head, as if protesting against the encroachment of civilization.

It is interesting that Agnes makes no mention anywhere of the Keeney family. Charles Keeney, brother of the town's promoter, J. F. Keeney, erected the first store in town and his daughter, Viola Frank Keeney, was the first baby to be born there, on December 16, 1878, "when the town was almost as new as the young lady herself".[109]

By the time Agnes was writing the article she was able to tell her readers: "In almost every direction, a mile or two out on the prairie, little unpretending farmhouses may be seen, like solitary ships anchored in a green ocean. The families within . . . come into the 'town', of course, to do their shopping, and so the business of the town increases". The population, by this time, had risen to "about 150" and there were "between thirty and forty houses of different kinds", whereas, "in the beginning of this year there was simply nothing at all here but the prairie, the sky, and the railroad!" By June the population of the County had reached 1,500 and on 21st of the month it was officially "organized by proclamation" of the Governor John P. St. John after the census. Wakeeney was designated the county seat which was considered pivotal to its prospects. A grand new limestone depot was opened too, described at the time as the most modern railroad facility between Kansas City and Denver. On July 4th there were grand celebrations in Wakeeney at which four hundred visitors from Topeka, including the Governor, were present. They had arrived, of course, by railroad. On July 26th the first county elections were held at which thirty-five county and township officers were appointed, one of whom was the Reverend James K. Wilson, appointed superintendent of "public instruction", i.e. of schools. The first school classes were taught in Wakeeney that summer but James, as superintendent, had eight districts to oversee. He would need the railroad for this work too.

---

109 Mary Michellich, *Our Heritage, First United Presbyterian Church, Wakeeney, Kansas, 1878-1978,* p.10.

It was little wonder that the railroad became so symbolic of the spread of "civilization" or that Agnes speaks of it with awe but also with something close to affection. It was the life-line that had already once snatched her away from the Indians; it was the means by which friends in other towns, other churches, could be reached within the day. Even more than this, in "story book" mode Agnes expands:

> But here comes the locomotive, with cup-shaped funnel and "cow-catcher" in front, thundering along the track and trailing a long train of cars behind it, laden with cattle . . . Isolation did I say? How can there be isolation where this wonderful creation of the mind of man, this mighty breathing creature, can penetrate? See, here are fresh fruit and vegetables, though we have none yet in our gardens; here is flour to make bread . . . though as yet no wheat waves in our fields; here are books and newspapers, though we are far from printing-press or office . . . [110]

The greatest excitement of the railroad, however, the writer reserves till last: "Ah, best of all, are letters, dear sweet letters from home, welcome as cold water to a thirsty soul".[111] Only the presence of God, Agnes reasons, is better than letters:

> And then, best and most reassuring of all, is not He with us? "If I take the wings of the morning and dwell in the uttermost parts of the (earth), even there shall thy right hand lead me and thy right hand shall hold me". We feel assured His hand has led us thither; our heartfelt prayer is that it may still lead us and make us the humble instruments of good in this uttermost part of the earth.

One cannot escape the impression that despite her vibrant faith that God had led them to this place so very far from home, Agnes, despite her protestations, did sense a great barrier between her and the comforts and securities

---

110 Not for long though. *Weekly World* was first published in Wakeeney on March 15th 1879 and *Kansas Leader* from August 6th. Ten years later there were 733 weekly papers being published in Kansas.
111 There are accounts of settlers riding 40 miles to pick up letters — often issued from a counter at the General Store. See Stratton, Op. Cit. p. 196.

she had grown up with. To a secular world her belief that James and she were led there by God would seem deeply ironic, given the bitter outcome of their brief stay. But for Agnes, this was not her view of the matter. And who knows what unseen chain of events in God's economy was enabled by their sojourn there, even at so great a cost?

Whatever our view of it, Agnes would feel the full force of "this uttermost part of the earth" by the time a year had past. "Even there thy right hand shall hold me" would be a reassurance she would have to fight to lay hold of and keep in her grasp.

CHAPTER SIXTEEN

A CHURCH ON THE FRONTIER

PLYMOUTH CHURCH, IN LAWRENCE, WAS the first church of any name formed in Kansas, except for missions among Indians.[112] Congregationalist services there were held in a "hay tent" and began in October 1854. The earliest ministers of such churches acted as architect, builder, sexton, and accountant as well as preacher and teacher. They also had to be circuit riders, the most robust of them on horseback for up to fifty miles on any Sabbath Nearly a quarter of a century later when the railroad had taken Kansas settlers as far as Wakeeney and beyond, it had taken the Church with them. One of the largest Christian influxes had been in 1874 when German Mennonites from Russia arrived along with Catholic, Lutheran, and Baptist families. Russell in particular had many Catholics. But it was the Presbyterians who "were the first denomination to form an organization in Trego County, having completed their organization April 17, 1878".[113] As we have seen, the local land agent's (A.H. Blair) connection with George Pierson at Solomon helped to secure James's appointment at Wakeeney. Presbyterians were active across the whole United States at this date. A map held at PCA, Lombard Street, shows that a single year's work resulted in 146 churches being founded — eleven of them in Kansas. In neighbouring Colorado there were four, and even further west in Utah there were two. It was not unusual for these churches to be comprised of people from many different denominational backgrounds. Cordley

112 Cordley, Op. Cit. p. 29.
113 Michellich, Op. Cit. p. 12.

mentions that in Leavenworth Congregational church seven separate group-
ings were represented in the membership[114] and we have seen that Wakeeney
was no different. Churches are notorious for splintering, but here, it seems,
is an example of the opposite. It was a gathering of Presbyterians, Methodists,
Congregationalists and Quakers who asked for James, as well as those from
two smaller groups, the Union and the American Reformation. This meeting
of March 31st was followed by that on April 17th for the election of a Ruling
Elder, Mr H. H. Hamilton, who, despite his reluctance, accepted the post and
was installed by Rev James Mitchell from Hays. The Home Missionary Board
then approved and sustained the choice of minister.

The earliest Presbyterian churches in the two enormous Kansas presbyteries of Highland and Topeka (stretching from the eastern to western boundaries of the state) had been only recently founded in Smith Center (1872), and in
the city of Hays (1873). The first church building was erected in 1878 in Norton,
close to the border with Nebraska. For his four years' labour, travel and un-
flagging ministry in achieving this, Rev Henry Albright (Doctor of Medicine)
received the rather astonishing wage of one dollar.[115] In the mid-eighteen-
seventies the territory of Central and Western Kansas was considered too vast
and too remote to sustain organized churches. Another Wilson (Rev John —
no relation) had explored the area and urged Presbytery to hold its spring
meeting of 1877 further west — at Beloit (a hundred miles east-north-east
of Wakeeney). The idea was rejected that year as impracticable, as it was an
inaccessible ninety-five miles beyond the railroad. Nevertheless, precisely a
year later, the meeting *was* held at Beloit and the preacher at that meeting on
Saturday 27th April was J.K. Wilson who chose Isaiah chapter nine, verse six
as his text: "And His name shall be called wonderful".[116] It was at this meeting
that James received his official appointment to serve the Church in Kansas.
Between 1877 and 1879 at least seven churches were organized in this huge

---

114 Cordley, Op. Cit. p. 6.
115 Michellich, Op. Cit. p. 7.
116 Solomon Presbytery Minutes, 1876-1884, p. 45.

area. One of them was Wakeeney, one hundred miles beyond Beloit, to which John Wilson's namesake was sent. James was, therefore, truly in the vanguard of the church's work on the frontier of the State.

As there were no church buildings it was an immense advantage that the Wilsons could immediately make use of the rather prestigious "Commercial House", the offices of Warren and Keeney, on the west side of a corner of Franklin street (now Main Street) for the services of the new little fellowship. The Wilsons did not take this usage for granted. Agnes wrote that Messrs. Warren and Keeney,

> who own about one hundred thousand acres of land, have from the first given the church their hearty support and encouragement. In this place we have not the difficulties and discouragements to contend with, incident to some other new churches in the west, where the powers that be refuse the use of a place of meeting or a site for the building of a church. Here, on the contrary, several of the firm with their wives are members of the church and among the most regular attenders.

The reality was, therefore, that even in a much godlier age than now, new churches were opposed or afforded no help whatever by powerful sections of the community — something we tend to forget today. The earliest records for this church were destroyed in a fire in 1925 which burnt the first dedicated building to the ground, but we have a surviving unique and priceless eye witness testimony to those very first Presbyterian gatherings: Agnes's second article or "Letter" written for *The Family Treasury*, published in Scotland the following year, 1879. Her description of the outside of their meeting place accords with a photograph of the time:[117]

> The land office of W . . . K . . . & Co., situated on the Franklin Street I have before described, is one of the principal buildings in our little frontier town. Its front rises up into a square top, hiding the sloping roof behind, and is nicely painted. Here, by the kind

---

117   See Michellich, Op. Cit. p.14.

permission of the members of the company, the First Presbyterian church of Trego holds its meetings every Sabbath, the said church having as yet no building of its own.

Mary Michellich's brief account states that it was James who "arranged for" the purchase of the "old frame depot" and its refit prior to the construction of a more permanent building.[118] But by the end of April 1879 plans were going ahead for the building of a stone church so that knowledge of the dates at which different buildings were used is inexact. "The site has been given" Agnes told Mary, "by W.K. & Co. and is on the corner of the block next to ours". Some of the stone had already been brought to the site and the cellar had been dug in readiness for further work. As at Cedarville, there was to be a concert to raise funds: "Mrs Warren is the M.C. and I have been asked to sing and intend to sing "With Verdure Clad" (provided I can get a good accompanist) and "Terence's Farewell to Kathleen". It will take place sometime in May".[119] We have no letter which confirms that the concert took place, but if it did, and Agnes was successful with the Haydn, there is no doubt that her reputation would have travelled widely among the towns on the KPR tracks.

At first sight, the lack of dedicated places of worship might be thought a hindrance to the faith of settlers who already had more than enough to contend with. Joanna Stratton, however, cites numerous cases where this was not by any means the case.[120] The earliest homesteaders met for worship in each others' cabins or even under a tree or in a borrowed store in town, as in Wakeeney. The social repercussions of this ought to be of interest to sociologists — at least of religion. The fact that so many of the immigrants brought their faith with them had a number of far-reaching results still felt in the United States today. In the first place, faith linked them with their past lives elsewhere and gave them a sense of rootedness which supported

---

118 Michellich, p.22.
119 These two songs show both the range of Agnes's repertoire and her ability. The former is from Haydn's oratorio, *Creation*; the latter is an old wistful romantic air from Ireland.
120 Stratton, Op. Cit. p. 172.

their need for perseverance against the odds. Second, the stories of the Old Testament enabled them to identify themselves as people on the road to the Land of Promise: they would be led through the wilderness to eventual prosperity. This meant that they built homes and churches to last which added to the stability of the community. Third, it was the glue in family life: parents taught their children to see the world as they did — a place perhaps of hardship but also of purpose and finally reward. Fourth, it created fellowship between neighbours and inculcated a sense of altruism and duty, sacrifice and courage which resulted not just in resilience but in hospitals and community care. Lastly, as has ever been true of Christianity, there was always the sense that second only to a place of worship, was the need for a place of education for the settlers' children. Many Kansas higher education institutions have a Christian foundation. All this and more has been the heritage, largely unacknowledged, of Kansas and the West direct from the spread of the Gospel across the United States.

Quite extraordinarily, of all the scores of places that might be mentioned by name in the mere dozen pages of the chapter that Stratton devoted to "The Frontier Church", Wakeeney in 1879 is one of them. What emerges from the reference, (the recollection of Mrs Stephen Osborn) is that "the townspeople gathered at the local drugstore for Sunday-morning worship". Each brought a chair and fifteen to twenty people were present. Of course, there were Osborns at Cedarville, as already seen, but it seems that this was a separate Union congregation, though perhaps not an organized church. When the KPR built their stone depot, this congregation moved into the relocated old frame building.

One little-considered effect of the Presbyterians, in today's much more secular age which devotes Sunday largely to shopping, was their strict adherence to the Sabbath. Agnes makes a great deal of this in her *Family Treasury* article, an insight to a way of living which in 1878 was on the cusp of disappearing from wider community life. Her description is evocative of both time and place and deserves substantial quotation:

It is Sabbath morning in our little Western town. The sun shines clear and bright from a dazzling blue sky over the almost equally dazzling green prairie. A decorous stillness prevails in the grassy streets; the stores are closed, the blacksmith's shop is empty and silent; but the usual number of loungers sit in front of the hotel and quite as many as usual are passing up and down, on foot or on horseback, intent on business and pleasure. Let us turn aside from them all and enter the building where "two or three are gathered together" to worship the Lord in this far-off land.

A large lofty room, unplastered, uncarpeted; several maps and advertisements hanging from the rough timber studding; a writing desk in a corner; bunches of Indian corn and millet, pieces of stone and chalk, lying about promiscuously under the windows, these last being specimens of the vegetable and mineral productions of Trego county; a half dozen or so of very plain wooden benches, minus backs, in the middle of the room; a small deal table for a pulpit and a plain wooden chair behind it; such is the meeting-place and its furniture.

After depicting those who come to the service, Agnes returns to her theme of the Sabbath, such a powerful punctuation point in her own life story:

Away out here on the prairies, far from all the settled institutions, habits, and associations of our former lives in older places, how easy it is to forget and let slip matters of first importance. The busy life, with so much work to be done and so little time to do it, fosters this tendency to forgetfulness, especially in matters of religion. During the week the whole being, mind and body, is absorbed in work, work: ploughing and sowing, digging and building, buying and selling and trading; and when the blessed Sabbath comes round, what more natural than to take a drive on the prairie to visit our "claim" or call upon that fine fellow who came into the place the other day and whom we have had no time to get acquainted with, or lounge about the hotel steps and pick up the gossip of the past week! Just here the little mission church steps in, with its modest and gentle reminder that this is "the Lord's Day" and must not be desecrated by attention to business or indulgence in pleasure. We "remember the Sabbath Day to keep it holy": the old habits resume their sway: and so the Home Mission gradually influences and leavens the whole community, and the gospel banner is upheld in this new region.

Agnes was, of course, writing for a converted audience — not just to her faith but to her views on the Sabbath: Presbyterians in Scotland had known nothing different. But it is interesting that she adopts such a non-confrontational tone here. Condemnatory finger-pointing is not foremost but rather a reminder that the old way is the better way for the whole community. And, of course, both she and James saw their presence in Kansas as being part of a larger, more dramatic picture:

> This is not a small matter, for it simply resolves the whole question, which none can consider trivial or unimportant, whether these vast new lands are to be populated by Christians or heathens, to be taken possession of for Christ, or given up without an effort to the god of this world.

Here then is the heart of James's and Agnes's motivation in moving to the frontier: a desire to take the light of the gospel to far-flung places which without it would so easily be taken over by "the god of this world". It is not fanciful to say that America is still in the grip of this battle for souls, though some of the terminology has changed. It is, by a huge margin, easily the most evangelically religious country in the western world, and yet it also suffers the worst gun murder rates and is the seed bed for so many facets of a lifestyle entirely in opposition to Christian values and beliefs. As G. K. Chesterton said, when people stop believing in God, they don't believe nothing, they believe anything with predictably damaging results for social cohesion. The fact that religious organisations in the United States have promoted cohesion by giving more to charitable causes in a year than the entire US government has is a fact that the media do not choose to broadcast.[121] The brief ministry of James and Agnes, along with countless thousands of others, helped lay the foundations of the nineteenth and twentieth-century church in America.

Agnes's article, *A Church on the Frontier*, has more to tell us about the nature of those who attended the services and the motives of those who led them. She described them entering the store, "dropping in by twos and threes" and then made her usual comment about how fashionable the wealthier ladies were, with their diamond rings glittering in the sunlight. They have bought properties but continue to live in the hotel — presumably because their houses are not yet finished. Their husbands, talking in a group by one of the windows were dressed for the day "in handsome broadcloth and faultless linen". Beside them were the farmers and their families who have come in from their claims,

> their hands and faces embrowned almost to the hue of mahogany by exposure to the ardent Kansas sunshine. Their wives, too, are sunburned and freckled, these sweeping prairie winds being fell destroyers of fair and delicate complexions.

Not everyone, however, was successful or prosperous and the life of many was often years of hardship:

> That bright-faced little woman, with two little boys beside her, is one of the pluckiest and most courageous creatures I have ever met. Her husband's business and health failed together in their former place of residence, and they have come out here to try the effect of this climate and to achieve an independency. They have suffered many discomforts, living at first in a rude shanty, through which the rain sometimes poured on their bed, compelling them to spread oilcloths and hold up umbrellas. Her husband, at first, rather grew worse than better, but through it all her hope and cheerfulness never failed her.

---

121 Rudyard Griffiths (ed.), *The Munk Debates, Hitchens v. Blair* (Black Swan, 2011), p.24. See also my book, *The Evil That Men Do* (Sacristy Press, 2016), p. 230.

Joanna Stratton's book shows this to be a prevailing attitude among so many immigrants, especially those connected to a church. In this particular case, the family escaped their devastating sod-house poverty and were able to move to a more permanent building. Agnes goes on to describe "a mere girl" — recently married — digging out the cellar of their future house alongside her husband. Others in the congregation included "young mechanics at work in the town". In fact, the majority of the congregation, by some margin, was male, and most of both sexes were young. "Scarcely one is past the prime of life" Agnes noted. That is likely to have been the case also in the community at large — an exciting place to be for the young minister and his wife, for, as she wrote, the church was led "by a pastor as energetic and lively as any of his hearers". Agnes had always enjoyed listening to James preach and looked forward to his "short, stirring sermon" each Sunday morning. Indeed, the whole business of church was "much more precious . . . than it used to be, somehow!"

Immediately after the short service "Sabbath school" was held,

> when the whole audience resolves itself into several classes, under different teachers and about an hour and a half is spent in the study of a portion of God's Word. Then all slowly disperse, lingering in knots and groups, those formerly acquainted asking after each other's welfare, the new arrivals getting introduced, for every Sabbath there are one or two new faces among us. They are greeted with cordiality and kindness . . . Our anxious desire is to get and retain a hold on all who come to our meetings.

The article captures something of the quiet strength and latent energy of a nascent frontier church — its long-term goals, desire for growth, social cohesion. The latter is made poignantly clear when Agnes describes those who attended the "sacrament of the Lord's Supper . . . celebrated *for the first time in Trego County*" using a "little deal table . . . and wine in a silver cup lent for the occasion by one of the ladies". The emphasis as well as the wording reveals just what a solemn occasion this is for the writer, as it must have been for all the communicants, for it was indeed a spiritual watershed, a dividing-point between the County's tribal "heathen" past and its global Christian future. The enthusiasm is strongly evident:

> And so, seated side by side, unknown to each other but a few weeks ago, gathered here by the providence of God from many diverse portions of the world: the rich lady from Chicago and the fair-haired mechanic from Bohemia, the young gentleman from London and the poor carpenter from Wisconsin: together we eat the bread and drink the wine, in remembrance of our dying Lord. We feel that a strong though invisible hand now unites us together; our hearts glow with love to our Lord and to each other; we form new and strong resolutions to live more entirely for Him and His cause, so that His Kingdom may be more firmly established in our midst.

The language and sentiments may be unfamiliar to a deeply secular twenty-first-century world but there can be no doubting either the joy of the experience or the sincerity and the social impact of the unifying experience that Agnes rather intimately describes.

Just as the congregation leave the Warren and Keeney building, the writer allows the everyday world to reassert itself for a moment — an abrupt reminder that life on the prairies was mostly not at all like the last two hours spent in church:

> As we are dispersing . . . a party of herd boys, mounted on their rough little Texas ponies, canter past the door. How picturesque they look, with their dark swarthy faces, broad flapping hats, loose shirts and top-boots, knives and pistols in their belts! But we know they are desperate characters and we think sadly how little they know of the heavenly joys we have been tasting.

Though the tone here may strike the modern reader as sentimental, the description is actually close to the mark. Of course, the Texas ponies are rightly named; the longhorn cattle had been driven up by the "herd boys" from the vast wild herds in Texas; but so are the faces, clothes and weaponry. It is also precisely right that these were often "desperate characters" who, in

Pressed prairie flowers from the frontier 1878

1878 or 1879, were in conflict with home-steaders every-where; who might have left Dodge City only days before, and only *hours* before been driving a herd in a world which operated beyond the reach of any lawman; a world where "justice" was more likely to be revenge and where a bullet or a noose was more frequent than trial by judge and jury. When in towns like Wakeeney, it was the barmaids and dance-hall girls who took most of the "herd boys'" or cowboys' money. The result was that, as Joanna Stratton remarked, "[M]ost pioneer women disdained any association with the cattle drovers and the fringe elements of the town's population".[122] Yet, as she also noted, even the trail riders had the religious notion of a controlling universal spirit, not unlike the belief of the Indians. Recognising this residual religious sense in most of those around them, the intention of James and Agnes was that "even they, in their distant camps on the prairies" should be encouraged into the Kingdom rather than shunned and ostracised, as others would prefer.

James's ministry, however, could hardly be primarily with those who were merely passing through, disappearing after an evening's entertainment in the saloons. His work was to nurture the infant church in Wakeeney and to organise other churches. He had told Warren and Keeney that he intended to devote his time to "establishing churches" and on April 24, 1879, he had been present at the Presbytery of Solomon in Hays City when Henry Albright

---

122 Stratton, Op. Cit. p.206.

preached. Albright, we have seen, was the pioneer who urged the church westwards, and built a church as far away as Norton. At the same Presbytery meeting, at some point after Albright's sermon, James was appointed to "organize churches at Grainfield, at Collier and on the Saline River".[123] It is reasonable to assume that he wanted to emulate Albright and pursue the calling which he first felt long before leaving Cedarville. The adventurer in him was as strong as ever. "To the West, to the West, to the land of the free" might, for James, have been modulated to "To the West, to the West with the Truth that sets free" but he had little time left for his ambitions.

---

123 See Presbytery of Solomon *Minute Book for 1876-1884* (p.63) in the Presbyterian Historical Society Library, Philadelphia.

CHAPTER SEVENTEEN

TRAGEDY ON THE FRONTIER

IN 1870S AMERICA THE PRACTICE of medicine was some way behind the centres of excellence in Europe, one of the foremost of these being Edinburgh. The frontier states, in particular, were often badly served insofar as those who failed their exams or could find no work in the East moved to the West for employment. Medical men frequently had to supplement their incomes with other, less mysterious, trades owing to the lack of ready money and great distances between homesteads. Moreover, state and national governments were less active in public health issues than were their European counterparts. Although the American Medical Association had been formed in 1846 to raise professional standards among doctors, in practice little standardisation resulted from this in its first half century. Qualified doctors were few and far between. For instance, in 1879, in Lakin, Kearney County, south-west of Wakeeney, the nearest doctor was seventy-five miles away in Dodge City. In Dickman's *Medical Directory* for 1881 only one is listed for the whole of County Trego: one H W Morgan, who we shall meet later.

It is easy, too, for us to forget how comparatively recently the germ theory of disease became widely known — it only being established by Pasteur and Koch in 1870. At Edinburgh, it was Joseph Lister who applied this theory to the practice of surgery and initiated the usage of antiseptics. Prior to these developments, diagnosing the cause of disease and saving lives through the prevention of infection was immeasurably more difficult. How malaria, for instance, was transmitted was discovered only in 1897, even though David Livingstone had noted the connection between mosquitoes and the disease forty years earlier.[124] Very few frontier houses had window-screens and "few Kansans in 1876 associated diseases with insect carriers".[125] Typhoid fever, it was known, could be spread by contaminated water but the bacillus that caused it was suspected only in 1880.

It was not only ignorance, but lack of money and the absence of technological advances which also contributed to high mortality rates and the rapid spread of disease through close-knit communities. Poor sanitation systems meant that wells and water sources could be easily polluted. In some places sewage was piped directly into the streets and it was said that some towns could be smelt before they could be seen. Everywhere the droppings of horses, pigs, and other livestock attracted clouds of flies. "Time after time, communities were ravaged by cholera, typhoid, diphtheria, pneumonia, pleurisy and smallpox".[126] Consumption, measles, croup, diarrhoea and, of course, malaria, were also frequent causes of death.[127] In the Trego County mortality schedule for 1880 in which James K Wilson is included (inaccurately), the most common cause of death is listed as "typho malarial fever", there being five instances among thirty-one in all, some sixteen percent of the total. Thirteen of the fatalities were among children.[128] The typhoid outbreak in Wakeeney was attributed to polluted water drawn from the town's well. Subsequently, drinking water had to be fetched from a spring and water for other purposes hauled from the creeks.

The young were particularly prone to malaria. Known as the 'ague' it produced headaches, severe chills and fever, often with diarrhoea and vomiting. In the days before capsules settlers kept the bitter natural quinine to hand, as an antidote, on a regular basis. Yet, in a survey of 1876, Kansas

---

124 See O. Ransford, Op. Cit. p. 79.
125 Socolofsky, Op. Cit.
126 K Wheeler, Op. Cit. p. 32.
127 Socolofsky, Op. Cit.
128 http://genealogytrails.com/kan/trego/1880mortality.html.

medics thought the state was as healthy as the one they had emigrated from and, naturally, the propaganda, as we have seen, claimed disease was largely absent from the prairies. That was a lie, or at the very least a misconception, which family after immigrant family must have reflected long and hard upon.

In the last week of May, the Wilsons welcomed a new arrival to their home. He had made the 4,700 mile journey alone after a severe illness back home in Scotland. It was Willie Arnot, Dr Arnot's son, from the family with whom they had shared so much in the Free High, now some five years earlier. He had been in America before but returned from Chicago ill. Now he was out again to try his hand as an apprentice on James's cattle farm. Agnes would, she told Mary, keep a watchful eye on him and see to it that he did not overdo it. But she had no doubts of the health benefits:

> The air is so pure, clear and light that it must be beneficial, and the open air work is the very best for him. At present he is serving a kind of apprenticeship to his new life here-learning to do what all men in this country need to know how to do — milking the cows, attending to cattle, horses and stock generally, hoeing in the field etc. . . . and gaining experience as a ranch man. In cattle rearing and trading more money can be made than in anything else. I am taking all the care possible of Willie, not letting him work too hard, and seeing that he is made as comfortable as possible. He gets lots of milk and cream to drink.

Two months later, in the heat of late July, "when it is a burden to do anything but what you have to do" Agnes described Willie as "keeping really well and strong" and she was surprised that the combination of extreme heat, change of climate and manual labour had not affected him more. But then he was "strictly enjoined never to overdo his strength, and to rest whenever he feels he needs it". He had had the encouragement of the generous gift of one hundred and sixty acres of the homestead portion of the farm from James, which prompted Agnes to say: "He will be a rich man yet, if he lives". In saying so, she betrayed the underlying awareness of so many in a previous age, especially when far from home, that life was an uncertain business, even at the best of times. Sudden death, the onset of irreversible disease, the occurrence of a crippling accident, were all everyday realities on the frontier at that time. None of these were predictable, such that one might be removed from earthly activity in the blink of an eye. Thus it was, even as things seemed to be settling into a fruitful pattern, that disaster struck, illustrating in real life the tragedian's device of allowing both audience and characters a brief moment of illusion: that just before the catastrophe, despite all the warnings and premonitions, things would eventually turn out for the best and the end of the drama be a happy one. It was not to be.

Willie wrote Mary a full account of "the work that is progressing out at the farm" and Agnes spoke for him, James and herself when she continued:

> It is a terrible business to begin at the very foundation in all our undertakings, as we have to do in a new country, but I think for us the worst is about over. For me, I know it is, for in our little house here I am as comfortably "fixed" as I can ever hope to be on the frontier, and a great deal better than many, many people here.

Of Willie she says: "Willie is a dear, good boy, it is a blessing to us to have him here and I feel certain that it will be a blessing to himself, both physically and temporally". Three times in these lines Agnes expects a future which never came to pass; three times the irony dramatically undercuts her words.

The summer heat caused a "lull in affairs . . . a quieting effect" though the building of "three handsome new houses" continued, and Agnes's "never mind" lets us know that by now some of the building was closer to their own little house than she could have desired. High temperatures always made it more difficult to preserve food and keep milk fresh and "Hammie" at the end of July had "about a week's siege of summer-complaint. This is his second summer", Agnes reminded her sister, "so I suppose he 'had to have something'. It has made him a little thinner, but he is fat and heavy enough yet, I can tell you". Agnes too, felt "quite bilious and headachy".

As summer gave way to fall, letter writing became increasingly onerous for Agnes as her time and energies were devoted to coping with a deteriorating situation at home. In October she knew she owed her sister a letter but did not sit down to write it until the 27th:

> My dearest Mary,
>
> I have been trying for some time back, to get my letter written which I owe you, but unsuccessfully. We are having such a time with sickness here, that I feel I can write about nothing else, and must just plunge into the subject at once. This malarial fever which I mentioned, I think, in my letter to Aunt, is still here, and our house and family has had their fair share of it.

Jim, the hired Irish hand on the farm, was the first to succumb and he was ill for four weeks. Sam had two bouts of the fever, almost constant diarrhoea, and intermittent teething sickness. Edina suffered least but Louise, the young servant girl, only two weeks into her employment, was very ill and had to go home, leaving Agnes with all the domestic chores until she was able to replace her with "a coloured girl very soon after". On the day that Agnes recovered from "a bad sore throat" James was taken ill and at the time of writing the letter was still incapacitated after a week. There had been some improvement in his condition but, Agnes wrote, "it is such a slow, lingering fever that he may be long in getting strong again". Lastly, while Jim and Edina were both suffering, Willie had to leave the farm (due to dysentery), where he had been struggling on alone for days without any help or company from Jim: "When I saw him come in, all thin and wan, my heart, which had been heavy enough before, sank like lead, and for a while I could scarcely keep up at all".

For the second time, therefore, Willie had been defeated by health issues in America, and was sent off to Russell where John Cassidy had bought
a butcher's business. There he would be able to keep the accounts for the
erstwhile farmer, and give other assistance, "which we think will be better for him than herding cattle", Agnes added. Willie was delighted at the
change, doubtless for the company in town (in exchange for the solitude of
the farm) as well as increased security and the more sedentary nature of the
job. The exposure, irregular and unsatisfactory meals "were too much for
him", Agnes opined.

One after the other each member of Agnes's household was developing
one or more symptoms of malaria, a killer disease then and now, which,
once established in the system, was very difficult to escape from. All
her predictions of future prosperity and fortune were collapsing around
Agnes's feet.

By Sunday November 2nd, James appeared to be "considerably better"
and decided that he would get up to preach that morning. It was a wrong
decision for as Agnes said, "he is the worse of it to-night. He is quite weak yet,
and so sensitive to cold, and so pale and hollow eyed that you wouldn't know
him. I will have to take the greatest care of him for a while". Nevertheless,
the tone and variety of topics in the letter reveal that Agnes was quite san-
guine at this point about James's recovery. The early cold spell with its keen
frosts "will effectually banish this fever" she feels sure. In preparation for
the winter she was, inevitably, doing a lot of sewing which had "fallen terribly behind of course". The letter contains extended descriptions of the pro-
cesses involved in the making of clothes for both children who had made
full recoveries from their illnesses. "Hammie" was now saying "'Mama', pro-
nounced of course in the American manner, with the accent on the first
syllable". His best dress was to be "Stewart tartan poplin, trimmed with
black velvet". Agnes shows some petulance in the letter, but she was suffering from exhaustion: "The truth is", she explained to Mary, "I think I am

worn out". Illness in the family under frontier conditions and with so little medical help surely excuses her exasperation.

In closing the letter, Agnes, quoting Romans 8:28, for the final time expresses with painfully unknowing irony her cherished hopes for the future:

> I trust that our present troubles are about over, and I trust that God, in His good providence, will grant us health and prosperity. But all things work together for good, you know, sickness, health, joy or sorrow . . . Write soon to me. With kindest love to you all, in which James joins me,

> Ever dearest Mary, Your loving sister, Aggie.

It was the last letter in which she could send James's love to anyone.

Exactly four weeks later, on Sunday 30th November, she was to send a very different sort of letter on its long slow journey back to Scotland:

> My dearest Mary,

> I feel that I must sit down and write to you though my heart is so sick and sore that I feel to-day as if I longed for death to put an end to my pain. Oh, darling Mary, if you could only be here, or if you could have been here with me during these terrible past weeks. It is wonderful to me that I am not dead too, and lying now in the grave with my dear husband.

Agnes then reminded Mary of the fact that James got up to preach that Sunday a month before and could now say:

> Now I know that that was the day he got his death-blow. He ought to have been in his bed. Next day his fever returned with increased violence, and he went upstairs to bed, never to come down again till he was carried down.

Understandably, Agnes wished that Mary could be with her, wanting somehow to purge the horror of those days by unloading every detail on to her sister; but she does the next best thing and tries to write an account which will help distance her from the ever-recurrent memories:

About Friday or Saturday typhoid symptoms began to appear and then the nursing and the care of him began to be more systematized as he had to get his medicine through the night as well as day. I had already lost much sleep, but from that time got assistance at night while I nursed him through the day. By Thursday we had secured as night nurse a very good Christian man, a Mr Johnson, an excellent nurse, and from that time he and I divided the nursing between us keeping careful records of all the symptoms and incidents of the disease. We had the best Dr in the place, Dr Morgan, and on four different nights he also sat up with James. I never saw a more devoted physician. He and James were very fond of each other and it was most affecting sometimes to see James, in his weakness, stroking the Dr's head and face and calling him pet names.

Despite Dr Morgan's encouraging remarks to Agnes, she felt that, as the days passed, James was getting no better. Later, the doctor confessed that he was merely "catching at straws". With only such rudimentary medication to palliate the disease, typhoid, with malarial complications, was very unpleasant to suffer:

> He suffered very much from diarrhoea, squeamishness and vomiting, so that he had to have all his medicine in capsules. But his patience, submission, tenderness of heart, and loving words and looks, became more and more noticeable as time went on . . . It seemed as if he could not say or do enough to show me how much he loved me. He would stroke and pet my head, and call me the tenderest pet names and was so concerned about my hurting myself in caring for him.

In the moments when the disease or pain was in remission James spoke of how, if he lived, he would devote himself "more entirely to the cause of Christ" but as the disease took firmer hold "there came a change when he talked more of his anxiety for my future":

> 'The Lord will provide for you my darling' he wd. say, and then once, 'I'm glad you've got Mary and Walter to think of you and my

good old father will never see you want.' Once he said, in bitter grief, 'My poor lamb, I've just brought her out here to kill her, and leave her a widow.'

Such words were to haunt Agnes continually in the days after James's death, but their agony was bitter-sweet:

> The mingled pain and yet pleasure which they give me is agonising, I cannot describe it. The joy that he loved me and showed it so fully and the bitter bitter grief that I shall hear that dear voice, those loving words no more. My heart at times swells almost to bursting with the longing to put my arms round him and pour out loving words in return, but now I cannot. And then the feeling of hopeless impotence that ensues is terrible.

As is characteristic of the condition James suffered, there were moments when it seemed he was on the mend:

> Last Sabbath, a week to-day, he seemed to be gaining, his symptoms were good, and the Dr felt encouraged about him but on Monday a change for the worse took place — nothing stayed in his stomach, not even stimulant. Then we began to give him everything by injection, medicine, food and all, and on Tuesday he was getting along better, the injections seemed to do him good, and he felt easier. Towards evening, he began to get a little restless, and I noticed his hands turning cold and his pulse feebler. I mentioned it to Mr Johnson and to the Dr when he came in. The Dr looked at him then laid down his hat and said he would stay.

It was at this point that Agnes knew, beyond doubt, that James was dying and yet her account of that process to Mary is detailed and unflinching. It continues to be (given that the letter was written less than a week after the event) an extraordinarily clear-eyed and matter-of-fact narrative:

> I knew my hour had come but I remained perfectly calm, and helped the Dr to give him an injection of the spirits of ammonia

which is given only in cases of extremity. While we were then kneeling at the bedside I said, in a low voice, 'Dr, is this the crisis?' He bowed his head. I said, 'Can you save him?' he replied, 'I'll do all I can.' And from that moment, all through that dreadful night, we worked unceasingly to save him — the Dr, Mr Johnson, and Mr M'Ginnis, a neighbour. We bathed and rubbed his feet, put mustard on them and on his bowels and wrists, gave him spirits every few minutes all to no avail.[129]

At this point in reading the letter archive, with its surprisingly un-agitated handwriting on the brittle, yellowing, lined note paper, it is easy for the reader to feel one should cease to read on, leave the room, allow this private grief to remain private. This most terrible of moments, I felt, should not be spied upon, even less written about. But the Wilsons and their children, especially Edina, had an acute sense of history. Agnes published a book about her father; Edina faithfully kept and organised the family letters. More importantly, Edina destroyed the documents which she did not see fit to share with posterity. This scene, however, she preserved so that others might enter into something of the struggles of their forebears. As noted earlier, "Faithful records," she later wrote, "illuminated by a sympathetic imagination, will bring before us the spirits and personalities that lived and moved in the past". This is Agnes's "faithful record":

> About 2 1/2 o'clock, utterly exhausted, I had sunk into a chair and as the Dr passed me I said, 'Dr is he dying?' 'He is dying' he re-sponded, and then my agony burst forth and all my forced calm-ness gave way. Shall I ever forget the terrible hours that ensued — they are scarred into my memory. After a time I asked the Dr if he thought I might make him try and speak to me. He said I might and he and Mr Johnson retired to the door of the room. I knelt beside him, took him in my arms, laid my lips to his ear,

---

129 Ammonia was used as a respiratory stimulant; mustard mixed with bread crumbs and vinegar was applied to soles of the feet to "rouse the system". See http://www.doctortreatments.com/19th-century-medicines-healing-drugs-chemicals-herbs.html.

his eyes were glazing, his pulse almost gone. I called in his ear, 'Jim darling, do you know me?' After a moment he said with difficulty, 'Don't I know my own wee kid' (his favourite pet name for me. He has called me kid for years). I said, 'Is Jesus with you, near you?' He replied, 'He is with me, and then added, clear and loud, 'Jesus Christ, the same yesterday, today, and forever'. Oh the joy and yet the agony of that moment. And so the hours wore on. We kept giving him stimulants every little while, but he was sinking fast. His last words were, very clearly spoken, 'He sees it all'. At about 9 o'clock on Wednesday morning the 26th Nov. he passed away, with his hands in mine, so sweetly and quietly that we could not tell when the last breath was drawn. It was a peaceful departure.

Agnes was not left alone in her grief. Kind friends had been gathering and led her from the room while others began the gloomy process of dealing with the deceased. That afternoon the widow asked a telegram to be sent to Russell informing Willie Arnot and John Cassidy of the news. Willie arrived in Wakeeney the next morning and was a great comfort and support to Agnes — a difficult task for a very young man. Even at this point Agnes's faith in the providence of God leads her to affirm that "God let him come to Kansas that I might not be entirely without my own friends in this time of sorrow".

The funeral took place the next day, as was usual in such communities, "and was the darkest and most terrible day in all my life" Agnes wrote. The cemetery was, of course, only a few months old and lay just south of the town "on one of the swells of the prairie". James had been asked to name it and called it "Mount Peace". He had bought a 'lot' in it himself already.

What follows in this last surviving letter from Kansas is a detail which many have forgotten or never known: Agnes never expected to go to the burial, or even perhaps, the funeral service. She was dismayed to have to do so:

It is the universal custom in this country for women to go to funerals, and so I had to undergo the fearful trial of following his remains to the Land Office, where the services were held. Dr Bishop of Salina preached the sermon, on "What I do thou knowest not now, but thou shalt know hereafter". Then we followed him to the cemetery and there with my own eyes I beheld my darling laid in his grave. But God gave me strength in my hour of need. Now that day of agony is over and I thank God can never be lived once again.

In nineteenth-century Scotland, the custom among many was that although women might prepare the body, they would not go to the church or to the cemetery. Some might go to the cemetery gates but then return home where their role was to look after the children and prepare food for the gathering afterwards. In England it was considered that only lower-class women would go. *Cassell's Household Guide* for 1878 discourages the practice. Agnes's words "with my own eyes" betray her shock at being expected to witness James's burial.

Despite the fact that only Friday and Saturday separate the funeral from the writing of this letter on Sunday, Agnes bravely stated, "I am growing calmer in my grief every day, but still waters run deep". Her mind, inevitably, was going unceasingly, exhaustingly, over the final hours, the days of sickness and their brief life together:

It seems as if the image and the thought of him are constantly with me. All through his sickness he took the greatest pleasure in repeating verses of Scripture, or hearing them repeated, and in hymns. Often he requested me to read to him, and would often say, as I sat holding his hand, 'Say a verse to me, Kid'.

Agnes then paid tribute to her friends in Wakeeney:

The people here have been very kind. I have much to be thankful for, for I have received the greatest sympathy. A dear lady, Mrs M'Ginnis, has been with me a great deal, and slept with me for three nights after his death. The Dr came to see me three or four times after too, in case I should be ill, after such a long strain of fatigue and mental distress, culminating in that fearful night.

Indeed, the folk were as generous and kindly as they had been in Cedarville — in such different circumstances. The empty, spiritually low, post-funeral moments had been anticipated:

> The terrible trial, too, of coming back to the desolate home was softened to me, for Mr and Mrs Cook, an elder of the church, had a bright fire in the sitting room and a cheerful teatable set. Mrs Cook met me at the door with a kiss full of loving sympathy, put me in a rocking chair, took off my things, and even knelt down and took off my overshoes. It was then I turned round to Willie and said, 'Willie, you can tell them at home what good friends I have here.'

As all thinking people know, the earliest days of bereavement can be the most desolate but during them it is often true that the bereaved remain in the forefront of the care of friends and relatives. "Mr Cassidy comes tomorrow and nearly all of the best and most reliable men in the place are ready and willing to help me in any way" Agnes believed, so she and the children would have been well supported within Wakeeney in the weeks following his death; but she knew immediately that without James there was no long-term future for them where they were. To return to Scotland was her only option. In the first few days, however, her mind could not always take in the enormity of what had happened. As convention required, mourning had to be visible in one's dress; so she wore her "widow's bonnet and long crepe veil" for necessary errands about the town, but she let Mary know, "I sometimes ask myself if it is really true, and if my darling boy has really left me for ever". Her strong faith was undaunted: "God, the Husband of the widow, is sustaining me and never, in all my life, have the promises of Scripture and the comfort of prayer been more precious to me".

Agnes's other precious gift was her children, and their very infancy was a relief to her: the "Dear lambs", she wrote, were "so unconscious of their loss". They were keeping well now the fever had passed, and though she had to admit that her "plans for the future" were "still unformed" she must have known that the journey home — unaccompanied this time, and with two toddlers — would be a massive undertaking. No wonder she concluded this letter, the last we have from Kansas, with:

Pray for your poor bereaved sister and write to me soon, soon.

Your loving Aggie

We do not know how long Agnes stayed in Wakeeney but James's business affairs must have taken some time to settle. There was the farm to sell as well as their house and the building lots in town. Nor do we know whether these sales were made before crops failed and prices fell as the first settlers began to abandon the settlement in search of more secure lives less far west. We do know, however, that James's death "came as a great blow to the church" where, as a result of it, "all was confusion and discouragement".[130] Michellich's research produced accounts of him as "a strong self-reliant man" who "carried almost the entire burden of the church up to the time of his illness". At that time the membership of the church was about forty, but there was neither the experience nor the financial means among the congregation to forge ahead with the planned stone church, though the move to the frame depot transported to "lots on the corner of 8th and Russell" took place in December 1879. This was used for some nine years, after which other denominations used it.[131]

At the meeting of the Presbytery of Solomon in Concordia, on April 23, 1880, the following "memorial of the death of Rev James K. Wilson" was "offered by Rev H. Bushell" and recorded in the minutes:

---

130 Michellich, p.22.
131 Michellich, p.15.

Two years ago in the full strength [of] early manhood, James K. Wilson left a church in New Jersey, where he was greatly beloved and where his labors had been owned and blessed of God, to cast his lot with those who were striving to plant the gospel standard on the extreme frontier. He united with the Presbytery of Solomon at the meeting in Beloit in the spring of 1878 and soon after removed with his family to Wa-Keeney where he continued to labor till his removal from these earthly scenes. By the death of Bro. Wilson we are again reminded of our own mortality — and of our obligation to redeem the time, for to us all the night is coming when no man can work. Remembering as we do this day our brother fallen, we extend to his wife and children our sympathy to pray that the Father of the fatherless and the widow's God may be theirs.[132]

The sombre tone of Mr Bushell's tribute is perhaps rather characteristic of the Presbyterianism of the time but is a reminder that in those days, early death — whether the result of disease, accident or exhaustion — was something all had to be prepared for. But it would have been more pleasing to read something of what he had *achieved* in his short time on the frontier. A better summary of his work was made in his obituary notice which can be found as an appendix to this book.

After the Wilsons' affairs in Wakeeney had been tied up, it would have been a reflective, perhaps rather mournful little party that made its way to the railroad depot one morning in order to reverse the journey undertaken in such hope just two years earlier. Goodbyes must have been said at the graveside as well as in church and in family homes. The community would miss this forthright, energetic and interesting family: the minister who had such vision for the Gospel on the frontier, his capable, musical wife and the two comely bright-eyed children. Those who had followed them out West from Cedarville would be especially at a loss as to what to make of the turn of events. Was the Promised Land turning

---

132 *Solomon Presbytery Minutes 1876-1884*, pp.87-88.

into another Wilderness experience? Where was God in all this? As the locomotive pulled away from the depot, so recently opened and to such acclaim, Agnes and Edina, perhaps even little Sam, would certainly have looked back, knowing they would never again see their father's grave or the freshly cut timber of the little town's buildings set so boldly in the endless green of the billowing prairie. But, I believe, Agnes would also have looked forward, beyond the smoke of the engine, in hope that where they were going would give them a new start and old friends to be with once again.[133]

After four days of travel eastwards, there would have been rising excitement as they approached Philadelphia, seeming unspeakably grand after nearly two years in Wakeeney. The majestic trees of Fairmount Park, the uplifting civic buildings and stately rivers would in themselves have lifted their spirits after the barren prairie winter. There they would be met, once again, by Dr Patterson and, after the initial tears, there would be old friends at his house on Frankford Avenue, and Agnes might have consented to play the piano there for them. Beyond the city, just three hours away, lay Cedarville, and although Agnes could no longer call it home as she once had, it was familiar, and probably the next best thing.

In the US Federal Census of 1880, the record shows that Agnes and the children were living in Cedarville with the Nixon family who had been exceptionally kind to Agnes throughout her time in New Jersey. The Nixons had at least three children of their own (and had lost two more in infancy)[134] and were the couple who Agnes cited as making her feel ashamed when she considered their workload — as we saw at the start of Chapter Three. Now she was truly dependent on their generosity of spirit and the tone Agnes had adopted (probably as a defence mechanism) in describing Mrs Nixon earlier may

---

133 In fact, Sam did return to Wakeeney in 1928 when in the US for a lecture tour — see Appendix B.

134 The Census gives the Nixon family as numbering seven, so presumably by this time there were the two parents, the grandmother, and *four* children in the household.

have come back to haunt her. It was indeed magnanimous of this Christian family to accept three more people under their roof when their lives were already under such strain.

By mid-August the Wilsons were aboard a steamship bound for Scotland. The children by this stage would have been more able to appreciate the adventure of being aboard such a vessel and it is impossible to imagine that their mother did not take every opportunity to educate her children about the ship and everything else that their active minds could absorb. Agnes's own fertile mind would have had to flit back and forth from what she had left behind to the necessities of the uncertain life ahead of her. One thing, however, she knew. Walter and Mary, especially dearest Mary, would be longing to see her and she could rely on their active protection and support. At the end of the month the steamer docked at Greenock and since Mary could not be there Agnes wrote to her the next day:

Wednesday, September 1st

My Dearest Mary,

Here I am once again in dear Auld Reekie and the relief and rest of mind that I am enjoying already is remarkable. Can you imagine what my feelings were when I saw Walter's face looking up at me from the tender as it came alongside the steamer. I was so glad, so overjoyed to see him that I just gave a sort of sob.

Brother and sister arrived at Walter's home, 12, Bruntsfield Place, Edinburgh, something before ten o'clock and the next day Agnes was "so giddy still with the motion of the steamer that my head spins round, round and round". The children, however, were unaffected and were, to Agnes's supreme delight, playing and running around with their new-found friends, Walter's children, the first cousins they had known.

Six and a half years after setting out for America, Agnes Legerwood Hately Kinnier Wilson, widow, was finally home again. Her story of romance, faith and tragedy now over. The final curtain seemed to have come down on Act V. How could Act VI ever be written or enacted? An answer was waiting in the wings.

Sam and Edina as young children

ACT VI

HENRY MACINTOSH, THE EDINBURGH MUSIC seller on George Street, had also suffered tragedy in his life. Ten years older than Agnes, he had, by 1880, already been bereaved of his wife and two children. Like many in the city he was a reader of Dr Arnot's *The Family Treasury of Sunday Reading* and there had found three articles written anonymously by "A Home Missionary's Wife" living on the Kansas frontier. They had a profound effect on him such that he knelt and prayed that God might grant *him* such a wife "as she who wrote those papers". Agnes, as a girl, had known Henry before his marriage and he had secretly admired her. Her marriage was, therefore, a bitter disappointment to him insofar as his unspoken love for Agnes had led him to hope that one day he might marry her. After her emigration he always enquired after her through Walter whom he knew professionally but it never crossed his mind that the author of *Letters from Kansas* was Agnes. Instinctively, however, Henry was strongly attracted towards someone who had the adventurous spirit exhibited in the articles along with the desire to take the gospel to the ends of the earth, a calling which exercised the imagination of so many godly Victorians even though only a small proportion of the Church could act on it.

When Agnes returned to Edinburgh her path soon crossed with Henry's through her need of sheet music and his shop's provision of it. To have Agnes back, as it were, on his doorstep must have both evoked his compassion and re-ignited his hope in equal measure. He was soon able to loan her a Chappell piano free of charge and then found music pupils for her. Owning the shop which was first port of call for musicians in the city meant that these things were not difficult for him. As the cold winter of 1880 set in, he sent her anonymous gifts to help provide winter clothing for the children and the following spring felt confident enough to declare his feelings for her. In August 1881, Agnes and Henry were married and the following year they had a son, Henry Walter, "a dear good infant and like the other two, not fractious and crying as some children are", as Agnes described him.

For both of them, widow and widower alike, there were scars of bereavement which at the time of their loss must have seemed irreparable. But just as in 1873 when Agnes reflected in her letter to James on the words of the hymn "God moves in a mysterious way/His wonders to perform", so now they must both have sensed that despite the vicissitudes of life — its deep troughs as well as moments of delight and unabated joy — God was in control in ways that surpassed their understanding. Agnes had certainly learnt so much through her suffering; things which perhaps she never could have understood about the needs and lives of others had her life and ambitions for her home in America been allowed to continue without setback. Her reliance on the grace and mercies of God had been deepened in a way perhaps — who knows — that simply would not have been possible by any other means. Could it be that, in the eternal perspective, so far beyond what we currently see, Agnes *needed* the severe mercy of her, sadly, brief time with James on a wild frontier so far from Ulster and Edinburgh?

So began, all unexpectedly, the gift of the God of surprises, of multiple blessings, "a quiet and uneventful period — peaceful quiet years, when I lived a very busy, happy life, much engrossed with my husband, my children and my household duties". She had no desire for further drama or upheaval and lived to be "full of years", grandmother to six boys and two girls. She kept up her wide interests and held her impassioned opinions well into her eighties.

As she grew older, Agnes continued to write and reflect, regretting her "very great fault" of being too judgemental when she was younger. Two things, however, she was very sure of:

> I know that the love we three bore to each other — Mary Walter and I — the brotherly and sisterly affection, is quite uncommon now. I most earnestly desired that my own three dear children should love each other and stand by each other all through life . . . I sometimes thought I had succeeded, I do not know; but God knows what my heart's desire ever was.

These, Agnes's faithful and almost final words are reminiscent of those spoken last of all by James nigh on half a century before on the distant prairies and are a reminder to those in suffering who might need reassurance: "He sees it all" and His plans for us are plans for good.

APPENDIX A

THIS OBITUARY, ALMOST CERTAINLY WRITTEN by Agnes, and placed in one of the local papers, is entitled "A Brief Sketch of the Life of the Late James Kinnier Wilson".

The Rev James Kinnier Wilson, Pastor of the Presbyterian Church in Wa-Keeney, Kansas, died at his residence, of typhoid fever, November 26, 1879. This, indeed, is a great loss to the church which he established and served so faithfully, and to the community among whom his labours were so highly appreciated. The following is a brief sketch of the life and character of Rev Wilson who was no ordinary man:

He was born in the county of Monaghan, Ireland, the 29th day of March, 1846. He was of Scottish ancestry. His father, Mr Samuel Wilson, who is still living, is a staunch Presbyterian, and has ever been remarkable for his pure Christian character and earnest piety. His mother, who died twenty years ago, was a lady remarkable for the kindness and benevolence of her nature, eminent in the Christian graces and is still remembered with love and esteem in the neighbourhood where she lived. At the age of seventeen, the subject of this sketch came to the United States to visit friends in Philadelphia, where he remained several years engaged in business. About this time the whole purpose of his life was changed and he entered upon a course of studies for the gospel ministry. He pursued his collegiate course at Princeton College. His theological training he received at Princeton, Chicago and the Free Church College in Edinburgh, Scotland. He travelled quite extensively abroad, making a tour through the continent of Europe, visiting the principal cities in France, Germany and Italy as well as Great Britain. On the 8th of April 1874, he was married to Miss Agnes L .Hately, of Edinburgh, whose father Mr T. L. Hately, was widely known in his native country, as a musician of high culture and attainments, especially in the department of sacred music. It is but justice to say that Mrs Wilson, now left a widow, with two fatherless children, proved, indeed, a "help meet for her husband" sympathizing and co-operating with him in all his efforts to build up the Kingdom of Christ. In May, 1874, Mr Wilson and wife came to Philadelphia, and in September, 1874 he received a call to the First Presbyterian Church in Cedarville, N.J. In the following winter, his labours were blessed by a revival of religion, during which he conducted meetings for nine weeks in succession, and at the ensuing Communion between fifty and sixty persons were added to the church. The news of his death will bring sadness to his many friends in that church. In the Spring of 1878, moved by the wants of the West, as presented by Dr Sheldon Jackson, the heroic Bishop of the mountains, he came to Kansas, and united with the Presbytery of Solomon at its spring session in Beloit, at which time and place he received his appointment to labor at Wa-Keeney and vicinity. About a month before his arrival, A Presbyterian Church had been organized with seven members. With characteristic energy he took hold of the work of laying deep and broad foundations for church and society. The church grew under his ministrations and he had a strong hold on the community. As a man he had a fine robust physique, with great executive ability, a vigorous intellect and scholarly attainments. He was just the type of man in the ministry, needed in the West, to mould into proper shape the formative elements in society. It was a sad Thanksgiving when he was borne by mourning friends to "the house appointed for all living".

During his sickness of four weeks, he gave evidence of the genuineness of his piety by his patient resignation to the will of God, under suffering. He was much engaged in prayer and his faith was sustained by the precious promises of the Bible. To the question

"Do you trust in Jesus?" he replied, "Yes! Jesus, the same yesterday, today and forever". His last words, seeming to refer to the Divine Providence in his affliction and prospective death inscrutable to the human mind, were "He sees it all!"

The funeral services took place at 3 o'clock P.M., November 27th at the Hall in which Brother Wilson had held religious services for some months past, and were conducted by the Rev William Bishop, D.D. of Salina, Kansas, whose remarks, based upon a portion of the 7 v. 13 ch. of John: "What I do thou knowest not now; but thou shalt know hereafter," were delivered with much force and earnestness. His admirations[135] to the church, now without a tender shepherd, were very earnest and tender, while he pointed them to the oft repeated calls to life, and warnings to prepare for death, which had been made to them by him whose remains they were now about to convey to their last resting place, there to await the dawn of the great resurrection morn".

---

135 This word is almost certainly a misreading of 'admonitions' in Agnes's sometimes difficult handwriting. "Kinnier" was also incorrectly spelt.

APPENDIX B

JAMES'S AND AGNES'S CHILDREN MIGHT have been traumatised by their mother's suffering and the loss of their father on the High Plains of Western Kansas. As it was, they both achieved distinction worthy of record.

EDINA WILSON

On returning to Scotland Edina attended Ladies' College in Edinburgh where, according to Agnes, she was noted for her intelligence "and gained prizes from the first". Like her mother she was musical and loved reading. From 1898 to 1901 she studied piano at the University of Leipzig in Germany, known as "The City of Music" and from there, like her mother, wrote a series of remarkable letters. (Six family members in all studied in the city which was not only home to Bach and Mendelssohn but also the birthplace of the Reformation and site of Martin Luther's great "Disputation" in 1519 — exactly 500 years ago). Edina described the city as "the place that once thronged with the learned of Europe and pulsating with a force that was to move the world". It was perhaps predictable that this elegant, articulate, educated, forthright and adventurous character should study, as a single woman, abroad for three years. She was very much her mother's daughter.

It was probably in Leipzig that she met a brilliant young academic from Ulster, Francis Paul, to whom she was married in September 1903 in Bushmills, Co. Antrim, where he was Minister at the Presbyterian church. While there she bore him three sons whom she fervently hoped would become missionaries. In 1911 Francis was appointed Professor of Church History at Magee University College, Londonderry.

When the First World War broke out in 1914 both Edina and Francis wanted to support Britain's cause. Edina, despite having three young boys to bring up while Francis was a temporary chaplain to the forces in France, managed to contribute to the war effort by working at the Hospital Depot in Derry and also by feeding, clothing and cleaning up after the thousands of sailors who reached Ireland's shores after their ships were torpedoed by German U boats. "I never felt brisker in my life", she wrote.

Francis's career next took him to Belfast where he became Principal, in 1924, of The Presbyterian College and later was awarded, among other honours, honorary doctorates for his scholarship by Glasgow University and Queen's University, Belfast where he was a member of the Senate. Sadly, ill-health forced him to turn down the Presidency of the General Presbyterian Alliance — a world-wide body. Edina, however, was not someone to bask in these glories and pursued her own path of Christian service. For many years she was editor of *Daybreak*, the official monthly children's missionary magazine for the whole Presbyterian Church in Ireland. She was also an indefatigable speaker and organiser, giving talks to the Mothers' Union, Women Citizens' Union and the YWCA. She wrote articles for a variety of magazines on a host of topics: "Disagreeable Goodness" and "Sandbags of Indifference" being two interesting titles. She became well-known, not just as the wife of an internationally re-puted scholar, but in her own right for her intellectual capability and her good works.

Francis died of a sudden heart attack in 1941 and with three sons all serving abroad during Second World War Edina was lonely and bereft. After the War ended, she emigrated to England where she lived first with Kinnier, her youngest son, and then in Bristol above the consulting rooms of Gordon, her oldest, who was a surgeon there. Walter was in the Colonial

Service in Nigeria. I, her only grandson, had the privilege of meeting her at home in Bristol on one memorable occasion.

Anne Edina Hately Paul died, after a rich and full life, in her 83rd year in 1959 and was buried alongside her husband in Bushmills. It is entirely due to her careful and admiring preservation of her father's and mother's letters, cuttings and artefacts that their inspirational story can be told today.

SAMUEL WILSON

Five years after his return to Edinburgh from Kansas, Sam entered George Watson's College in Edinburgh. He won scholarships from the start and from early days was attracted by classical studies; he said he wanted to be a Professor of Greek. His school essays are in remarkably fluid handwriting and illustrated with fine line-drawings. He enjoyed public speaking at school — a foreshadowing of his later, dramatic lecturing style.

In 1894 he was awarded an Entrance Bursary in Arts to Edinburgh University and graduated from there M.A. in 1897. Immediately he changed tack and studied medicine, graduating MB ChB in 1902 and BSc the following year with First Class Honours. Edinburgh was considered perhaps the finest medical school in the world at the time. Sam then went on to obtain a Carnegie scholarship to study in Paris (1903-1904) — a mecca for neurologists. His letters from this time give the reader the impression of someone immensely quick-minded, coming to a considered and perceptive judgement with breath-taking speed and definiteness. He enjoyed words and his capability in multiple European languages became legendary among medics.

From Paris Sam went more briefly to Leipzig, and later in 1904 became resident medical officer at the National Hospital for the Paralysed and Epileptic, Queen Square, London — an association that went on for 33 years to the end of his life. International fame came to him through his monograph to *Brain* in 1912. It not only gained him his MD but also the gold medal of Edinburgh

University for its ground breaking thesis on 'progressive lenticular degenera-
tion', or Wilson's Disease as it became known, and still is.

In 1912 he also joined the honorary staff of Westminster Hospital where
he was first Assistant Physician, then two years later Dean, resigning in 1919 to
take up the post of Junior Neurologist and Lecturer at King's College Hospital
where he became Senior Neurologist in 1928.

Meanwhile, he had married, in June 1913, Annie Louisa Bruce, daughter
of the late Dr Alexander Bruce of Edinburgh, himself another distinguished
neurologist. The couple lived at Harley Street, London, where they had three
children — Muriel, Bruce, and James (who has kindly written the foreword
to this volume).

In 1920 Sam founded the *Journal of Neurology and Psychopathology* and became its first editor. He was also neurologist to the Metropolitan Asylums
Board and London County Council. His reputation was by the mid-1920s
firmly established as an academic, as a lecturer, and as a brilliant and highly
individual practitioner so he was the obvious choice to deliver the 1925
Croonian Lectures of the Royal College of Physicians of London. In 1930 he
gave the Morison Lecture in Edinburgh. By 1933 he was President of the neurological section of the Royal Society of Medicine. In 1934 he became DSc
of the University of Edinburgh and in 1935 Secretary–General of the second
International Congress of Neurology.

As well as contributing to many journals, Sam wrote three books.
One, *Aphasia* (1926) was a concise overview, the second was fuller: *Modern
Problems in Neurology* (1928); the third, *Neurology*, published posthumously
in two volumes in 1940 — edited by his brother-in-law, Alexander Ninian
Bruce,(another Edinburgh doctor and Alexander Bruce's son) — has been
frequently described as one of the most important neurology textbooks
ever published.

Sam was honoured all over the world, the obituary in *The British Medical
Journal* calling him "a neurologist of world-wide reputation". He was *Officier*

de l'Instruction Publique de la République Francaise and became an honorary fellow or member of medical academies or neurological societies in Paris, Belgium, America, Turin, Italy, Poland, Paris, Vienna, Philadelphia, Germany, Japan, and Copenhagen.

The Dictionary of National Biography stated that his clinics at Queen Square were popular with students across the globe, and abroad his name was probably the best known of all British neurologists.

When on a lecture tour of the United States in 1928 he visited his birthplace, Cedarville, New Jersey, and made the extra effort of the long journey out to Kansas to visit Wakeeney. He photographed the plot of his father's grave there, though no headstone can be seen in the rather poor exposure. The tour began in Montreal and took in New York, Philadelphia, Chicago, Kansas City, Denver, Los Angeles, San Francisco and the Canadian Rockies. In Los Angeles he stayed with Charlie Chaplin with whom he and Nancy were good friends.

He described Cedarville as a "one-street country village with maize fields, peach orchards, trees and a lake. It was quiet and old looking. Rockers on the verandahs, fly-nets on all the doors and windows". The parsonage he found "entirely unchanged".

Samuel Alexander Kinnier Wilson died after a short illness (cancer) on May 12, 1937, at the height of his powers, just after two colleagues (both Nobel Prize winners and past presidents of the Royal Society) had put him up for the high honour of being elected FRS. He was buried at Longside, near Peterhead, close to the Bruce family home.

In 1988, Macdonald Critchley, a senior neurologist who had served under Sam as a close colleague for fourteen years, was asked to write a conference paper, "Remembering Kinnier Wilson" and it was published in the journal *Movement Disorders* Vol. 3, No. 1, 1988. He began: "Do we, I wonder, sufficiently realise today his sheer magnitude in the pantheon of neurology? . . . in the 1920s and 1930s there were two supreme figures among the world's neurologists, and Kinnier Wilson was one of them".

In February 2013, King's College, London, ran in their magazine a full page article about Sam "a century on" in honour of the publication of the "famous thesis" considered a "milestone in the history of neurology". His book is described there as "widely regarded as the greatest single-author text on the subject ever written".

SELECT BIBLIOGRAPHY

BOOKS

Bilby, J.G., James M. Madden, Harry Ziegler. *350 Years of New Jersey History.* (The History Press, 2014).

Bodine, L. T. *Kansas Illustrated. An Accurate and Reliable Description of This Marvellous State for the Information of Persons Seeking Homes in the Great West.* (Kansas Pacific Railroad, 1879).

Buchan, John. *The Kirk in Scotland 1560-1929.* (Hodder and Stoughton, 1930).

Cordley, R. *Pioneer Days in Kansas.* (Dodo Press reprint from 1903).

Dickson, N. *The Kirk and its Worthies.* (T. N. Foulis, 1912).

Griffiths, Rudyard (ed.). *The Munk Debates, Hitchens v. Blair.* (Black Swan, 2011).

Handbook for the Kansas Pacific Railway. 1870.

Love, James. *Scottish Church Music.* (Wm. Blackwood, 1891).

Michellich, Mary. *Our Heritage, First United Presbyterian Church, Wakeeney, Kansas, 1878-1978.* (Private Publication).

Pascal, Blaise. *Pensées*, translated by M. Turnell. (Harvill Press, 1962).

Patrick, Millar. *Four Centuries of Scottish Psalmody.* (Oxford University Press, 1949).

Paul, F. J. *Romanism and Evangelical Christianity.* (Hodder and Stoughton, 1940).

Paul, M. K. *The Evil That Men Do*. (Sacristy Press, 2016).

The Picturesque Tourist: A Handy Guide around the World. (Adams and Co., 1877).

Ransford, O. *David Livingstone, The Dark Interior*. (John Murray, 1978).

Riley, Karen F. *The Pine Barrens of New Jersey*. (Arcadia Publishing, 2010).

Stratton, Joanna L. *Pioneer Women, Voices from the Kansas Frontier*. (Touchstone, 1982).

Wheeler, Keith. *The Townsmen*. (Time-Life Books, 1975).

REFERENCE BOOKS

The Century Cyclopedia of Names. (The Times, 1894).

The Century Dictionary. (The Times, 1899).

The Concise Dictionary of National Biography. (Oxford University Press, 1961).

Encyclopaedia Britannica, Eleventh Edition. (The Encyclopaedia Britannica Company, 1910-11).

MAGAZINES, NEWSPAPERS, ARTICLES, MINUTES

Cedarville N. J., First Presbyterian Church minute books. 1874-1878.

Frank Leslie's Illustrated Newspaper for 18th December 1875.

Harper's New Monthly Magazine: August 1870, vol. XLI, no.242.

"The Irish Church". *Quarterly Review* Vol 124. (John Murray, 1868).

Movement Disorders Vol. 3, No. 1. 1988.

Presbytery of Solomon *Minute Book for 1876-1884*.

Professor Socolovsky. *Kansas in 1876.* http://www.kancoll.org/khq/1977/77_1_ socolofsky.htm.

Rules for Sessions. 1906. The Presbytery of West Jersey.

The Western Star for July 4, 1885 and January 23, 1920.

A.E.H. Wilson. *Letters From Kansas* in *The Family Treasury.* (T. Nelson and Sons, 1878–1879).

INTERNET SITES

https://christianheritageedinburgh.org.uk/2016/08/23/ the-peak-years-and-the-moody-revival-1865-1900.

http://www2.hsp.org/exhibits/Balch%20resources/phila_ellis_island.html.

http://www.gjenvick.com/SteamshipArticles/TransatlanticShipsAndVoya ges/1870-08-TheOceanSteamer-HarpersMagazine.html#axzz4bflmbhID.

http://www.proclaimanddefend.org/2014/07/25/moody-and-sankey.

http://www.kansasmemory.org/item/220006. *The State of Kansas and Irish Immigration.*

https://en.wikipedia.org/wiki/WaKeeney,_Kansas.

http://history.hanover.edu/courses/excerpts/336RR.html.

http://www.kansasmemory.org/item/1441/page/3.

http://www.kansasmemory.org/item/209737/page/38.

http://www.kansasmemory.org/item/218972.

http://www.kansasmemory.org/item/210684.

https://en.wikipedia.org/wiki/Fort_Robinson_massacre.

http://genealogytrails.com/kan/trego/history1.html.

http://genealogytrails.com/kan/trego/1880mortality.html.

http://www.doctortreatments.com/19th-century-medicines-healing-drugs-chemicals-herbs.html.

http://scholarship.law.berkeley.edu/cgi/viewcontent.cgi?article=1077&context=californialawreview.

http://www.kancoll.org/khq/1977/77_1_socolofsky.htm.

For more information about

Marcus Paul
and
Ireland to the Wild West
please visit:

www.marcuskpaul.co.uk
www.goodreads.com/author/show/14938095.
Marcus_Paul

For more information about
AMBASSADOR INTERNATIONAL
please visit:

www.ambassador-international.com
@AmbassadorIntl
www.facebook.com/AmbassadorIntl

If you enjoyed this book, please consider leaving us a review on Amazon, Goodreads, or our website.

Also from Ambassador International:

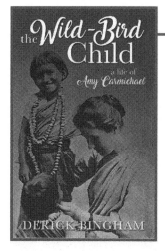

The Wild-Bird Child: Brilliant, personable and passionate, Amy Carmichael is arguably the most gifted of all Irish woman writers of Christian literature. For this biography, Derick Bingham carefully researched Amy Carmichael's original letters now placed by the Dohnavur Fellowship and Miss Margaret Wilkinson in the Northern Ireland Public Records Office.

Women of the Frontier: American frontier women of the 18th century were an extraordinary people whose contribution to the creation of the United States is one of the most enduring stories in history. *Women of the Frontier* tells the stories of more than 50 heroines who were part of the making of America from the 1700s through the early 1900s.

Christian Men of Science: In the short biographies in *Christian Men of Science*, readers are presented with a distilled version of each man's scientific accomplishments and the evidences of his Christian faith. These testimonies demonstrate that true scientists can be genuine Christians, and that faith in God and the authority of the Bible is not a sign of inferior intellect.

Printed in Poland
by Amazon Fulfillment
Poland Sp. z o.o., Wrocław

62408067R00148